When Daylight Comes

THE GOLDEN STAIRS

" BEHOLD THE TRUTH BEFORE YOU: A CLEAN LIFE, AN OPEN MIND, A PURE HEART, AN EAGER INTELLECT, AN UNVEILED SPIRITUAL PERCEPTION, A BROTHERLINESS FOR ONE'S CO-DISCIPLE, A READINESS TO GIVE AND RECEIVE ADVICE AND INSTRUCTION, A LOYAL SENSE OF DUTY TO THE TEACHER, A WILLING OBEDIENCE TO THE BEHESTS OF TRUTH, ONCE WE HAVE PLACED OUR CONFIDENCE IN, AND BELIEVE THAT TEACHER TO BE IN POSSESSION OF IT; A COURAGEOUS ENDURANCE OF PERSONAL INJUSTICE, A BRAVE DECLARATION OF PRINCIPLES, A VALIANT DEFENCE OF THOSE WHO ARE UNJUSTLY ATTACKED, AND A CONSTANT EYE TO THE IDEAL OF HUMAN PROGRESSION AND PERFECTION WHICH THE SECRET SCIENCE (*Gupta Vidyá*) DEPICTS—THESE ARE THE GOLDEN STAIRS UP THE STEPS OF WHICH THE LEARNER MAY CLIMB TO THE TEMPLE OF DIVINE WISDOM." [1]

H P Blavatsky

---

[1] [This is the original form of this statement of the ideal before the occultist, given by H.P.B. to her esoteric students. When later the statement was issued to Theosophists in general, the words "a loyal sense of duty . . . in possession of it" were omitted, as seeming to impose a blind "occult" obedience on unwilling students. Also "a brotherliness for one's co-disciple" was changed to "a brotherliness for all," and "secret science" changed to "sacred science."—C.J.]

When Daylight Comes

A Biography of Helena Petrovna Blavatsky

by

HOWARD MURPHET

A QUEST BOOK

Published under a grant from The Kern Foundation

THE THEOSOPHICAL PUBLISHING HOUSE
Wheaton, Ill., U.S.A.
Madras, India / London, England

Original edition 1975 published by The Theosophical Publishing House, Wheaton, Illinois, a department of The Theosophical Society in America

Murphet, Howard.
  When daylight comes.

  1. Blavatsky, Helena Petrovna Hahn-Hahn, 1831-1891.
I. Title.
BP585.B6M87   212´.52´0924 [B]   74-18958
ISBN 0-8356-0459-4

Printed in the
United States of America

And not by eastern windows only
When daylight comes, comes in the light,
In front the sun climbs slow, how slowly,
But westward, look, the land is bright.

—ARTHUR HUGH CLOUGH

. . . if a man does a useless thing, none reproves him;
if he does a harmful thing, few seek to restrain him; but
if he seeks to imitate the gods and to encourage others,
all those in authority accuse him of corruption. So it is
more dangerous to teach truth than to enter a powder
magazine with a lighted torch.

—TSIANG SAMDUP

The Book of Sayings

CONTENTS

PART I
THE SEARCH

PART II
THE SUN CLIMBS SLOW, HOW SLOWLY

PART III

WESTWARD GLIMMERINGS

ILLUSTRATIONS

ACKNOWLEDGMENTS

In a search over many years for significant data and light on the mysterious life of Madame Blavatsky, I have received kind assistance and co-operation—often quite unexpected—from many individuals. These include Mr. N. Sri Ram, late International President of The Theosophical Society, and other members of the Society in India, America, Britain and Australia. I would like to express my sincere gratitude to all of these, and also to the following in particular: the late Helen V. Zahara, formerly Publications Manager of the Theosophical Publishing House, Wheaton, Illinois, U.S.A.; Mr. Boris de Zirkoff and Mrs. Camille Svensson, both of Los Angeles, California, U.S.A., for the many rare and useful biographical items they so generously supplied; to Mrs. Lina Psaltis for preparation of the index; and, finally, to my wife, Iris Murphet, for her valuable help and constant encouragement in my research work at the Adyar Archives and Library in India.

H.M.

FOREWORD

In every major epoch in the progressive unfoldment of mankind upon the stage of history, one or more individuals have stood as witnesses to that Mystic Knowledge which universal tradition has either loudly proclaimed or cautiously whispered about, as cycle followed cycle in the ebb and flow of historical life-waves.

Our own epoch is no exception. The reawakening of the ancient Gnosis and the resurgence of long-forgotten truths—buried for centuries and stolidly denied a voice upon the forum of human affairs—have seen the appearance of such a witness—H.P. Blavatsky—whose flaming torch was lit upon the altars of ancient gods, and whose starlike thoughts rent the Cimmerian darkness of our entrenched ignorance and superstition, driving a wedge of fire between those who preferred to remain blind and those who dared to see!

The spiritual life of our planet has its ebb and flow as do all manifestations of cosmic life throughout nature. Cycles of spiritual and intellectual fertility, when the tides of natural inspiration run high, are followed by periods of spiritual barrenness and intellectual somnolence. It is then that inspired Teachers appear among men, to strike the keynote of the Spirit and help mankind to keep unbroken the mystic link which binds it to its Divine Home. The appearance of Teachers is therefore governed by Law, and their work among men is subject to the cyclic sequences inherent in the very nature of Cosmic Being. They act as direct Messengers from their own Superiors in the Hierarchy of Compassion and are entrusted with a specific mandate. Though varying in their spiritual status and occult knowledge, most of them are at various periods of their lives embodiments or vehicles of the consciousness of still Higher Beings who, to a greater or lesser extent, manifest themselves through them for the upliftment of the human race.

Who was H.P. Blavatsky? And what of H.P.B.? . . . .
Misunderstood and reviled, attacked and slandered, adored
by some and hated by others, she is today as much, if not
more, alive than she was a hundred years ago, and her
name arouses a storm of feelings in various quarters
wherein other individuals of her own day have become
but mere entries upon the roster of historical annals.

Some centuries from now, she may become a legend;
a dimly outlined figure of bygone cycles, whose origin
and aims may have become blurred by the passage of
time, and around whose image may center innumerable
stories of both wonder and horror.

But now, while facts are known and eyewitness accounts are yet on hand, while family records and personal correspondence are extant, it is easier to present a
factual record of the many vicissitudes in her career, and
to draw some obvious deductions from the imposing
array of data which are still available to the historian
of today.

It is to this impartial record that we now turn and
bid the reader to an exciting journey through a vast
labyrinth of people and events.

Our guide being our good friend Howard Murphet,
we are assured of a safe passage. Keen observer and unbiased historian, experienced in literary ventures, he is
a dedicated Theosophist and an entertaining story-teller.
His friendly and at times humorous pen carries the reader
over from the suspense at the end of one chapter into the
unforeseen adventures of the next.

We commend this work to the attention of those who
may desire to have some light thrown upon the dynamic
and mystery-packed life of the nineteenth century "Sphinx"
—Helena Petrovna Blavatsky. May it receive the wide-
spread distribution throughout the world which it de-
serves, and may its perusal stimulate a deeper search for
Truth on the part of the readers.

—BORIS DE ZIRKOFF

INTRODUCTION

Two Legends

On the life and character of Helena Petrovna Blavatsky two conflicting legends exist. According to one, from pens dipped in the garbage cans of Victorian gossip, she was either the mistress or the bigamous wife of Agardi Metrovitch, a celebrated operatic singer of the day, but also had many other lovers and at least one illegitimate child. Several men were nominated as the father of this, but the most favored choice was Prince Emile von Sayn Wittgenstein, a cousin of the Empress of Russia.

The story goes that at times she earned her living in the Paris demimonde, and at other times by riding horses in a Turkish circus, engaging in shady commercial ventures, giving pianoforte concerts in London and Paris, and—though ignorant of the theory of music—conducting a large orchestra. She is even credited with managing the Royal Choir for the King of Serbia.

Her remarkable talents, it is said, included those of writing satirical poems, and she once pasted insulting verses on the doors and walls of the old Kiev, lampooning its Governor-General, Prince Dondukoff-Korsakoff. This resulted in her leaving the city in a hurry.

Later when Spiritualism became popular in America, she exploited it for money. Then, after meeting Colonel Olcott in Spiritualistic circles, she began the most daring, ingenious, and infamous impostures of the century. She launched The Theosophical Society and, to support it, invented Mahatmas—adepts in the occult arts—whom she credited with many of the miraculous phenomena that went on around her. The so-called miracles were, however, produced by clever tricks and conjury which she had evidently learned somewhere in her checkered career.

She even invented handwritings for several of her imaginary Mahatmas, and in this guise carried on a long correspondence on abstruse matters with Mr. A. P. Sinnett, Editor of *The Pioneer,* considered the most influential newspaper of British India.

The great theosophical and Mahatmic imposture was at first a cover for Russian espionage, and later for making money.

Well, that is the essence of the colorful legend, and it makes good grist for the mill of the writer of popular biographies. But how much truth is there in it? The origin of most of its features can be traced back to Victorian drawing-rooms, particularly those of Russia. Considering the circumstances, this is, in a way, not so surprising.

For one thing Helena Blavatsky broke most of the strict social conventions of her time. She deserted her husband almost immediately after the marriage ceremony and wandered off into the wide, wicked world of the mid-nineteenth century, a woman alone. Any woman who did this—and there were not very many— was automatically suspect and the target of malicious, inventive tongues.

To add fuel to the fires of slander, Helena shrouded her movements in mystery. Furthermore, she even encouraged the rumor that she was living a wildly unconventional life. She did not want members of her family in Russia to know the actual reason for her nomadic life. They would not really believe, she hoped, the stories of immorality that were being circulated, but, knowing her early interests, they *would* believe the truth if they heard it, and, being conservative, orthodox Christians, they would be horrified.

Caring nothing, at this time, for the empty talk of fashionable society, she used its rumors as a smoke screen to cover her tracks. "Had I been a common p - -," she wrote, [one did not spell out "prostitute" for the eyes of Victorian prudery] "they would have preferred it to my studying Occultism." Later on Helena brought about a change in their outlook, and they came to accept some of the ideas of higher Occultism. But in the years when she was on her great search among the world's hidden, off-beat cults, had her family known about it, they would have considered her "sold to Satan."

Another thing that added to the spicy rumors about Helena was the fact that the public often confused her with a popular fictional character of the day. This was the infamous villainess Madame Heloise Blavatsky who was the leader of an anti-Semitic cabal called the "Black Hundred." The fictional exploits of Heloise were apparently often credited to Helena.

Scandalous tales of Helena emerged in due course from behind spread fans into the glare of newspaper columns. One Russian paper, for instance, came out with the stupendous statement that the authoress of *Isis Unveiled* (written by Helena in America) was "the same Mme. B. who at the age of 17 had murdered her venerable husband, and then disappeared from Russia."

A later generation of muckraking authors, intent on making money out of the lurid legend, thought they had found a reliable source of evidence in the *Memoirs* of Count Serguey Y. de Witte, published as a book in 1921. This was 31 years after the death of H.P. Blavatsky, and a few years after the Count's own demise.

Serguey was Helena's first cousin, but a baby less than a year old when she first left Russia on her travels. His mother, Katherine de Witte, never had much of an opinion of her niece Helena, and perhaps the boy imbibed something of her attitude. When Helena first returned to Russia at the end of 1858, after a nine-year mysterious odyssey, Serguey de Witte was still only about 10 years old.

One would expect an eminent ex-Prime Minister of Russia, writing on matters concerned with national history, to ply a reliable pen. But the truth is that, in facts which can be checked against historical records, he makes many incredible errors and self-contradictions.

A few of these, connected with his own life, are: he gives wrong and conflicting dates (sometimes years off the mark) concerning his appointments to high official positions; his statements about his relations with Czar Nicholas II are self-contradictory; and he even fails to give the correct date for his own marriage.

With regard to his cousin Helena, the Count dishes up much of the old toxic tittle-tattle of the drawing-rooms, but adds some poison of his own.

His reliability and veracity, however, are not helped by his incorrect statements on easily-checked facts of Theosophical Society history. For instance, he has it founded in England, instead of in New York, and states that Helena settled down in Paris at the head of her Society, whereas she settled in London, and the recognized, nominal head of The Theosophical Society was Colonel H.S. Olcott, as President-Founder, with Headquarters at Adyar, Madras, India.

It seems hard to believe that the old statesman, known as the Czar's ablest Minister, could have been so careless about statements of fact in his *Memoirs*. He wrote the manuscript in Paris during vacations and after retirement. As he died at the reasonably early age of sixty-six, he could scarcely have been senile. It is possible, of course, that his mind was becoming confused, but some people have suggested a more sinister explanation.

Victor Endersby in his book, *The Hall of the Magic Mirrors*,[1] gives as his opinion that, after the Count's death, Russian secret police got hold of the manuscript and altered history to suit the imperial requirements of propaganda. In other words they aimed to discredit Count de Witte's veracity and reliability.

There were sufficient Machiavellian reasons for such a move. Count de Witte had been opposed to Russia's war with Japan, and he was opposed to the Russian machinations and maneuvers that led toward World War I. He was a reformer and a liberal, creating a legislative *Duma,* a parliament with "the voting franchise almost universal and elections free of Cabinet control." The Czar thought this was going much too far, dismissed him, and soon afterwards dissolved parliament.

So it would be greatly feared that the Count's *Memoirs* might reveal too much of Russian power politics. It is known that attempts were made by Czarist agents to get the manuscript back to Russia for censorship, both during the Count's lifetime and after his death. The theory is that after his death Russian secret police succeeded in "borrowing" the manuscript from a bank vault in France for long enough to make alterations, and thus undermine its value as a historical document.

At the same time, the theory goes, the Czarist agents took the opportunity to falsify the section on Helena Blavatsky, whose writings were inimical to the Russian Establishment, religious and secular.

Apart from the childish errors of fact, it does seem odd that a Russian aristocrat and figure of history should wish to shake his family skeleton before the eyes of posterity, even if he himself did believe the rumors concerning the scandalous, immoral, and dishonest career of Helena Blavatsky.

Beatrice Hastings, writing years before Endersby, considered that the Count's *Memoirs* "bear marks of adulteration."[2] Truth is often stranger than fiction and this real-life spy story may be true. But whatever the reason for its obvious factual misstatements, the point here is that the *Memoirs* cannot be taken as a reliable source of information on the life of Helena Petrovna Blavatsky.

The story of Helena being the mother of a bastard child was spiked on medical evidence. In 1885, when the rumor was proving a liability to the ten-year-old Theosophical Society, Madame Blavatsky was asked by her followers for a medical certificate on the matter. She was living at the time with the Countess Constance Wachtmeister at Würzberg in Germany.

The Countess requested Doctor Leon Oppenheimer, in Madame Blavatsky's presence, to make the necessary examination. He did so and furnished this certificate.

MEDICAL CERTIFICATE

The undersigned testifies herewith, as requested, that Madame Blavatsky of Bombay-New York, Corresponding Secretary of The Theosophical Society, is at present under the medical treatment of the undersigned; she suffers from *Anteflexio Uteri,* most likely congenital, because as shown by a minute examination, she has never given birth, nor has experienced any gynaecological illness.
Würzburg, 3rd November, 1885.

(Signed) *Dr. Leon Oppenheimer*
Women's Physician

The signature of Practicing Physician, Dr. Leon Oppenheimer, is hereby officially attested.

Würzburg, 3rd November, 1885

(Signed) *Dr. Roeder*
Royal District Physician

The certificate was sent by the Countess to Colonel Olcott in India, and was published during the lifetime of Dr. Leon Oppenheimer, who died in 1912.

Helena had friendships with men, certainly, and sometimes traveled with them in her wanderings around the world. "I loved one man deeply, but still more I loved occult science. . . . I wandered with him here and there, in Asia, in America, in Europe."[3] But all indications are that her friendships were Platonic. "Every word and action proclaimed her sexlessness," wrote Colonel Olcott who knew her well.

The man named by most as the father of "her illegitimate child," Prince Wittgenstein, wrote in a letter to her, dated April 20, 1878, "I should have been glad and proud to have had you stopping under my roof to introduce my wife to you, and to have my children kiss your hands; I hope this is clear and explicit, and I assure you that I am not more given to mere polite phrase-making now at 54 than I was when you used to know me as the frank, joyous, honest boy I was then."[4]

The Governor-General who was supposed to have hunted her out of Kiev for publicly insulting him, Prince Dondukoff-Korsafoff, was during the 1880s in amicable correspondence with Madame Blavatsky. Mlle. Smirnoff, a viperish tongue among the ladies-in-waiting at the Court of the Czar, was spreading poison about alleged swindles and thefts by Helena Blavatsky. In one of Helena's long letters to the Prince,[5] she asked him (then Governor-General of Odessa) to initiate an inquiry into police records "all over Russia," to clear her reputation, for the sake of The Theosophical Society. No records of any dishonest enterprises were ever found.

Actually, all of the gaudy bubbles of anti-Blavatsky slander that form the basis of Legend Number One were pricked and deflated in a test case toward the end of the last century. As will be shown in the penultimate chapter and epilogue of this book, the accumulated, character-damning rumors were all paraded in a long article by the New York *Sun*.

Madame Blavatsky sued for libel; the powerful newspaper, with all its resources, was unable to substantiate any of the charges and retracted them.

The second legend began in the last years of her life, and gathered strength after her death. It was born of the human desire to deify, to place someone of extraordinary knowledge and power on a pedestal of infallibility and ultimate authority beyond question, beyond criticism. She, who spoke and wrote against the concept of a personal God, was to become almost one herself in the eyes of devout disciples.

So this second legend goes to the opposite end of the pole from the first, and paints Madame Blavatsky as an immaculate saint. The one who never claimed perfection and infallibility even for her great Masters, let alone her humble self, would be the first to shatter the "plaster saint" image with the hammer of her contempt.

Madame Blavatsky was—and was never ashamed to show it—a robust, forthright, straight-shooting character, often quite shocking to polite society, both for her language and her trait of saying exactly what she thought. Rolling endless cigarettes, vigorously denouncing all hypocrites, fools, rogues, and "flapdoodles," she strode into the world's far-off, dangerous places, sometimes dressed as a man, usually alone, but at times in the company of men, those interested in the same search that she was and able to face the risks and rigors involved.

The legend that dehumanizes the great Russian Occultist and turns her into a paragon of perfection is unreal and untrue. It serves her almost as badly as does the image of a crafty charlatan, adventuress, free-lover, and courtesan.

This biographer has struggled to find and project the true Helena Blavatsky that existed somewhere between the two legends. This is not an easy task. Perhaps it can never be done with complete success because her life had motivations and dimensions beyond man's familiar horizons.

Mahatmas, Yoga, ESP

The western world began to believe, after Darwin, in the evolution of forms, but not in the evolution of soul and consciousness. The soul—to those who accepted its existence at all—was a static entity, born in sin along with the body. If not redeemed through Christ, it suffered in hell eternally; otherwise it rejoiced in heaven eternally. There was no concept of a dynamic, evolutionary progression for the man within.

Consequently, the west had no logical basis for a belief in Mahatmas, progressed yogins with consciousness and extrasensory faculties beyond the normal. Miracles, if they ever existed at all, belonged to Biblical times, and the Biblical men of God. That age had passed; this was the age of science.

And so the world welcomed a document that confirmed its own unbelief—the *Report of the Committee appointed to investigate phenomena connected with the Theosophical Society,* published by the *London Society for Psychical Research.*[6]

The writer does not propose to give a critical appraisal of the *Report* in this volume. Such an appraisal, to be just and adequate, requires a book in itself, and indeed books have already been published, analyzing the *Report* and revealing the inadequacy of the investigation and the falsity of its conclusions.

In 1968, in a letter to *Time* magazine, the S.P.R. disclaimed all responsibility for the *Report,* pointing out that, "Responsibility for both the facts and the reasonings in papers published in the *Proceedings* rests with their authors." The authors in this case were the Committee, made up of founders and early leading members of the S.P.R.: E. Gurney, F.W.H. Myers, F. Podmore, H. Sidgwick, and J.H. Stack, along with their special investigator who visited India, Richard Hodgson.

Hence, in the public mind, the conclusions of the Committee have been—and no doubt will continue to be—identified with the Society for Psychical Research, itself.

"Poor Myers! and still more poor Hodgson! How terribly they will be laughed at some day," wrote Madame Blavatsky to Mr. A. P. Sinnett at the time.

Even then the *Report* must have been comic in many ways to theosophical leaders; but they were afraid that its effects on the work might be tragic. Colonel Olcott, for instance, who had been the leading Special Investigator and exposer of fraud and corruption in the conduct of the American War between the States, and who had been officially commended for his success, was written off by the callow young investigator Richard Hodgson as credulous, gullible, and a poor observer. But Olcott had been observing theosophical phenomena for years at close quarters, and had himself met several of the Mahatmas and their high *chelas* (disciples), in the flesh.

Then there was Damodar K. Mavalankar, the hard-working young Brahmin at The Theosophical Society Headquarters. According to the *S.P.R. Report* he was an accomplice of Madame Blavatsky in the production of letters in the handwriting attributed to various imaginary Mahatmas. But oddly, in private letters to each other, these two partners in the invention wrote as if they believed in the actual existence of their own inventions.

The sardonic-faced Damodar, with T. Subba Row and some other chelas, looked on R. Hodgson's investigatory efforts in India with Brahminic contempt, unfortunately withholding cooperation. For this national and caste pride Damodar suffered when he set out to reach the Tibetan Ashram of his Sadguru, Mahatma Kuthumi Lal Singh, whom he had earlier met in the flesh.

According to a letter from the Mahatma K.H., received phenomenally by Olcott, Damodar did reach the Ashram, but "He had to undergo the severest trials that a neophyte ever passed through, to atone for the many questionable doings in which he had over-zealously taken part, bringing disgrace upon the sacred science and its adepts."[7] Incidentally, this Mahatma letter to Olcott was precipitated in India when the arch "Mahatma inventor," Madame Blavatsky, was in Europe.

The Report must also have been a kind of tragicomedy to a number of Theosophists who had met, or received communications from, Mahatmas when neither Madame Blavatsky nor Damodar was within many miles of the locale. Two brothers, Narasimhalu and Subbiah Chetty, for instance, had met the Master Morya in his physical body when he was passing through the city of Madras in 1874; at this time Madame Blavatsky was still in America, and The Theosophical Society had not been formed.[8]

Even the ultracritical Britisher, A.O. Hume, agreed that he had received phenomenal letters from the Mahatma K.H. under circumstances that forced him to believe in the existence of that particular Adept.

Now, a century after the early theosophical controversies, the tapestry of psychic phenomena has greatly enlarged, and the climate of thought has changed. It does indeed seem that the Western mind was not prepared for the avalanche of paranormal phenomena that came in the last quarter of last century, through both Spiritualism and Theosophy.

One great investigator, Sir William Crookes, who had a foot in both the spiritualistic and theosophic camps, tried to get his fellow scientists to take seriously his experiments, materializations, and hypotheses in psychical research. But he tried in vain, achieving only contemptuous laughter.

Yet many years later, Professor Charles Richet, world-renowned physiologist, apologized publicly for his own ridicule, and confirmed all that Crookes had claimed for the phenomena of materialization. He wrote: "The idolatry of current ideas was so dominant at that time that no pains were taken either to verify or to refute Crookes's statements. Men were content to ridicule them, and I avow with shame that I was among the wilfully blind. . . . And so was Ochorowicz. But he repented, and said, as I do, smiting my breast, 'Pater, peccavi!' " [Father I have sinned.][9]

If, however, there is another high tide of psychic phenomena in the last quarter of this century, as prophesied, the Occidental mind should be more ready for it. The organized psychical research begun tentatively last century has flowered into departments of parapsychology in many western universities. Experimental and statistical methodology is being employed to test and demonstrate the existence of extrasensory perception (ESP) and its more elusive sister, psychokinesis (PK). These are only modern terms for powers exercised in a much greater degree by chela Madame Blavatsky and her great Adepts.

Some parapsychologists are struggling hard to find the key for bringing these latent human faculties under conscious control of the will, as, to a large extent, the five senses and the thinking mind are.

But the key lies in the philosophy and science of yoga. To begin to understand this, we must think of man's consciousness in evolutionary terms. Back along the chain of evolution such powers as abstract reasoning and creative imagination, for instance, were merely dormant and potential in animal consciousness. Likewise today ESP and PK are mainly dormant, but give occasional indications of their existence in the human consciousness.

Through the practice of higher yoga (or else the long passage of time) human consciousness will expand, a greater spiritual understanding will open and, as by-products of this, ESP and PK will develop naturally. In other words, as mind evolves into supermind it acquires some extra instruments to add to its normal kit of sensory tools.

Once we accept the idea of dynamic individual souls, evolving over long periods of time—through lifetimes on earth or elsewhere—it is logical to postulate the existence of men higher up the ladder than the normal human. They have been longer on the evolutionary climb and have helped their own progress by the self-disciplinary practices called yoga. If they choose, for reasons of their own, to work behind the scenes, helping men to a higher knowledge and understanding, and sometimes influencing great events, through the use of telepathy and other extrasensory powers, they are usually called Adepts, Masters, Elder Brothers.

The fact that the masses—not seeing them—do not believe in their existence does not worry them. In fact, in many ways, it is an advantage, helping in the conservation of their powers.

The existence of Adepts is a logical, inevitable assumption to serious students of yoga, the esoteric philosophy, or the Wisdom-religion on which Theosophy is based. But the existence of the particular Adepts concerned with the launching of the Theosophical Movement becomes much more than an assumption to the conscientious researcher into the theosophical archives. Anyone who delves deeply into the files of documents, diary entries and private correspondence of the Founders and early theosophical workers must inevitably come to the conclusion that Madame Blavatsky's Mahatmas were real, living individuals.

To the theosophical phenomena or "miracles" the same remarks apply. For most of these Madame Blavatsky gave the credit to her invisible Masters, or their high and equally invisible chelas. Though unseen, they were often present, she claimed, in their *mayavi rupas* (mental-astral bodies). But she was a trained-in-Tibet lay chela herself, and we have the Master K.H.'s word for it that she actually performed many of the phenomena independently.[10]

Again, while to the yoga student such *siddhis* are acceptable logically, to the painstaking researcher into the documents the fact that they were frequently demonstrated through theosophical leaders—Madame Blavatsky in particular—is beyond all reasonable doubt. Any student who studies the records and sees the whole picture (Richard Hodgson saw only a small fraction of it), will assuredly decide that Madame Blavatsky's phenomena could not possibly have been all fake, as her traducers claimed.

And if the archives researcher is also a student of Indian spiritual philosophy, he will understand the situation as the S.P.R. investigators did *not,* for they were conditioned by the static-soul concept of both the classical and Christian cultures.

But through Madame Blavatsky's work, and other forces, the West has now imbibed more of the Eastern culture, and the current of world thought has left the inadequate and misleading *Report* stranded along its banks, a sad reminder of past Occidental arrogance.

Living Mahatmas and psychic phenomena were a vital part of Helena Blavatsky's life, and this biography deals with them as such, and as actual realities. It makes no attempt to prove to the reader that which can never be definitely proved, except by personal experience. The tale is told simply as it has been recorded by many witnesses of the remarkable and significant events in the life of the Mahatmic Messenger Extraordinary, Helena Petrovna Blavatsky.

PART I

The Search

". . . the coming of Christ," means the presence of *Christos* in a regenerated world, and not at all the actual coming in body of "Christ" Jesus; this Christ is to be sought neither in the wilderness nor "in the inner chambers," nor in the sanctuary of any temple or church built by man; for Christ—the true esoteric *Saviour—is no man,* but the *Divine Principle* in every human being. He who strives to resurrect the Spirit *crucified in him by his own terrestrial passions,* and buried deep in the "sepulchre" of his sinful flesh; he who has the strength to roll back the *stone of matter* from the door of his own *inner* sanctuary, he *has the risen Christ in him.* The "Son of Man" is no child of the bond-woman—*flesh,* but verily of the free-woman—*Spirit,* the child of man's own deeds, and the fruit of his own spiritual labour.

"The Esoteric Character of the Gospels," *Lucifer.*
Vol. I, November, 1887, p. 173;
Collected Writings, Vol. VIII, p. 173.

CHAPTER 1

In the summer of 1831 the ghoul of cholera was haunting the Ukranian steppe, decimating towns and villages in its insatiable greed for corpses. Not excluded from its terrifying itinerary was the town of Ekaterinoslav[1] (Glory of Katherine) on the banks of the Dnepr, some hundred leagues from where that great river meets the Black Sea.

Catherine the Great had laid the first stone of the town some fifty years earlier, and Prince Potemkin had built a magnificent palace there, as a resting place for the amorous empress during her fantastic journey from St. Petersburg to the new wonders of the Crimea, which Potemkin had conquered for her.

A French visitor to the town, in the 1830s, writes that it "is built on such a gigantic plan as makes it a perfect wilderness, in which the sparse houses and scanty population seem lost, as it were. Its wide and regular streets, marked out only by a few dwellings at long intervals, seem to have been planned for a million souls. It contains, however, some large buildings, numerous churches, bazaars and charming gardens. But for the absurd mania of the Russians for planning their towns on an enormous scale, it would be a delightful abode, rich in its beautiful Dnepr and the fertile hills around it."

Now there seemed to be constant funerals moving along its wide streets, and a pall of fear hung over the town. In the great mansion of Andrey Michailovich de Fadeyev there had been several deaths, but on the night of August 11 (Gregorian calendar) a different kind of event was taking place. At 1:42 a.m. of the twelfth, his delicate daughter, Helena Andreyevna von Hahn, gave premature birth to her first child. The baby, a girl, was so weak and puny that her sojourn in the world of cadavers and coffins threatened to be a very brief one indeed.

The father of the child, Captain Peter von Hahn was away in Poland, where his battery of artillery had been busy quelling the first Polish revolt. But many members of the mother's family were present, and it was decided, as the little weakling seemed likely at any moment to join the stream of corpses, that for the sake of her soul, there must be an immediate baptism.

So before the baby was twenty-four hours old, all the members of the great household—relatives, friends, and the numerous servants—gathered in the largest room of the house. Each bore a consecrated wax candle for the baptismal ceremony. Among the candle-bearers was a three-year-old child, an aunt of the new-born baby. She was being made to stand as a proxy godmother for someone absent, and was, therefore, placed close behind the officiating priest who stood in the middle of the room in his long flowing robes of golden cloth.

The ceremony droned on monotonously, while the room grew hot and heavy with the smell of burning wax. The child-aunt, standing erect like all the others, became drowsy; she sat on the floor; her head nodded; her candle flame slanted toward the old priest's robe. In the baptismal rites the invisible Evil One was just being renounced and spat upon; the hem of the officiating priest's robe swung over the candle and caught fire. Before anyone had noticed it, he was enveloped in flames.

The priest was, of course, badly burned, as were several others who rushed to his rescue, and the ceremony came to an abrupt end. But not before the infant, unaware that she had started life with some inadvertent priest singeing, was duly christened Helena Petrovna von Hahn.

It was a bad omen, said the superstitious townsfolk, and her life would henceforth be stormy and filled with vicissitudes. According to popular Russian superstitions the date of her birth (July 30-31 by the old Julian calendar, still in use then in Russia) made her outstandingly psychic. She would have second sight, power over the demovoy (house goblin) and other sprites, and be wise in the ways of witches.

But the child's 17-year-old mother, Helena Andreyevna von Hahn of the delicate oval face and almond-shaped eyes, was above such superstitious nonsense. She was the daughter of a princess whose ancestry went back deep into Russian history through a long line of princes of the Dolgorukov family. The name Dolgorukov itself meant "long armed." It also could mean a man who grasped more, or knew more; and, centuries back, it had a mystic connotation.

Writing of his travels in Russia in 1858, Alexandre Dumas, has this to say about the Dolgorukov family, some members of which he met: "One, Prince Gregory, defended the convent of Saint Sergius from 1608 to 1610 against 30,000 Poles and Cossacks commanded by the four greatest leaders of the time . . . In 1624 a princess of the house of Dolgorukov was married to the Czar Michael Romanoff, founder of the dynasty that rules Russia today. . . . Peter II made Prince Ivan A. Dolgorukov his closest companion."

Dumas goes on to say that, when power came into the hands of the infamous Biren who caused the death of 11,000 Russians, Prince Jean and his family were exiled to Siberia. Nine years later he was brought back and killed by torture. Then his wife Nathalie climbed to a steep cliff overhanging the Dnyepr river and cast her wedding ring into the water. Next day she became a nun at Kiev and spent the last 30 years of her life praying for the soul of the man she had loved.[2]

Accounts of the historic doings of the Dolgorukovs can be found in many sources; all show that a fiery, turbulent, imperious spirit ran through this princely family.

But not all members of the family were cast in the warrior mold. No one could have been more gentle and romantic than Helena Andreyevna, the new-born baby's mother. She had dreamed of an ideal marraige to a man who would have the same deep soul interests as herself.

But with the tall, handsome Captain von Hahn of Horse Artillery such hopes were swiftly and rudely shattered. Peter Alexeyevich von Hahn was, like herself, of noble family: the Counts Hahn von Rottenstern-Hahn of Mecklenburg, Germany, who had emigrated to Russia about a century earlier. Peter's father was an army general of distinguished career, and his mother had been Countess Elizabeth Maksimovna von Probsen.

Well educated, brilliant, gay, and twelve years older than his wife, Peter should have made a good companion. But his interests were only in horses, dogs, guns, dinner-parties, and the like; he regarded with indifference, even hostility, his wife's literary and spiritual aspirations.

She writes: "All that I aspired to from my childhood, all that was sacred to my heart was either laughed at, or was shown to me in the pitiless and cynical light of his cold and cruel reasoning."

She took refuge in writing novels on the theme of women's unfortunate social position with regard to marriage. Critics have called her the "George Sand" of Russia, and traced the beginning of the modern feminist movement to the writings of Helena A. von Hahn, George Sand, and a woman novelist of Germany.

So the young mother was not overwhelmed with joy when Peter of the red, pointed moustache came riding back down the dusty road through the ripe wheat and sunflowers. The war and his duties in Poland were over. It was summer, and baby Helena, still frequently sick and near to dying, was a few months old.

Now there began a period of moving here and there to wherever Captain von Hahn's regiment was temporarily stationed, mainly in "small, dirty provincial towns," where boring social activities were expected of an army officer's wife.

But to little Helena or Lyolya, as she was called, the life was great fun. She watched from a window the soldiers maneuvering to the sound of drum and trumpets, and the big guns hurrying about on wheels that thundered as they moved, while her father galloped around on his fine horse, shouting orders with animated gestures.

Lyolya became the pet of the rough soldiery and learned from them to call a spade a spade when she could not think of something stronger. The penchant for robust, soldiers' language stayed with her to the end.

But on frequent visits to her grandparents the child learned something quite different. To the serfs she was that very special person born on a date that gave her power over unseen beings, particularly the demovoy of the house, and also the roussalkas, or nymphs, along the river's bank.

The demovoy was a kind of unseen caretaker who watched over the affairs of the household, guarded against malevolent witches, and made sure that all ran smoothly, that is, except on one day of the year. On March 30, for some reason, he became a mischievous poltergeist. To keep the household from harm he had to be propitiated. This was where Lyolya was thought to be of tremendous value. On the appropriate date for the propitiation ceremony she would be carried by the serfs around house, stables, and cowsheds. She had to sprinkle holy water from her own small hand, while a servant repeated the mystic sentences and charms that had been used by the peasants for a thousand years.

It was natural that the child should gain not only a keen interest in the folklore of invisible beings, many of which, indeed, seem to have been quite visible to her, but also a sense of power with regard to them.

Family records tell a story of her childhood which illustrates this. In one of her walks by the reedy river with her nurse, a boy of about fourteen was dragging her carriage. Through some slight disobedience he incurred little Helena's displeasure. "I will have you tickled to death by a roussalka," she shouted. "There's one coming down from that tree . . . here she comes . . . see, see!" She pointed upward.

The terrified boy took to his heels and disappeared along the sandy banks. Grumbling about how she would have the boy punished for running away, the old nurse herself pushed the carriage home. But the boy did not return, and some weeks later the fishermen along the river caught his body in their nets.

"Drowned by accident," was the verdict of the police, and so it may have been. But the domestics of the household, and peasants of the locality, passed a different verdict. Lyolya, they said, had withdrawn her protection from the boy and thus he easily became the victim of some roussalka on the watch. Helena, herself, gravely corroborated the charge: yes, she agreed, she had handed over the disobedient serf to her servants the water-nymphs. The family was horrified with this gossip and the child's ready acquiescence.

Yet, despite such Dolgorukov imperiousness, little Helena was really a warmhearted, affectionate child. Though quick to fly into a passionate rage, she was even quicker to forgive, and never bore malice or resentment.

One thing, however, that worried her aristocratic parents was her strong preference for the children of the lower classes. "She always preferred to play with the servants' children rather than with her equals, and had to be constantly watched lest she escape from the house to make friends with ragged street boys," writes one of her aunts.

Even more disturbing to the family was the fact that she claimed to have a troupe of invisible playmates with whom she spent much of her time. To her, it seemed, they were quite as real as if they had been flesh and blood, and it annoyed her exceedingly that nobody would believe in their existence. It is interesting, in view of a later event of her life, that the most beloved of these "spirit" companions was a little hunchback boy. With him she talked and laughed and went on adventures, and he seems to have led her into endless mischief.

In 1835, when Helena was nearly four years old, her sister Vera was born. And the next year brought a happy event for the young mother. Peter von Hahn was transferred to St. Petersburg, taking his wife and two children with him. There in the exciting, colorful life of the capital city the novelist enjoyed theaters, art galleries, new books, and conversation with many Russian writers, including Alexander Pushkin. This stirred again a soul stifled by dull provincial life, and she decided in future to devote all her time to creative writing.

Consequently, she parted temporarily from her husband when he was reassigned to a station in the Ukraine. Instead of going with him she accompanied her parents to Astrakhan, romantic half-oriental city on an island of the mighty Volga where it emptied into the Caspian Sea. Her father had been appointed to that center as trustee, or curator-general, of the Kalmucks.

There, while nursemaids took care of her two little daughters and breezes stirred sand in the streets of Astrakhan, from hushed noon to the chatter of evening bazaars, Helena Andreyevna wrote and wrote. She signed her writings with the pen name Zeneida R-Va.

In her novel, *The Ideal,* she said: "The position of a woman, who has been placed by nature itself above the crowd, is verily desperate. The hundred-headed monster of public opinion will declare her immoral, will throw dirt on her noblest feelings, her purest aspirations, her most elevated thoughts; it will soil them by the mud of its comments . . . she will be like a criminal rejected by society. . . ."

Her words were, no doubt, born of bitter personal experience, but they were also strangely prophetic of what life would bring to her daughter, Helena Petrovna.

During the next few years the novelist alternated her residence between her parents' home, her husband's military stations, and mineral spas, where she hoped to improve her deteriorating health. She engaged two governesses for her daughters, one of them a Miss A. S. Jeffers from Yorkshire, complete with provincial accent. Young Helena was taught French and English, music and dancing.

Meanwhile the ailing, unhappy mother battled on with her writing against all obstacles. Vera recalls: "I remember . . . that my mother was a great sufferer, but that she spent long hours writing, behind a partition covered with green cloth. The little nook behind this green barrier was called mother's workroom, and never did either my elder sister Lyolya, nor I, venture to touch anything in that room, which only a curtain separated from our own.

At that time we did not in the least understand what our mother could be occupied with in this retreat in which she passed whole days. We only knew that she was writing at her table, but we did not in the least suspect that she was working there to earn money to pay our tutors and governesses."[3]

When Helena Petrovna was eight years old her maternal grandfather, A.M. de Fadeyev was appointed Governor of the province of Saratov and took up residence in the city of that name on the banks of the Volga. It was not long before her novelist mother agreed to go there in the hope of getting better treatment for her lung disease. The trip across new territory to the grandparents was an exciting adventure to the two little girls. Vera, who was only five at the time, recalls some impressions: "It was night. Our closed coach swung gently from side to side. Worn out by the long journey and weary of looking for a city which never appeared, we were all half asleep. My sister and I were lulled to sleep by our smooth progress over the snow, by the whistling of the wind, and by the monotonous cries of the coachman encouraging his horses. My mother alone was not asleep. She held me on her knee . . . with one hand holding my head pressed against her breast, seeking to protect me against the jolting of the coach. . . .

"All at once I was awakened by a more vigorous jolt, and an intense ray of light, shining in my face, made me blink my eyes. . . .

"Our coach passed through a great stone gateway, and stopped before the brilliantly lit steps."

She then describes how a tall, stately lady—their grandmother, the princess—clasped them all in her arms, how a tall, thin gentleman in a gray frock coat—their grandfather—kissed her several times, how inside the mansion she looked at the big ancestral portraits hanging on the walls, and drank hot tea.

A few months later, in 1840, at Saratov, their brother Leonid was born.

But the medical facilities of the city of Saratov (30,000 population at that time) did nothing to help the sickly young mother, and she returned to her husband in the Ukraine for a time. But the end was drawing near.

In the early spring of 1842 she went to Odessa for mineral water treatments, taking her three children, two governesses, and personal physician who was now always in attendance. Odessa, swiftly growing as a Black Sea port for the agricultural steppe, was a painfully long way from the grandparents at Saratov. But though coaches were uncomfortable and roads rough in those days, the Russian nobility seem to have traveled frequently over immense distances, especially when family affairs were at stake.

It was a very strong family reason which now, in May 1842, drew the Governor of Saratov and his wife to Odessa. The seemingly endless steppe still wore its green cloak of luxuriant grass and young wheat when the de Faydeyev couple, both now fifty-three years of age, made their arduous journey from Saratov to see their daughter in Odessa.

As yet only twenty-eight years old, with nine novels to her credit, the fine-spirited Helena Andreyevna von Hahn was dying. Her black, eloquent eyes looked larger than ever in the pale face, and it seemed certain now that nothing could be done to combat the dread tuberculosis. Nothing but pray, and try to hide their sorrow from the little girls (Leonid was only two) and wait for the end.

This came in midsummer, on July 6, 1842. Soon afterward eleven-year-old Helena, Vera (aged seven), and baby Leonid were taken by their grandparents over the treeless, brown expanses of the autumn steppe to Saratov.

A new life was to begin for the child Helena Petrovna. After the nomadic existence with an unhappy, preoccupied mother, and a romantic, but usually absent, father she was to come under the influence, and discipline, of one of the most outstanding women of her times.

CHAPTER 2

Lady Hester Lucy Stanhope, whose brains Mr. Pitt, her uncle, had admired, whose beauty Mr. Brummell praised, who played the secret game for England in Syria, had seen most of the world and met many of its interesting people. Often she traveled dressed as a man—sometimes, in the East, magnificently—with gold embroidered pantaloons, satin vest, and gold burnouse, carrying a sabre.

She wrote of the people who impressed her most, and in her book about Russia, this haughty, pipe-smoking English aristocrat said: "In that barbarian land I met an outstanding woman-scientist, who would have been famous in Europe, but who is completely underestimated due to her misfortune of being born on the shores of the Volga river, where there was none to recognize her scientific value."[1]

Helena Pavlovna de Fadeyev, nee Princess Dolgorukov, spoke five languages, was a student of natural science, especially geology and botany, kept a private museum of rare specimens and wrote books on her studies in natural science, archaeology, and numismatics.

Nor, despite what Lady Stanhope said, was she entirely unrecognized by the leading *savants* of her day with whom she carried on a correspondence. Mr. Ignace-Xavier Hommaire-de-Hell, geologist and traveler, who met Madame de Fadeyev, wrote of her as an outstanding scientist who helped him in his researches;[2] the President of the London

Geographical Society, Sir Robert Murchison, paid her a visit in the remote Ukranian steppe, and, it is said, named a fossil shell in her honor. It is not stated whether she regarded this as a compliment.

This remarkable Dolgorukov princess, noble in mind, manners and appearance, became the dominant influence in the life of her granddaughter, Helena Petrovna von Hahn.

The house they lived in at Saratov also had its powerful influence on the child's mind. It has been described as an "immense old castle-like mansion, where the long lofty halls were hung with portraits of the Dolgorukovs and Fadeyevs." Under the house were gloomy corridors and caverns, said to be haunted by the ghosts of serfs beaten to death by a former tyrannous steward.

These subterranean corridors seemed to have an irresistible attraction for little Helena. Often the child walked in her sleep, and after a fruitless search everywhere else, a party of terrified servants would have to brave the haunted caverns. There they would be sure to find Helena engrossed in conversation with someone invisible to everyone but herself. Frequently in her waking hours she would go there, too, to dream in solitude, or to play with her invisible companions, including the little hunchback boy.

From early childhood Helena lived in two worlds. One was the mystical world to which no one around her had a key, not even her wise old grandmother. But it was intensely vivid and real to her, though it held many strange mysteries.

The other was a tomboy world, a world of huge enjoyment where she must have her own way at all costs. It was in this man's world that she had learned to swear roundly with her father's soldiers, and to ride any Cossack horse, bare-backed or using a man's saddle. But even in her most daredevil tomboy escapades the other world sometimes intruded itself. Once, for instance, she was galloping wildly across the steppe when the horse got out of hand. It bolted and suddenly swerved sharply, throw-

ing her out of the saddle. Her foot caught in the stirrup,
and she hung down, head and shoulders reaching the
ground, while the horse galloped homeward. Many riders
have been badly injured or killed in this kind of accident,
and it seems nothing short of a miracle that this 14-year-
old girl was not. She felt distinctly around her, she relates, "a strange sustaining power" which seemed to hold
her up in defiance of gravitation. She was quite unhurt
when the horse was finally stopped.

Her two worlds were united beautifully when she entertained her young friends—and sometimes her older
ones—with colorful, often terrifying, tales woven around
her grandmother's fossils, stuffed animals, skulls, skele-
tons.

"She used to dream aloud," recalled sister Vera, "and
tell us of her visions, evidently clear, vivid and as pal-
pable as life to her. How lovely the description she gave
us of the submarine life of all those beings! . . . How
vividly she described their past fights and battles . . .
assuring us that she saw it all!"

Sometimes she would tell her stories lying on the
ground in the open; then she would draw in the sand
with her finger the fantastic forms of long-dead monsters,
some bone fragments of which were lying in the sand
around her. She would describe their colors and surroundings with such striking clearness that her listeners
would be transported to a savage prehistoric world, and
the children would shiver with fright.

She had a wonderful imagination, said her elders, but
perhaps it was something more than that—an inborn
faculty of psychometric clairvoyance that opened the
door to an akashic picture gallery of the long-dead past.

In the everyday world Helena was impatient of all
restraint. It was as if the Dolgorukov strain in her found
it very difficult to take orders—except where she felt the
greatest respect for the one commanding. Such respect
had nothing to do with a person's station or position of
authority. In her grandmother she seemed to recognize
an inherent wisdom, and mostly she bowed to the old

lady's will—but not always, especially if her curiosity was piqued.

High up on a wall in the old house was a picture covered by a curtain. What was behind that curtain, she wanted to know. Just a portrait of one of her ancestors, she was told. *Why* was it hidden, then, and could she see it? No, she could *not!*

Little Miss Hahn decided that, in that case, it must be something very intriguing indeed. She awaited her opportunity to find out for herself. One day when the coast seemed clear, she dragged a table up to the wall, set a smaller table on top of it, and a chair on top of that. Then she climbed onto this shaky scaffold, and found that she could just reach the curtain that hid the mystery. Leaning with one hand against the dusty wall for balance she drew the curtain aside.

The effect of what she saw was evidently quite startling, she made an involuntary backward movement, and upset her precarious equilibrium. In the fright from the situation or the fall itself she seems to have lost consciousness. For the next thing she knew she was lying on the floor, quite unhurt. More amazing still, the tables and chair she had used were neatly back in their accustomed places, and the curtain was again across the face of the picture.

Had she dreamed it all? she wondered. No, for there was the imprint of her small hand, high up on the wall over the picture.

What strong arms had caught and saved her? Certainly, none of the elders, otherwise there would have been a great lot of fuss. It must have been, she thought, the very tall, dark man she sometimes saw in visions. Perhaps too, it had been his arms that had held her up when she was dragged by the horse. She felt that it was. Surely he must be her guardian angel, her invisible protector!

A flesh-and-blood character who appealed to her deep yearning for a "wise old man" to answer the many riddles about life was a centenarian who lived in a forest ravine not far from the banks of the Volga. In popular estimation this man was a real magician, but in the main of the benevolent kind. He cured the worthy ones who came to him but punished with disease those who had sinned. He could also foretell the future, it was said.

Certain it was that he had a way with bees, and also with the birds and animals of the forest. Helena would find him walking among his hives, covered from head to foot with swarms of buzzing bees. Or he would plunge his hands into their dwelling places, talking to them in a strange language which they seemed to understand. They never stung him.

Helena would sit with him by his hut, listening earnestly to his explanations of how to understand the language of bees and wild life, and the occult properties of plants. She would put questions to him on all manner of things, showing great eagerness to learn.

Her governesses did not find however, that Helena was as eager for formal learning, though she did have a gift for languages and music. The only books she read avidly, when she could get them, were not regarded as the business of a young lady being groomed for a suitable marriage and her rightful place in high society. Of what value were magic, alchemy, and such to a lady of noble birth?

Fortunately there were places in the cellars and attics of the old house and the dense woods near the Volga, where she could hide away from her tutors and spend hours reading books full of strange lore. Such volumes could be found, if one knew where to look, in the great library at her grandfather's house.

Much later in life she wrote about this to Prince Dondukoff-Korsakoff, then Governor-General of the City of Odessa: "My great grandfather on my mother's side, Prince Paul Vasilyevitch Dolgorukov, had a strange library containing hundreds of books on alchemy, magic and other occult sciences. I had read them with the keenest interest before the age of 15. All the devilries of the Middle Ages had found refuge in my head and soon neither Paracelsus, Khunrath nor C. Agreppa would have had anything to teach me."[3]

The years passed. The year 1845 brought a month's visit from her father, now forty-seven, and a Colonel, with patches of grey at the temples and few wrinkles on his handsome face. Later in the same year Helena spent some time with an uncle near the Ural mountains, along the borders of Mongolian lands.

Next year her grandfather was made Director of the Department of State Lands in Transcaucasia, and set off with his wife to live south of the Caucasus mountains, in Tiflis. The Hahn children did not accompany them immediately, but instead went with their Aunt Katherine—their mother's sister now married to Yuliy F. de Witte—to vacation at a country house on the farther side of the Volga. The two inevitable governesses were of the party, but cousin Serguey de Witte, the future Prime Minister of Russia, and alleged traducer of Helena Petrovna, was not yet born.

Early in May 1847 the children, with Aunt Katherine and a governess, started on the long journey to Tiflis. From Saratov they traveled by boat down the Volga to Astrakhan at its mouth, thence by another ship over the Caspian Sea to Baku. Disembarking at this port, they set off in horse-drawn coaches up the valley of the Kura river and through the mountain passes to Tiflis.

Helena's grandparents, and 19-year-old Aunt Nadyezhda, came part of the way to meet the travelers, and then all enjoyed vacationing together at several places on the homeward journey. It was nearly two months after the party had set off from Saratov when they finally reached Tiflis.

Here Helena's grandparents lived in the Chavchavadze Mansion, formerly the home of Prince Alexander Gersevanovich Chavchavadze, the well-known Georgian poet, whose eldest daughter, Nina, married the great Russian writer Griboyedov.

But it was not a happy home for teen-age Helena; she suffered much from what she regarded as the tyranny of stuffy governesses and the firm discipline of her grandmother. She was constantly in a state of rebellion at their restrictions, concerned mostly with social conventions, which she regarded as meaningless and stupid. She sometimes cooled her violent resentments by a long, wild gallop on the most spirited horse she could find in the stables. At other times she buried herself for hours in some old book on travel, magic, alchemy, or some other branch of occult lore.

One of the many visitors who came to the de Fadeyev home in Tiflis was Nikifor Vassilyevich Blavatsky. Mr. Blavatsky was losing his hair and to young Helena he seemed a very old man; she called him a "plumeless raven." In fact, however, he was only forty. There were some things about Mr. Blavatsky that she found mildly interesting. He knew Transcaucasia well, having served there for some years in various Civil Government posts; he had just returned from a short residence in Persia, and had been appointed Vice-Governor of the newly-formed Province of Yerivan which lay farther south in the mountains of Armenia. In effect he governed the province in the absence of its Military Governor.

Another point in Blavatsky's favor was the fact that he never laughed at her profound interest in things occult, as did the young men of her acquaintance. Moreover he told her most interesting stories about the sorcerers of Armenia, about the mysterious sciences of the Kurds and the Persians, and he claimed to have a collection of rare occult books himself. Yes, Nikifor V. Blavatsky, even though rather a fool, was better company than the young bloods who thought of nothing but drinking, hunting, and sex—three things Helena held in absolute horror.

But, in another man who often called on the family and had long wonderful talks with her, she recognized a much more serious and much better informed student of the occult. This was Prince Galitzin, a relative of the Viceroy of the Caucasus, and popularly regarded as "either a Freemason, or a magician, or a fortune-teller."

It was sometime during the winter of 1848-49 that Helena—then seventeen—became betrothed to Nikifor V.

Blavatsky. Research has established with fair certainty that this was the period of the betrothal, but the reason for it still remains a mystery.

However, it does seem that the maiden had strong misgivings during the next few months, and, as rumor had it, ran away from home following Prince Galitzin who had left Tiflis some time earlier.[4]

The story originates in a biographical sketch written by Madame Pissareva for the Russian public. She asserts that it was told to her by Madame Yermolov who was the wife of the Governor of Tiflis between the years 1840 and 1850. All the Yermolovs were intimate friends of the de Fadeyev family at the time of the betrothal and the events surrounding it.

It is not difficult to imagine the scandal this must have caused in provincial social circles, and the consternation in family circles. The grandparents would be more than ever anxious to get their wayward charge married off as quickly as possible. Would Blavatsky still be willing?

It has been suggested, too, that Prince Galitzin gave the earnest young student of occultism some vital information at this time, including the address of an occultist in Egypt, and that he made arrangements for her to travel abroad in the company of another Russian lady.

But first there was the little matter of the marriage with Vice-Governor N.V. Blavatsky.

CHAPTER 3

Several reasons have been advanced by biographers for Helena's willingness to marry a man she neither loved nor really admired. Some say she was pressed into it gently and hopefully by her family. But she was hardly the kind of young lady who could be forced into anything against her will, for the sake of appearances. She evidently accepted the idea; it has even been suggested that she saw marriage as a gateway to freedom from the irksome restraints imposed by tutors, grandparents, and other relatives. She was virtually an orphan, as her father was always away with his regiment, and every grown-up relative was ready and anxious to tell her just what she ought to do. Marriage would lift her above all that and initiate her into the greater independence of womanhood. These considerations may have been in her mind.

Her Aunt Nadyezhda gives another reason and writes of an incident at the great house in Tiflis one day when Helena's stormy temper had been even more trying than usual to one of her governesses.

"You'll never find a man to marry you; even the 'plumeless raven,' as you call him would not take such a spitfire as you for wife," taunted the governess.

"That's all you know," Helena retorted, "I could make him propose anytime—the next time I see him, in fact."

The governess gave an incredulous laugh: "I'll believe *that* when it happens."

Three days later Mr. Blavatsky called and, before he left the house, had proposed to the seventeen-year-old Miss Hahn—and had been accepted.

No doubt her acceptance was necessary, initially, in order to prove to her challenger that the proposal of marriage did, in fact, take place. But, had she really wanted to, there must have been some way in which she could have broken the engagement before the wedding, even with relatives applying considerable pressure to get her safely off their hands into matrimony.

Perhaps the escapade with the Prince was an expression of her fear at the thought of marriage to Blavatsky, and an attempt to break the engagement. If so it did not work. Apparently Mr. Blavatsky was unaffected. His ego may have been flattered that an attractive, spirited young seventeen-year-old had agreed to be his wife.

On Helena's side the perceptible reasons—escape from family restraints and access to new areas for occult study —do not seem strong enough motives to take someone of her character into a loveless marriage. So it may be there were occult reasons for the marriage which she never revealed.

Whatever the facts, to the pleasant surprise of her elders, the betrothal held. In June of 1849 she was taken by a large family group, including the de Wittes and Uncle Rostislav (her mother's brother), to Gerger in the vicinity of Yerivan. Aunt Katherine de Witte was pregnant and, just before the wedding, gave birth to Russia's future Prime Minister, Serguey Yulyevich de Witte.

The baby was only eight days old when all gathered in the church at the settlement of Kamenka, on July 7, for the colorful marriage ceremony. Everything went according to plan, except that when the bride was told she must obey her husband, one standing close by saw her turn pale and heard her mutter: "Surely, I shall not!" But apparently the priest heard nothing amiss, and her family members breathed a sigh of relief when the young rebel was formally pronounced the wife of Vice-Governor Nikifor V. Blavatsky.

On the same day the bridal couple left for Darachichag (Valley of Flowers), a mountain resort near Yerivan. Here amidst the great beauties of nature the couple began what must have been a very unhappy honeymoon. They had entirely different and opposing ideas about the meaning of the nuptial bond. Nikifor expected it to be a normal marriage, with its consummation to take place in the lovely, remote mountain valley. But the poor man was married to a strong-willed occultist who was quite determined to remain a virgin.

Helena tried to forget the nightly emotional battles of will—and the matrimonial trap into which she had walked —by going for long rides through the valleys at the foot of Mount Ararat. Sometimes she thought of escape, but always behind her was a member of the Governor's body-guard, a Kurd tribal chieftain by the name of Safar Ali Bek Ibrahim Bek Ogli. The Kurd was respectful and very protective—far too protective and far too good a horseman—for Helena to carry out her ideas of quick escape.

Unhappy days dragged on into weeks, with no improvement in the tense situation. There were no interesting books to read at this holiday resort; there were only the mountains—like prison walls—and Blavatsky her jailor. It was ironical that what she had anticipated as a way of liberation from restrictions was proving a worse and more loathsome restriction. As her Yorkshire governess would have said, she had jumped out of the frying pan into the fire.

Temporary respite came with the arrival of her grand-parents and aunts after about two months of honeymoon horrors. It was then the end of August, and after a few days the whole party set off for the town of Yerivan.

It proved to be a poor, straggling city of the plains, whose only beauty was Mount Ararat of eternal snows, some forty miles off, brooding in majestic calm, a contrasting background to the mean, dingy streets.

About the only thing that pleased Helena about her new home was the fact that in the garden there was "an enormous column, a ruin from the palace of Tyridates, all covered with inscriptions." She had these translated and explained by a learned monk from the Echmiadzin monastery. Here, she believed, was part of the cradle of the Akkadian tribe that had left Armenia to become the ancient Chaldeans.[1]

But apart from this diversion, and the pleasure of some new occult books in the library the city was an ugly cage. Grandparents and aunts had returned to Tiflis, over a hundred miles away across the mountains; she was alone again with Blavatsky.

Despite the utter failure of the honeymoon, Nikifor had not given up hope of gaining his conjugal rights. The foolish moods of a young bride would pass, he thought, and it was high time that they did pass. He became more forceful and dominant, more insistent. The battle of the wills became more and more intolerable and exhausting.

Her desire for escape, for flight, grew more urgent. She began to feel as if she must get away from a mortal danger. One morning, following a night of quarreling more violent than usual, Helena tied her crinkly blond hair in a tight knot behind her head. In the mirror she observed the cold light that had replaced the usual vivacity in her blue eyes. The time had come to act. She put on her riding hat and packed a few personal requirements in a saddlebag.

As soon as she heard her husband leave for his office, she went straight to the stables and ordered a groom to saddle her favorite Cossack horse. He was a strong, hardy animal and would, like herself, do the journey over the mountains in the hours of a long day.

It was important that she get away quickly as at any moment the Vice-Governor was likely to send Ali Bek to accompany her wherever she might go. And from him she could never escape. So she told the groom at the stables that she intended to ride southward, and set off in that direction. Then, when out of his sight, she turned north and galloped across the plain toward the hills and mountains that stood between her and Tiflis.

No one at the Tiflis mansion, except perhaps her young sister Vera, was overjoyed at the sudden and dramatic appearance of the travel-stained Madame Helena Blavatsky. What to do with her now was the big question. At a family council next day it was decided that her father must solve the problem.

But Colonel Peter von Hahn was in the far north, near

St. Petersburg. Furthermore, he had only just remarried, to a Baroness von Lange. Still, the problem woman was genuinely *his* problem. The grandparents had done their best, they thought, in getting her safely married; they would have taken her back to her husband now, only they knew full well by her threats that she would simply find a way of escaping again and go somewhere else, which would be worse.

They wrote a letter to her father, asking him to see her, talk with her, and decide on the best course of action. He replied in due course that he was unable to come as far as Tiflis, but would meet his errant daughter at Odessa if they could arrange to have her suitably escorted to that City on the Black Sea coast.

Helena gathered from the tone of his letter, part of which was read to her, that the Colonel was not likely to take a very lenient line with his troublesome daughter. He would most probably order her to return to Nikifor Blavatsky. Such a thing could not be tolerated. So it was better that she did not see her father, much as she loved him. Nevertheless, she must pretend to go along with the plans of the elders.

Thus while her grandparents made thorough and detailed arrangements for her journey, she was busy hatching her own plans. It was a long trip to Odessa, the best route being through the mountain valleys to the port of Poti on the Black Sea, and from there on by ship. The grandparents chose two trusty, reliable servants (one an old retainer) to accompany Helena all the way until she met her father.

But Helena intended, at some point along the route, to give her escort the slip. This was to be the big break, the departure from Russia, the beginning of the great search. It was, of course, an incredibly daring adventure for a young lady of eighteen to contemplate at that time. And it seems likely, as some say, that her plans were linked with information and help given her by Prince Galitzin, the occultist, and that he arranged for her to meet a Russian traveler, Countess Kisselev, soon after leaving Russian soil.

CHAPTER 4

In a letter to Prince Alexander Dondukoff-Korsakoff written over thirty years after these events, Helena stated: "What I wanted and searched for was the subtle magnetism that one exchanges, the human 'salt', and father Blavatsky did not have it; and to find it and obtain it, I was ready to sacrifice myself, to dishonour myself!"[1]

Her great search was, basically, for the symbolic philosopher's stone, that which transmutes the lead of human nature into the kingly gold of divine nature. Dr. Franz Hartmann, in his book, *Paracelsus,* calls it the solid rock upon which the foundation of one's spiritual house is built. "It is the Christ in man; divine love substantialized. It is the light of the world; the very essence of that of which the world has been created; it is not mere spirit but substantial."

H.P.B. realized before leaving Tiflis that once aboard the steamer at Poti there would be no escape. It would take her directly to Odessa where Colonel von Hahn would be waiting to receive her. So she must somehow miss the steamer.

But the old retainer thought only of his master's orders, and was determined to get to the port on time. Helena tried in every possible way to delay progress, without letting the old man guess her intentions; and so the 200-mile journey through the hills of Transcaucasia became a battle of wits.

She won by a narrow margin. When they reached Poti the vessel had just sailed. But there was in port a small sailing vessel, the *Commodore,* flying the English flag, and Helena consoled the old servant by saying that she would inquire if that would take them to Odessa.

She went aboard and saw the captain. He told her that he was sailing to Kertch on the Crimean peninsula, on to Taganrog at the far north of the Sea of Azov, then back through the Straits and across the Black Sea to Constantinople.

"Good," said the eighteen-year-old aristocrat, "I will go with you to Constantinople."

But that was impossible, he informed her, he had no accommodation for passengers. The Yorkshire governess had not managed to equip her with a ready supply of fluent English, but she carried what she imagined was an endless supply of roubles. She offered the captain a large sum to take her and the two servants as passengers. He succumbed.

At Kertch, where the servants imagined the party was disembarking, she sent the old retainer and maid-servant ashore to find and prepare suitable accommodations for her. She would leave the ship next morning, she told them, and then all would stay at Kertch until they found transport to Odessa, either by land or sea. Having no suspicions of her true intentions, they dutifully went ashore.

That night the *Commodore* sailed out of the port with Helena aboard. Next morning she stood on deck feeling light and free, as free as the seagulls skimming over the Sea of Azov.

On the voyage Helena learned that not all men would treat her as she wished to be treated—as one of themselves. The captain evidently found her physically alluring and seemed to think she was very much in his power. She decided that this, the first Englishman of her acquaintance, was more of a pig than a skipper.

Their ship anchored some distance offshore at Constantinople, but the captain made no attempt to put her ashore. It was very difficult and too risky, he told her. There were evidently to be no more favors until *she* gave some. And he did not mean roubles this time.

So she decided to try her luck with the steward who had been friendly and seemed a decent fellow. Could he hire one of the caiques in the harbor? She would pay for it, of course, and pay him well for his trouble. The steward was afraid of the captain and hesitated. But with a handful of roubles, she finally persuaded him.

One evening several days later when the captain was ashore, a caique carried Helena and her luggage from the *Commodore* and landed them at a quiet spot. The fascinating, if somewhat frightening, city of Constantinople lay before her.

She tells of an event in Constantinople which may have taken place during this first visit, as she was probably already getting short of funds. But it could have been on a later visit to the city.

"At Constantinople I was in need of money and I wanted to earn the 1000 offered to the one who won the *steeplechase*—18 fences to jump with a wild horse which had just killed two grooms. I jumped 16 but at the 17th my horse reared and fell backwards and *crushed* me. I saw a man, a giant, dressed differently from the Turks, who lifted my tattered and bloody garments from under the horse and—nothing more, nothing but the memory of a face I had seen somewhere."[2] He was the same mysterious Protector who had previously appeared at times of great need.

In other ways, too, she either had unseen help in the dangerous Turkish capital, or previous arrangements *had* been made, as suggested, for her to meet with an old family acquaintance, Countess Kisselev. Anyway, accounts of the next few years, admittedly vague, show her traveling with the Countess in Turkey, Greece, Egypt, and France. In Egypt, Helena met the Copt occultist, Paulos Metamon, whose address she had from Prince Galitzin. He was a man of considerable property and influence, "and of a great reputation as a magician."

Next we hear of her in the company of another Russian aristocrat and friend of her family, the Princess Bagration-Muhransky. With this lady she toured various European

countries and went to London, where they stayed for a
time at Mivart's Hotel (now Claridge's). Some versions
of her story state that her father spent time in London with
her in 1851, but in a letter to Sinnett, Helena herself
says she was not with her father but, after the Princess
left, alone "in a big hotel somewhere between City and
Strand or in the Strand, but as to names or numbers you
might just as well ask me to tell you what was the number
of the house you lived in during your last incarnation."
The past, especially dates and numbers, seemed to put on
the insubstantial cloak of dreams in her memory.

A highly significant event in her life took place at about
this time in England, though again the facts of time
and setting are confused. In a travel sketchbook she records it as happening at Ramsgate on August 12, 1851.
But later she told friends that it actually took place in
London, and that the mention of Ramsgate was a "blind"
to mislead anyone looking through the sketchbook. She
had, she indicated, good reasons for not writing down
the actual facts.

She relates that one day while walking in the street,
her attention was attracted to the colorful and pleasing
sight of some Indian princes. One of them was exception-
ally tall. Gazing at his face, she recognized with a leap
of her heart the very man she had so often seen in visions,
the one she called her Protector. Here he was, unbelievably, in the flesh, and in a fine uniform, walking in a
London street. Her first impulse was to rush forward and
speak to him, but he made a sign that held her back, and
she stood spellbound while he passed on with his friends.

The next day some inner urge made her go for a walk in
Hyde Park, which was just across the street from Mivart's.
She sat down on a park bench alone, thinking about the
thrilling encounter of the day before. Could she have
dreamed it? But no, for, unbelievably again, here he was
now, walking with long strides across the grass toward
her. Had he known she would be here? The whole of
her being seemed to lift up toward him, and she was
flooded with a tremendous joy. She knew at that moment

that she would do anything in the world for this Great One. On the surface he was a handsome, majestic, heart-stirring Indian Prince. But she knew he was much more than that.

She tried to stand, but he gestured her back gently and sat beside her. He told her that he was in London on an important mission with some other Indian princes and, of course, knew that he would meet *her* here and be able to talk to her.

Helena could scarcely believe her ears.

He went on to tell her that he had some important things to impart about the future and wanted to request her cooperation in a great work for mankind that he, and others, would be starting.

She did not care very much about mankind at this time, but she was willing to do anything he asked.

He warned her, however, that the task would be far from easy and gave her some idea of the tremendous problems and troubles that would surely come. She must think about it well before deciding, he said, and he would see her again somewhere. Meantime he would help her whenever necessary, as he had before. Eventually, if she was willing to assist in the great work, she would have to spend time in Tibet in order to prepare for her unique role.

From that day her life took on a new significance. Now she began to understand that she was not seeking occult knowledge for its own sake alone, but in preparation for special work assigned to her from some high level. And she had found the man she could truly love, honor, and *obey*. He was not a figment of her mind, but *real!* To others' eyes he might appear to be just another Indian prince, but she knew he was no ordinary mortal.

CHAPTER 5

There is no guidebook to the centers of esoteric knowledge; occult gold is where you find it. Realizing this, Helena set off from London on a world-wandering trail.

This took her first to the Red Indians in Canada, but from them she learned only that they were first-class thieves. Then she went in search of the Mormons in Illinois. But here again her "occult nose" failed, and she found that the Mormons had just fled, under the leadership of Brigham Young, into the western wilderness.

Helena's next throw was a rash one. She went straight to the center of sorcery in New Orleans, planning to look into the secrets of Voodooism. But before she got too far involved in this dark aspect of witchcraft, her Guardian took a hand. Suddenly appearing—extracorporeally this time—he warned her that she was meddling with sinister forces that should be left alone.

So she traveled farther southward through Texas to Mexico and on through Central America to Peru. Remnants of ancient civilizations in those places were to her purpose.

By 1852 we find her in the West Indies with a "certain Englishman" who is mentioned in several documents on her life, but is never named. We know that she had met him on the first occasion in Germany, soon after leaving Russia, and discovered that he was on the same kind of search as herself. Now she joined forces with him and a Hindu she had met in Mexico, who, she thought at the time, was a pupil of a hidden brotherhood of Adepts.

The three decided to go to India together. They sailed around the Cape to Ceylon and thence to Bombay. This was Helena's first visit to the land of her great destiny. Dates in the stories are vague, but this was probably toward the end of 1852.

The trio soon broke up, however, each apparently having different exploration plans. Helena had her eyes set on Tibet where she hoped to see her Protector. She made a bold bid to reach the forbidden land, but the time was not yet and, the Protector giving no help, her attempt failed.

Foiled in this ambition, she went down to southern India for a time, and then returned to England by way of Singapore and Java.

Most chroniclers of her life agree that she was in England some time in 1853 and stayed there through part of 1854, possibly until after Czar Nicholas I declared war on England in April 1854 and the Crimean struggle began in earnest. Her sister Vera, writing of this period, says that Helena was a member of the Philharmonic Society of London and had been retained there on a contract. Many have spoken of Helena's outstanding ability as a pianist.

She says herself that during these months in London she saw her "mysterious Hindu" again "in the house of a stranger." He had come over to England this time in the company of a dethroned native prince. This would probably be Prince Dhuleep Singh Maharaja of Lahore who was later presented to Queen Victoria. He and party arrived at Southhampton in June 1854, so Helena's meeting with her Protector must have taken place just before she left the country. At this interview her tall, turbaned Guardian told her, she relates, that her destiny lay in India, seat of the mission to come, but later, "in twenty-eight or thirty years." However, in the meantime, there was no reason why she should not spend time there and get to know the country.

It may have been during this period in London, or the earlier one, that, feeling terribly depressed by her failure to find what she sought, she stood one day on Waterloo Bridge contemplating suicide. "The muddy water of the Thames seemed to me a delicious bed."[1] But before she could jump, the mysterious figure of her Guardian stood beside her (she does not say whether or not in the physical body). He cleared away her depression by assuring her that her search would not be in vain, that she would find the "philosopher's stone."

Although it was some five years since she had set out on the fateful flight from Yerivan, and had already encircled the globe, she had no desire to return to Russia. Better the rigors of world travel in odd places than the security of the Blavatsky mansion.

The summer of 1854 found her in New York, then Chicago, then in a covered wagon with a caravan of pioneers going westward. On this journey she finally made contact with the Mormons at Salt Lake City, Utah. There she was the guest of Mrs. Emmeline Blanche (Woodward) Wells, Editor and Publisher of *The Woman's Exponent,* who told the tale to her granddaughter, mentioning the fact that Madame Blavatsky was wearing heavy men's shoes.

From California Helena may have made another journey to Mexico and South America. At any rate, sometime in 1855 she crossed the pacific to Japan where she met some members of the Yamabushi brotherhood. From Japan she sailed to India and began the enthralling task of getting to know that mysterious country.

Here we find another witness whose shoes trod the same dust as Helena's for a time. This was a German ex-Lutheran minister, Herr Kuhlwein, probably related to her old governess of that name. He had come to India on a mystic quest of his own and was actually on the lookout for the young Madame Blavatsky. Colonel von Hahn had asked Herr Kuhlwein to try to make contact with his wandering daughter. The Colonel was supplying her with money as occasion allowed, but was still, no doubt, greatly concerned about her safety and welfare.

The German did manage to meet her, perhaps not such a difficult task, as Russian travelers would be a rarity in

British India during the Crimean War. They met at Lahore where Kuhlwein and two companions, "the Brothers N - -," were hatching a plot to penetrate Tibet under various disguises. Helena, eager to make another assault on the forbidden land, joined the project. They went together into Kashmir to Srinegar, and through the Sind valley to Leh, 11,550 feet up toward the sources of the Indus. From Leh, the chief city of Kadakh, there are several routes into Tibet proper, while to its northwest and west lies the territory sometimes called Little Tibet.

According to A.P. Sinnett, the three men were unable to get into Tibet, but, with the valuable aid of a Tartar shaman, Helena managed to cross the border into either Tibet or Little Tibet.[2]

In her book *Isis Unveiled* H.P. Blavatsky writes about some of her experiences with the shaman who had marked telepathic and other extrasensory powers. She tells how he used these powers to call a party of twenty-five Lamaist horsemen to her rescue on one occasion when she was in a critical situation.

Another story says that it was on the other side of India, near Darjeeling, that she made an attempt at about that time to reach Tibet. But she did not get through because a British army officer, Lieutenant Murray, who was commanding the frontier there, turned her back.

Murray, himself, many years later when he was a Major-General (retired) told Colonel Olcott and another witness the story of how one of his guards had found Madame Blavatsky somewhere near the frontier. She was conducted to Murray's home where she met his wife and remained for about a month as their guest.

Beatrice Hastings[3] attempts to remove the apparent contradiction between the two stories with the credible theory that when Murray's soldier found Helena alone near the border, she was not going into Tibet, but returning from it. If so, she may have made her entry earlier in the northwest through Kashmir as other accounts state.

After leaving Lieutenant Murray's house, she disappeared into the great Indian subcontinent. Her experiences of that time, she told Sinnett, would make a whole book.[4] And she did, in fact, later write a book about it, or at least a series of pieces for the *Moscow News* that were later published as a book, *Caves and Jungles of Hindustan.* Her pen name for this, and other Russian writings, was "Radda-Bai." But the book is not a strictly factual account of her experiences; it is rather a highly imaginative concoction of fact-and-fiction, written in a style that established her literary reputation with Russian editors.

To a friend she says about this period in India: "I was in a dream. I stayed nearly two years, traveling about and receiving money each month—from whom I have no idea, and following faithfully the itinerary given to me. I received letters from this Hindu [her Protector], but *I did not see him a single time during those two years.*"[5]

The India of that day—Kipling's India—was full of grave dangers to the traveler. But Helena had her invisible Protector, and furthermore, she often traveled as a man, dressed in men's clothes (for "I was very thin then," she states).

Before the outbreak of the Sepoy Mutiny in 1857, she was ordered by her mysterious Hindu, by letter, to go to Java "for a certain business" and then return to Europe.

Back in Europe she traveled in France and Germany. Then toward the end of 1858, nine years after she had left home, she felt an overpowering urge to see her family once more. She was twenty-seven years old by then, a mature woman who had twice circumnavigated the globe, living in outlandish places, seeing and learning things far beyond the wildest dreams of the home-keeping folk she longed to see. Surely there was no danger, now at last, that they would try to dominate her life, or return her to N.V. Blavatsky! Perhaps by now Nikifor's ardent passion for her had cooled off, anyway. She fervently hoped so as her nostalgic footsteps turned toward the soil of Russia.

CHAPTER 6

When he knew where to reach her, Colonel von Hahn would send money to his daughter Helena, but sometimes for long intervals he would hear nothing from her and wonder whether she was still alive. He knew that Vera never received a letter from her, either, and he understood this was true of the whole de Faydeyev family.

Although the family never heard *from* her, they sometimes heard *of* her, through some scandalous rumor that reached as far south as Tiflis. But most of them preferred not to believe such stories. Some thought that the long silence meant she was dead. Otherwise surely she would have written a line to those she loved!

Vice-Governor Nikifor Blavatsky had tried to get his marriage annulled, but the Church had refused. So he had accepted his fate as a grass widower, hoping soon to retire to his country estate "in that hidden corner which nobody knows of, and live there surrounded by the delights of a lonely life. . . . I have got used to a joyless life at Yerivan," he wrote to Helena's favorite aunt, Nadyezhda.[1]

A few years after Helena's flight from Russia, her sister Vera had married a man named Nikolay de Yahontov. But he had died and, on Christmas night, 1858, the young widow, with her two infant sons, was staying with her father-in-law, General de Yahontov at Pskov in northern Russia. Colonel von Hahn, still erect and handsome, was there, too. He had not heard from his prodigal daughter for a very long time, and there was no thought of her as the Christmas guests gathered.

The party was a special one, for, at the same time the wedding of Vera's sister-in-law was being celebrated. Troikas and sleighs full of guests, with bells jingling merrily, kept arriving over the snow; servants scurried to answer the hall bell that seemed never to stop ringing. A babble of greetings and conversation filled the great reception rooms. Champagne corks popped under the glittering chandeliers.

Finally, all were sitting at the banquet, and a happy but solemn moment had arrived. The best man stood up with a glass in his hand to propose a toast to the bridal pair. He waited for silence and was about to launch into his carefully prepared speech when the front-door bell rang again in a commanding tone.

A sudden and strange intuition came to Vera; she was certain that the person ringing the bell was her long-lost sister. It was a crazy idea, she knew, but her heart leaped with excitement, and, before a servant could move, she had left the table and rushed to the entrance door.

There, incredibly but surely, wrapped in a snow-flecked cloak, stood Helena. Too overcome to speak, but with tears of joy in their eyes, the sisters embraced. Then Vera led her sister to the wedding feast.

A great hush fell over the company. A moment later Colonel von Hahn, wiping his greying moustache, leaped to his feet, and everyone began talking at once. Helena's eyes shone with love for her countrymen, and with delight at the drama of her entry. It was quite a time before the best man got back to his speech and his toast.

Before her sudden appearance at Pskov, Helena had made contact with her grandparents and her Aunt Nadyezhda at Tiflis in the South. She had evidently written to them from somewhere in or near Russia, for Mr. N.V. Blavatsky, at Yerivan, had received a letter from Nadyezhda on November 12, 1858, to which he replied on the next day, saying: "Until now I knew nothing of H.P.'s return to Russia. To tell you the truth, this ceased to interest me long ago. Time smooths out everything, even every memory. You may assure H.P. on my word of honor that

I will never pursue her."

According to family memoirs, written later by both Vera and Nadyezhda, when Helena Petrovna Blavatsky arrived back in Russia she was even more of a "haunted woman" than the girl who went away.

"Raps and whisperings, sounds mysterious and unexplained, were now being constantly heard wherever the newly-arrived inmate went . . . knocks were heard and movements of the furniture perceived nearly in every room of the house, on the walls, the floor, the windows, the sofa, cushions, mirrors and clocks; on every piece of furniture, in short, about the rooms."[2] Although from childhood strange things had happened around Helena, the phenomena were now much more frequent and insistent. It seemed as though she were surrounded by invisible beings for whom she provided a ready source of psychic power. To some extent she could control these manifestations by her will, but they were largely quite beyond her control. She found them a great nuisance and often very embarrassing; she knew that she must gain complete power over them, or have them exorcised— or go mad. She was striving to bring the entities involved under the domination of her will and was making some progress in that direction.

It had been about a decade since the beginning of modern spiritualism in America, with rappings on the furniture in the home of John Fox at Rochester. The cult had spread to Europe and, in 1854, was introduced in Russia by people who had witnessed the phenomena abroad. In the fashionable drawing rooms of St. Petersburg, many were amusing themselves with the new craze, though it was condemned by the State Church and the "scientific authorities." The Church called it the work of Satan and the scientist brushed it off as "physiological disturbances."

The folk of Pskov—180 miles from St. Petersburg—had heard of these things but had never witnessed any spiritist phenomena. Now the news that Helena was a "medium" spread rapidly, and people became very excited and curious. The hall bell at the de Yahontov mansion rang frequently.

Most of those who came suspected that they were being fooled by some kind of chicanery. It all seemed too fantastic to be genuine. They demanded to search the "medium," as they termed her, to tie her arms and legs, to put her through every test they could devise. Helena submitted graciously.

Still many would not believe. "How do you *do it?*" they would ask, or "What *is it* that raps?" "How can *you* guess people's thoughts so well?" "How could *you* know that I had thought that?" And so on.

The men were the hardest to convince. Even her brother and father thought that Helena had, somewhere in her travels, learned to play these advanced parlor tricks for social entertainment.

One evening the drawing-room was filled with visitors, some playing cards, some occupied with music, but most of them badgering Helena for some psychic tricks. Her brother Leonid, now a strong, muscular youth, "saturated with the Latin and German wisdom of the university," stood behind his sister's chair, listening superciliously to her discourse on the subject of how magicians can change the weight of objects.

"And you mean to say that *you* can do it?" he scoffed.

"I *have* done it on occasions, but I can't always answer for its success."

There was an immediate chorus of requests for her to try.

Finally she consented, warning them that she promised nothing. Then getting one of the young men present to test the weight of a small chess table nearby, she fixed her large blue eyes on the table with an intense gaze. After a while she motioned to the same young man to try the weight again. This time he was unable to move the little table from the floor.

Everyone was impressed except Leonid, who, from the look in his eyes, evidently suspected that his sister was acting in confederacy with the young man.

"May *I* try?" he asked sardonically.

"Please do, my dear."

He approached, smiling, and seized the chess table with one muscular arm. The smile vanished when the table refused to budge. He stepped back and carefully examined it. Then he gave it a tremendous kick; but it remained as if glued to the floor. Next he encircled it with his arms and tried to shake it from side to side. The wood creaked but the table did not move an inch. Finally Leonid straightened up and looked with astonishment at his sister.

"How strange!" he muttered.

All agreed that the situation was at least that.

After a number of people had tried the experiment and failed, Helena said to her brother, with her usual careless laugh:

"Try to lift the table now, once more."

He approached the little thing slowly, cautiously, paused, took a deep breath, grasped a leg and pulled upward with all the force he could muster. He almost lost balance and dislocated his arm for now the table came up, feather-light.

After that episode Leonid no longer scoffed at his sister's "alleged psychic phenomena."

Colonel von Hahn, known to his contemporaries as an old "Voltarian," believing in nothing, would not deign to take the slightest interest in such "superstitious nonsense," as he called the new craze.

One evening he had as guests two men he had known for many years—one as a fellow student at the *Corps de Pages*. Much to his surprise and disgust, both of them were taking an active interest in the silly psychic parlor games in which the women were, as usual, indulging. His guests in their turn upbraided him for his indifference. One of them, a General; said:

"I don't know how you can close your eyes and your mind to these wonderful phenomena your daughter is producing!"

"Stuff and nonsense!" retorted the Colonel. "It's not worthy of consideration by serious people." He continued to lay out his cards for *"grande Patience."*

But his old friends would not be silenced so easily, and finally they challenged him to a simple experiment. He was to go into another room and write any word he liked on a slip of paper; then it would be seen whether the invisible intelligent force could repeat the word through raps.

To please his friends the Colonel complied. He went to his desk in an adjoining room, took a slip of paper, wrote a word, put the paper in his pocket and returned to his cards. But, smiling behind his moustache, he listened to what was going on.

Someone was repeating the alphabet, the raps would indicate the correct letter when reached, and the General would write it down. Helena, as usual, seemed to be doing nothing. In fact she was sitting back away from the table. Whatever trick she was up to was a clever one!

Finally the raps would say no more. But none of those at the table seemed satisfied with the word they had got; there was much agitation and whispering. They have failed, of course, as I knew they would, thought the Colonel. Looking over his glasses he demanded:

"Well, have you any answer? It must be something very elaborate and profound!"

He stood up and approached the group. Vera, with some confusion and embarrassment, handed him a slip of paper, bearing the word produced by the raps.

Looking at it, the Colonel's eyes bulged and his ruddy face turned pale. He adjusted his spectacles, cleared his throat, and in a strained voice read the word aloud:

"Zaitchik! Yes, Zaitchik; so it is. How very strange!"

Taking from his pocket the piece of note paper he had written on while in the adjoining room, he handed it in silence to the group.

They read: "What was the name of my favorite war horse which I rode during my first Turkish campaign?" Lower down the page in parenthesis he had written the word "Zaitchik."

After that episode the Colonel plunged into the region of psychic phenomena with zeal. By means of it he set out to check and, if possible, restore the missing links in his family genealogical tree—right from the Knight Crusader, Count von Rottenstern who, legend said, had been awakened in his tent by the crowing of a cock (hahn) to find a Saracen intruder there, intent on murdering him. For thus saving his life the rooster was incorporated into his family coat-of-arms, and the name became Hahn von Rottenstern-Hahn.

Helena's uncle, Mr. J. A. von Hahn, Post Director at St. Petersburg, whose ambition was to settle the title of Count on his eldest son permanently, took the greatest interest in this mysterious work. To confirm the information received from the unseen sources, documents were consulted in the dusty archives of both Russia and Germany. On all points that could be checked by the records the mysterious *intelligence* behind the psychic messages proved unerringly correct.

Part of this work was probably done at St. Petersburg where the Colonel took Helena, Vera, and his daughter Elizabeth by his second wife. Elizabeth (Liza) was now, in the spring of 1859, about nine years old. They all stayed at the Hotel de Paris in St. Petersburg. From there they eventually moved to Rugodevo, in the Province of Pskov, where Vera's estate, inherited from her last husband, was located.

As the Rugodevo estate, with its village of several hundred serfs, had been purchased by her husband only a short time before his death, neither Vera nor any member of her family had ever been there before. They knew nothing whatever of the former owners, nor of the serfs or the neighborhood.

The old mansion, surrounded by hills of dense pine forest, large parks of ancient trees and steely lakes, proved to Helena to be haunted in an interesting way. In one room in particular she saw a group of figures, some of them quite remarkable and unusual in their appearance and attire. She described the strange ghosts and their dress to Vera, who was unable to see them. In fact, the only other person in the house to whom these phantoms were visible was little Lisa; but she, seeing them in occasions moving along corridors, took them to be real people, other inmates of the big house.

Some discreet questioning of one or two old retainers on the estate revealed that these apparitions were, from appearances, people who had formerly lived and died in the house. The room where they were mostly concentrated had been for all of them, it was said, either the death chamber, or else the mortuary chamber where their bodies had lain for from three to five days before being carried for burial to the old chapel across the somber lake.

About these phantoms Helena made some interesting comments, revealing her attitude and the progress of her own occult knowledge and development at the time. Vera, who was both frightened and curious, wanted to "call out" the spirits in a seance. To this Helena replied:

"We may, but what of that? Can any one of them be relied upon or believed? I would pay any price to be able to command and control as *they*—some personages I might name, do; but I cannot. I must fail for years to come," she concluded, regretfully.

"Whom do you mean by 'they'? Vera asked.

"*Those who know and can*—not mediums!"

Later she remarked: "It is very interesting, the more so *since I now see them* [apparitions] *so rarely* . . . not as I used to years ago, when a child."

She explained to her sister that the shadowy figures seen were lingering reflections of the dead, but not the immortal souls.

"Why is it never—or rarely—possible to contact those near and dear to one?" Vera asked; "I mean loved relatives and friends, instead of hosts of strangers!"

"A difficult query to answer," Helena replied. "How often, how earnestly, have I tried to see and recognize among the shadows that haunted me some one of our dear relatives, or even a friend. How I longed from the bottom of my soul—but, all in vain!"

She went on to say that these "reflections of the dead" were attracted, not to living people, but to localities where they had lived and suffered, and where their personalities and outward forms had been most impressed on the surrounding psychic atmosphere.

Soon after these experiences and discussions Helena became very ill. A profound wound opened in the region of her heart, she suffered intense agony, sometimes going into convulsions, followed by a deathlike trance. Mystified and greatly frightened, Colonel von Hahn and Vera sent to a neighboring town for a physician.

When, on his first visit, the doctor was examining the wound, with Helena lying prostrate and unconscious before him, he suddenly saw a dark, ghostly hand slowly moving at intervals from the patient's neck to her waist. At the same time the room was filled with a chaos of noises and sounds from the ceiling, the floor, the windowpanes, and every bit of furniture. The poor man was so horrified that he refused to stay alone in the room with the unconscious patient.

In a few days, however, the wound healed, leaving only an old scar. Helena never told her family, or anyone else, how she had come by this strange wound, which opened on occasions.

In the spring of 1860 Helena and sister Vera with her two young sons, left Rugodev to visit the grandparents in faraway Tiflis. Vera writes of the many strange adventures the two sisters had on this three-week journey by coach and post horses across Russia. Most of the episodes had to do with Helena's remarkable psi faculty, and they were sometimes quite embarrassing.

At Zadonsk, for instance, they were invited to visit the learned Isodore, one of the three Metropolitans (highest at that time in the ecclesiastical hierarchy of the Russian Orthodox Church). At this time Isodore was Metropolitan of Kiev, but the sisters had known him as a friend of the family when he was Exarch (prelate in charge of several dioceses) in Georgia. He was, in fact, also the man to whom Nikifor Blavatsky had applied, without success, for annulment of the marriage with Helena.

At the Lord Archbishop's house Isodore received the ladies with great kindness. "But", writes Vera, "hardly had we taken our seats in the drawing room of the Holy

Metropolitan than a terrible hubbub, noises, and loud raps in every conceivable direction burst suddenly upon us with a force to which even we were hardly accustomed; every bit of furniture in the big audience room cracked and thumped—from the huge chandelier under the ceiling, every one of whose crystal drops seemed to become endowed with self-motion, down to the table, and under the very elbows of His Holiness who was leaning on it.

"Useless to say how confused and embarrassed we looked —though truth compels me to say that my irreverent sister's embarrassment was tempered with a greater expression of fun than I would have wished for."

But the old man was only momentarily startled. He seemed to understand the causes behind the phenomena and questioned the ladies about their beginnings. He then asked some mental questions of Helena's invisible entity, and appeared to receive such interesting and satisfactory answers that he entirely forgot about his dinner; he kept the visitors with him for over three hours.

When bidding them goodbye and giving them his blessings, the venerable old man said to Helena:

"Let not your heart be troubled by the gift you are possessed of, nor let it become a source of misery to you hereafter, for it was surely given to you for some purpose, and you could not be held responsible for it. Quite the reverse! For if you but use it with discrimination, you will be enabled to do much good to your fellow-creatures."[3]

His Holiness, Isodore, apparently did not, personally, hold the same hostile views toward psychic powers as did his Church. He seemed, also, to want to assure the young woman, whose family he had long known, that her powers were not of darkness, but of light. Yet there was a note of warning; she must use them with discrimination, discretion, restraint.

Unfortunately for herself, discretion and restraint were the last things Helena was at that time likely to employ.

CHAPTER 7

In Tiflis Helena found her 71-year-old grandmother still working hard. The former Princess Dolgorukov had learned to write with her left hand after a stroke deprived her of the use of her right arm. She was in the midst of a series of botanical studies and was not only writing, but was drawing and painting beautiful botanical specimens. Her health, however, was rapidly deteriorating, and later in the year 1860 she died.

The following year saw the emancipation of the Russian serfs, but apparently this made little difference to life at the Chavchavadze mansion where grandfather Andrey de Fadeyev and Aunt Nadyezhda still resided. A regular visitor to their home, General P. S. Nikolayeff, wrote in a memoir:[1]

"The whole enormous host of their *valetaille* [ex-serfs], having remained with the family as before their freedom, only now receiving wages; and all went on as before with the members of that family. I loved to pass my evenings in that home. At precisely a quarter to eleven o'clock, the old general, [A. M. de Fadeyev] brushing along the *parquets* with his warmly muffled-up feet, retired to his apartments. At that moment, hurriedly and in silence, the supper was brought in on trays, and served in the interior rooms; and immediately after this the drawing-room doors would be closely shut, and an animated conversation take place on every topic. Modern literature was reviewed and criticized, contemporary social questions from Russian life were discussed; at one time it was the narratives of some visitor, a foreign traveler, or an account given of a recent skirmish by one of its heroes, some sunburnt officer just returned from the battlefield (in the Caucasian mountains), would be eagerly listened to; at another time the antiquated old Spanish mason (then an officer in the Russian army), Quartano, would drop in and give us thrilling stories from the wars of Napoleon the Great. Or, again, 'Radda Bai'—H. P. Blavatsky, the granddaughter of General A. M. de Fadeyev—would put in an appearance, and was made to call forth from her past some stormy episode of her American life and travels; when the conversation would be sure to turn suddenly upon the mystic subjects, and she herself commence to 'evoke spirits' . . ."

During this time at Tiflis Helena appears to have become reconciled with her husband. She states in correspondence[2] that she lived for a year with him at Yerivan at the house of Mr. Kobrzhausky in Golovinsky Avenue. "But" she says, "I lacked the patience to live with such a fool and I again went away."

However, in other writings she contradicts this, and says that she spent only three days with him. Whatever the truth, relations between the pair at this time appear to have been amicable. One indication of this is the fact that Mr. Blavatsky petitioned to the right authorities for a passport for a little boy named Yuri. The passport—still in existence—was issued in Tiflis in August 1862 and described the child as the infant ward of Mr. and Mrs. Blavatsky.

A mystery surrounds the origin of this little boy. Some of Helena's enemies later declared that he was her own illegitimate child. At the time even her father, she said, was suspicious until she produced a "doctor's certificate" that proved her innocence. Apparently, however, Nikifor Blavatsky entertained no such suspicions of improper involvement by his legal spouse.

Pernicious gossip kept reviving, however, and many years later while she was staying in Germany, to protect her reputation for the sake of The Theosophcial Society, she obtained another medical certificate. (Introduction)

When Mr. Sinnett was writing Helena's memoirs in the 1880s, he tried to obtain from her the facts about Yuri, but she would tell him very little, saying that she was in honor bound to keep silent and never reveal the name of the boy's mother. It evidently involved scandal in high European society. The father she referred to as the "aristocratic Baron," and rumor named Baron Meyendorf of Estonia.

Yuri was a hunchback—strangely reminiscent of the little other world hunchback she had played with in childhood. She felt a tremendous compassion for Yuri, describing him as a "being whom I loved according to the phraseology of Hamlet as 'forty thousand fathers and brothers will never love their children and sisters.'"

Passports were at that time required for travel between certain parts of Russia, and she obtained one for the boy, but there is no record of where she took him in 1862. Later that year she wandered—apparently alone—in different parts of Georgia and along the Black Sea coast. Probably her motive for this journey was the same as that which took her to other out-of-the-way places around the world, namely, the desire for occult knowledge, the passionate yearning to learn the secret of the philosopher's stone, and the effort to control the psychic forces now strengthening around her like a curse.

Her travels took her through the wild mountain terrain of Transcaucasia, with its immense crags like giant, isolating walls. Much of the area was at that time covered with thick virgin forests, and inhabited by untamed warlike people. But deep in the great forests there were also those who appealed to Helena's curiosity and sympathy—the native *kudyani* or magicians.

She was now in the ancient, half-legendary land of Colchis where Jason, with his Argonauts, had come to remove a family curse by securing the Golden Fleece and was helped in his search by the powerful resident sorceress, Medea.

Some of the people of the region, it was said, were descendants of those Argonauts. At any rate, there was a

great mixture of races, though the social structure was
the simple feudal one of proud landowners and poor
peasants. The landlords, when Helena rode by their
fortress-like castles, were as ignorant and superstitious
as the peasants, and as violent as Corsican brigands.

Generally she ignored them, and reined her horse
toward the smoky huts of the thaumaturgists and fortune-
tellers, people with unusual knowledge and powers out
of the ordinary.

Word soon spread through the region that a Russian
noblewoman was roaming the mountains alone, and dwelling among the socially taboo portion of humanity. Moreover, this woman, it was said, possessed extraordinary
powers; she was able, for example, to communicate with
spirits, offset the deadly effects of the "evil eye," and
solve any personal problem. The upper classes disapproved
of her way of life but were anxious to take advantage of
her powers.

They came from far and wide to consult this new
"witch" of the forest.

Helena's technique of communication with the unseen had now moved into a new phase. Instead of raps
on the furniture she would use automatic writing, sitting
with pen in hand, outwardly relaxed and abstracted, but
inwardly in "a state of intense concentration." Her hand
holding the pen would move without her volition, directed
by a will working through her nerve and muscular mechanism.

It is reported that the results were astounding and satisfactory to her visitors. Not *always* *s*atisfactory, however,
for although she was ever ready to relieve distress she
would never use her powers to bring harm to anyone.
But that was just what many of her clients wanted! They
regarded magic as essentially a tool for confounding their
enemies. To enlist her aid as a sorceress they offered
her large bribes, but these she scorned contemptuously—
and seldom diplomatically.

One way and another, with her unceremonious treatment of those who sought to use her powers for selfish
ends, and her open preference for the company of peas-

ants and native magicians, she made many enemies among the powerful families of the region.

The monetary temptations for the practice of her occult art were really a great test of her character, because she often needed money rather desperately. Not that her simple mode of life was expensive, but she was inclined to spend recklessly, and often more than she could afford, to help the unfortunate and poverty-stricken around her.

At one time she must have written to her aunt, Katherine de Witte, asking for financial help, for she received an angry, scolding letter[3] in which her aunt wrote: "One could believe that you have not even a kopek, like other poor people. And one would be much surprised learning that you receive 100 roubles every month. Because I am *quite sure* you are receiving them, with the exception of one of the winter months when Blavatsky did not get his salary either. I have a letter from Alek. Fed. [Major Alexander Fyodorovitch von Hahn] in which he says that he sent my letter and the money of Blavatsky to you . . . This happened in July; now we are in August, and Blavatsky sent you money some days ago again, in the presence of the husband of N - -."

Extant correspondence from Madame de Witte indicates that she was always very critical of her niece, but this letter is of special interest because it tells of Nikifor Blavatsky giving financial assistance to his wife—so perhaps their relatoins *were* better at this time.

Helena's years in the wild lands of Transcaucasia came to an abrupt and unexpected end. She had bought a house in the military settlement of Ozurgety in Mingrelia, probably from proceeds of "the floating of lumber and the export of nut-tree-spunk," a commercial enterprise in which her biographers say she was engaged for a while.

One day she fell ill. The symptoms were strange, to say the least. Physically, she had a mild fever and a complete loss of appetite. She refused everything except a little water and was most of the time in a half-dreamy, disinterested state, though not completely unconscious.

But mentally she appears to have reached a great crisis, so that she became a double personality. When a friend or servant called her name, she opened her eyes and answered—as Helena Blavatsky. But as soon as left alone, she closed her eyes and became, she said, somebody else in "another far-off country, a totally different individuality," who seemed, indeed, even to live in a different dimension of time. Helena later described it in this way:

"In cases when I was interrupted, during a conversation in the latter capacity (in my *other self*), say, at half a sentence either spoken by me or some of my *visitors*, invisible of course to any other for I was alone to whom they were realities—no sooner I closed my eyes than the sentence which had been interrupted continued from the word it had stopped at. When awake and *myself*, I remembered well who I was in my second capacity, and what I was doing. When somebody else, I had no idea of who was H. P. Blavatsky!"[4]

The army surgeon, the only doctor in the small town, found himself completely out of his depth. He knew only one thing—that she was declining rapidly and would certainly die if she remained in Ozurgety. But no roads led out of town and the patient could not go on horseback or by cart over the rough tracks. Finally he decided to send her in a native boat down the narrow river Rioni (the Pharsis of the Argonauts) which was navigable but seldom used.

Gliding silently between steep banks, hedged in by the ancient forests, Helena lay close to death, and the boatmen went through an eerie, terrifying time. During the first night they saw—they vowed—the patient glide off the boat and cross the water toward the forests, but at the same time her body was lying prostrate on the bed at the bottom of the boat. When the same ghostly episode occurred on the second night they were ready to abandon both the boat and the patient. Only the courage of the man in charge kept them at their posts. He wavered, himself, on the third night when he saw *two* phantom figures while his mistress, in flesh and bone, was sleeping before his eyes. But he steeled his nerves, calmed his terrified companions, and brought the boat safely to Kutais. There Helena was met by friends, and taken by carriage to the family home at Tiflis.

Under the care of her loving aunt, Nadyezhda, Helena recovered. She had been through a great battle with occult forces that had almost killed her, but she emerged from the crisis complete master of those forces. In a letter to a relative she wrote: "I am cleansed and purified of that dreadful attraction to myself of stray spooks and the ethereal *affinities*. I am free, free, thanks to those whom I now bless at every hour of my life." Somehow in "ancient Colchis" she had thrown off the curse of unwanted mediumship and become a magician. Now psychic phenomena would be subject to her own will, and not to the mischief of "stray spooks." Between the pre-1865 and the post-1865 Helena Petrovna Blavatsky there was, she declared, "an unbridgeable gulf."

After the complete recovery of her health, she left Russia—apparently taking her ward Yuri with her. Then two years later, in 1867, she was back on her last visit to her own country.

We find her standing by an open grave, under a pale autumn sky, in a small town in southern Russia. The last rites are being said as the body of the little hunchback, Yuri, whom she loved above all human beings, is lowered into his grave. There are no members of her family present. Her only companion at the graveside is the celebrated basso, Agardi Metrovitch. How did this come about?

Metrovitch was a friend of her family and, on their travels, his and Helena's paths sometimes crossed, usually dramatically. The first time this occurred was in Constantinople in 1850. Late one night she was on her way, with a guide, to Missire's hotel when she saw a body lying in the deserted street. It proved to be Metrovitch with three stab wounds in his back. She sent her guide for help, and stood guard over the body for nearly four hours, she states, before her guide "could get *mouches* to pick him up. The only Turkish policeman meanwhile who chanced to come up asking for a *baksheesh* and offering to roll the supposed corpse into a neighboring ditch, then showed a decided attraction to my rings and bolting only when he saw my revolver pointing at him."[5]

She had Metrovitch carried to a nearby Greek hotel where he was rcognized and given medical care. He was conscious the next day when Helena visited him. At his request she wrote to his wife who was in Smyrna. The latter came as quickly as possible and took care of her husband.

"I lost sight of them after that for several years," wrote Helena,[6] "and met him again at Florence, where he was singing at the Pergola, *with his wfie*. He was a *carbonari,* a revolutionist of the worst kind, a fanatical rebel, a Hungarian, from Mitrovitz,* the name of which town he took as a *nom de guerre.* . . . Then I found him again in Tiflis in 1861, again with his wife, who died after I had left in 1865 I believe; then my relatives knew him well and he was friends with my cousins Witte. Then, when I took the poor child to Bologna to see if I could save him, I met him [Metrovitch] again in Italy and he did all he could for me, more than a brother."

The boy had died without documents to show his name or parentage. Helena did not wish to give her own name for his burial—"as food for the gossips." So Metrovitch came to her aid, accompanied and buried the *aristocratic Baron's* child—*under his,* Metrovitch's name, saying "he did not care," in a small town of Southern Russia in 1867.

"After this, without notifying my relatives of my having returned to Russia to bring back the unfortunate little boy whom I did not succeed to bring back alive to the governess chosen for him by the Baron, I simply wrote to the child's father to notify him of this pleasant occurrence for him, and returned to Italy with the same passport."[7]

In the two previous years, between leaving Russia in 1865 and returning, during the autumn of 1867, to bury Yuri, Helena was traveling in the Balkans, and perhaps in other parts of the world, though this is not definite. The only travel notebook she left behind undoubtedly

---

*Now Sremska Mitrovica in Yugoslavia.

belongs to this period. Typically, she has not put a date in it, but she notes that during a visit to Belgrade, a "horrible, dirty city, Turkish, ugly, badly paved but full of ducats . . . The Turks were busy evacuating the fortress. Rezi Pasha was about to leave by order of the Sultan, and the Serbs celebrated their freedom. Michael Obrenovic was going to Constantinople to thank the Sultan. Cannons were fired 101 times."

History relates that Prince Michael Obrenovic (1823-68) received keys of the Fortress in Belgrade on April 13, 1867 from Al Rezi Pasha. So Helena must have been in Belgrade sometime just before this date. The notebook shows that she (and presumably Yuri, though he is not mentioned) traveled, before and after this, to many different towns in the Balkans. Journeys were made by train, coach and steamers on the Danube.

Just before her return to Russia, she had been in Bologna, Italy, where she vainly hoped to get the little boy cured of whatever ailment he had. After the burial she returned to Italy.

On November 2, 1867, she was definitely at the battle of Mentana as a soldier in Garibaldi's army. In the fighting her left arm was broken in two places by a sabre stroke, and she was badly wounded by musket shots in the right shoulder and one leg. When she fell in the heat of the battle, her companions thought she had been killed, and left her behind. Later she was found.

Part of 1868 she spent in Italy, and it may have been at this time that she sojourned in Bari on the Adriatic, "studying with a witch." It may also have been somewhere about this period, or earlier, that she "lived with the whirling Dervishes, with the Druses of Mt. Lebanon, with the Bedouin Arabs and the Marabouts of Damascus."[68]

Sometime during the year 1868 she received a letter from her Hindu Protector, directing her to wait in the Serbian mountains until she had definite word from him to go to Constantinople and meet him there. She had high hopes that the meeting would be soon, and that he would take her to India and Tibet.

CHAPTER 8

Helena lifted her eyes from the old manuscript of Senzar characters that she was struggling to translate into English, and looked through the window. She never failed to get a wonderful lifting of the heart from the mass of snowcapped mountains guarding the peaceful valley, from which no sound came save the occasional tingle of a distant cowbell or the warble of a bird in the trees near the house. This, she thought, must be *the* abode of perfect peace and happiness.

Sometimes she had to pinch herself to prove that she was really there in the flesh, and not suffering another of those double personality experiences; that she was actually near Shigatze, Tibet, living in the house of the Kashmiri Adept, Kuthumi Lal Singh. His sister and sister's child were there too and, wonder of wonders, most of the time under the same roof as herself was the great Protector of her visions, the Master Morya!

A lifetime ago, it seemed, since he had sat with her on a bench in Hyde Park, London, and told her that some day she would be in Tibet, training for the special work she had to do. Years and years it seemed, too, since he had met her in Constantinople and brought her across the snowy range to this roof of the world. As to how long ago it *actually* was she had little idea and no concern. She knew only that the sun shone brilliantly in the clear, clear air; or else all was grey, with black storm clouds rolling weirdly over the mountains. And then for an eternity the world would be Christmas white-and-tinsel in a cloak of snow, adorned with trees of glittering glass. Then again would come the sunshine, the bird-song, the gurgling streams. Seasons passed, but time itself stood still in the aura of peace that the Masters seemed to weave around this divine place.

She had not spent all her time in Tibet at the house in the valley near Shigatze. With the help of her Protector, whom she now knew to be her Guru, she had gained entry to certain Lamaistic convents, ancient seats of learning where no European, male or female, had ever before set foot.

This had been part of her training but, most important, she felt, was the personal instruction she had from her Guru himself. When he was away from the house, she still had plenty to do, practicing her *sadhana* (spiritual exercises), talking with the beautiful, intelligent sister of the Master Kuthumi (usually called K.H.) or learning something valuable from that great Adept himself. Much of this was concerned with the Sacred Science, but there was another, a mundane subject, too, on which he gave her instruction.

Since, in London, people had laughed at Helena's Yorkshire accent, a legacy of her Yorkshire governess, August Jeffers, she had hated the language and had spoken it only when forced to do so, which was seldom. But the Master K.H. had been educated at some European universities. Like Helena, he was a linguist; unlike her, he spoke reasonable English. And for some reason he was most insistent that she should improve *her* stumbling English.

From the shining mountains beyond the window she turned back to her translation of the passage of archaic Senzar. Master K.H. had given her this exercise—as he had others—to improve both her English and her knowledge of the Secret Sacerdotal language.

She had finished the translation and was about to go out in the sunshine, and perhaps have a game with K.H.'s adorable niece, when she heard his footsteps outside the window. He had returned from his ride, and she could see him strolling under the trees in his riding clothes. She took her translation out and handed it to him.

Anxiously, she watched his thin, sensitive face, with its almost transparent skin. How young he looked, yet the very soul of mature wisdom! Now his soft blue eyes turned on her, and she heard his gentle voice saying:

"Your English is becoming better."

Unexpectedly, he put his hand on her forehead, in the region called by phrenologists the seat of memory (the middle of the brow about an inch above the root of the nose) and said:

"Try to pick out of my head the little I know of the language."

She felt a trifling pain and a cold shiver went through her.

Every day, for about two months after that, the Master K.H. gave her these telepathic lessons in English. He also insisted on that language in conversations, though she much preferred talking in French, which he also spoke well.

In November 1870, just before Helena left Tibet, Master K.H. wrote a letter in French to her family in Russia. Some changes had taken place at the old home since her departure in 1865. Her grandfather, Andrey Mihailovich de Fadeyev, had died in 1867 and her maiden aunt, Nadyezhda A. de Fadeyev, had moved to Odessa. In that city there were other relatives, such as Katherine de Witte and her family.

Even if Helena had wanted to write from Tibet, it would have been impossible by ordinary mails. And what could she write about? Loving them as she did, she knew that no member of her family would understand what she was doing and what was happening to her.

So no word from Helena had come for five years. The family had tried all means of locating her through inquiries, and by asking travelers of their acquaintance to look for any sign of her in foreign parts. But, wrote her maiden aunt, "All our researches had ended in nothing. We were ready to believe her dead . . ."

Then on November 7, 1870, a man of Asiatic appearance came to Nadyezhda's house with a letter. The envelope bore no postmark, only her name and the simple address: "Odessa." She tore it open and unfolded the page. It was written in French, with no signature, but only a strange sign at the bottom. She looked inquiringly toward the messenger who had delivered it, but he was nowhere to be seen. He "disappeared before my very eyes," she wrote later.

In translation the letter read:

"The noble relations of Madame H. Blavatsky have no cause whatsoever for grief. Their daughter and niece has not left this world at all. She is living, and desires to make known to those whom she loves that she is well and quite happy in the distant and unknown retreat which she has selected for herself. She had been very ill, but is so no longer; for under the protection of the Lord Sangyas [Lord Buddha] she has found devoted friends who guard her physically and spiritually. The ladies of her house should therefore remain tranquil. Before 18 new moons shall have risen, she will return to her family."[1]

There was no indication from where the letter had come, or by what means, save for the vanishing Asiatic. But it certainly brought some reassurance to the family.

Nadyezdha carefully preserved the mystifying, but comforting, letter. It was written in the K.H. script which was to become famous in the Master's correspondence with Mr. A. P. Sinnett, the English journalist and early member of The Theosophical Society.

At about the same time, across the world in the high valley near Shigatze, Helena was bidding farewell to her hermitage of peace and contentment. There were several Masters and other *chelas* at the house. The *chelas* were smiling brotherly good-byes; the Masters giving kindly advice. Mahatma K.H. suddenly dispelled her feelings of gloom and sadness by laughing at her, in his kind way, and saying jokingly:

"Well, if you have not learned much of the Sacred Sciences and practical Occultism—and who could expect a *woman* to—you have learned, at any rate, a little English. You speak it now *only a little worse* than I do!"[2]

Her own beloved Guru took her away, guiding her safely out of Tibet and setting her on the route back to Europe. But there were several things to be done, and some trials to be met, before she would see the old familiar sights of the Ukraine again. The Adepts had, in fact, forecast with amazing accuracy the number of moons that would wax and wane between her departure and arrival.

In December 1870, she sailed through the Suez Canal (which had opened for traffic the year before) to Cyprus and then on to Greece where she saw Hilarion, another member of the Great Brotherhood. Several months later, on July 4, 1871, she embarked, for reasons unknown, on the S.S. *Eunomia,* from the port of Piraeus, for Egypt. Like many merchant ships of the day, *Eunomia* mounted guns and carried ammunition and gunpowder as a measure of protection against pirates.

Helena was standing on deck watching the Greek islands, pearly and pinkish, rise out of the incredible blue of the Aegean. The outline of Spetsai was just beginning to show over the port bow when a tremendous explosion shook the ship and burst its bows asunder. A powder magazine had exploded, destroying the whole fore part of the ship, killing thirty passengers and wounding many others. Fortunately Helena escaped injury, although she was badly shaken and lost her baggage and money. The dead were taken to the Island of Syros; the survivors to Spetsai, from where the Greek Government provided them with other means of reaching their destinations.

So eventually, Helena found herself in Alexandria, Egypt, with few possessions and very little cash. She writes that she extricated herself from this predicament by winning a sum of money on "No. 27"—probably at roulette.

Toward the end of the year 1871, she was in Cairo staying at the Hotel d'Orient. There she met a Miss Emma Cutting who, some thirteen years later, was to prove the Judas Iscariot of Helena Blavatsky's crucifixion. But at this time Miss Cutting was seeking to contact her brother who had recently died, an alcoholic. She had heard of Madame Blavatsky's psychic powers and sought her acquaintance. Helena was short of money again, and Emma Cutting befriended her with a loan. Thus the wind was sown for the whirlwind to be reaped.

Hilarion, too, seems to have gone to Egypt from Greece at this time, for she writes of seeing him there.[3] She also renewed her contact with the well-known Coptic mystic and occultist Paulos Metamon. Either with the assistance of these men, or alone, Helena seems to have performed some psychic wonders in the land of the Pharoahs that brought her a mixed reputation and set tongues wagging again in the international set of that day.

"She is a marvel, an unfathomable mystery. That which she produces is simply phenomenal. . . . If it is after all but jugglery, then we have in Mme. Blavatsky a woman who beats all the Boscos and Robert Houdins of the century," wrote, typically, a Russian gentleman from Cairo to a brother-officer of his regiment in Russia.[4]

But Helena demonstrated at this time in Egypt what seems a strange lack of judgment of people and circumstances. She seemed overeager to begin her world mission, to use the current popular interest in spiritist phenomena as a channel for the introduction of Eastern esoteric philosophy.

Against the advice of Paulos Metamon, who knew Egypt intimately, she started a Spiritist Society for the investigation and study of psychic science. She tried, but failed, to get a good medium from England or France, so she employed amateur mediums—"French female spiritists, mostly beggarly tramps, when not adventuresses in the rear of M. de Lesseps' army of engineers and workmen on the canal of Suez," she wrote to her aunt in Russia.

"I caught them cheating most shamefully our members, who come to investigate the phenomena, by bogus manifestations. I had very disagreeable scenes with several persons who held me alone responsible for all this. . . . I got nearly shot by a madman—a Greek, who had been present at the only two public seances we held, and got possessed I suppose by some vile spook."

So Madame Blavatsky dissolved her fortnight-old fiasco of a society, changed her address, and went to live in Boulak near the fine Cairo Museum.

Back in Odessa, Nadyezhda A. de Fadeyev was very worried about her niece. Now that Lyolinka (as she called her) had left Tibet and India, why did she not come straight home? What was she doing there in Egypt.

Simply getting herself into needless dangers, it seemed, by the sound of the letters she now wrote.

One day Agardi Metrovitch called to see Miss de Fadeyev and happened to mention that he was shortly making a journey to Alexandria, Egypt, on business. This was an opportunity she could not miss.

"Would you go to Cairo and see Lyolinka there, and beg her to come home? It would be doing me a very great service if you would," she pleaded.

Metrovitch readily promised to do so. And so it was that he once again crossed Helena's path to enact the final, terrible drama of his life.

Helena had, she said, been warned by Hilarion that Metrovitch was coming, and that he was in grave danger of his life in Egypt: "Some Maltese instructed by the Roman Catholic monks prepared to lay a trap for him and kill him." Metrovitch, it seems had made many enemies in the Roman Catholic Church. "He was," she said, "a Mazzinist,"[5] had insulted the Pope, was exiled from Rome in 1863."[6]

Now Helena who, with the assistance of Countess Kisseleff, had saved Metrovitch from the gallows some years earlier in Austria, once more decided to help her friend, at the grave risk of her own life and reputation.

She sent a message to him that he should come directly to her house in Cairo. When he arrived, she told him to stay in hiding there, and not to go outside at all. But— a restless, courageous man—he could not bear the confinement, so in a few days he left the house and returned to Alexandria. Hilarion again warned Helena that he saw death for her friend there. Immediately she set off after Metrovitch, planning to persuade him to return to Europe on the very first ship.

But when she reached Alexandria, she was told that he had gone to Ramleh (a few miles along the coast) on foot. Later she learned that he had stopped on his way to drink a glass of lemonade at the hotel of a Maltese who was seen talking to two monks.

When he arrived at Ramleh, he fell down senseless. Countess Lydia A. de Pashkoff heard of it and sent word to Helena. "I went to Ramleh," she says, "and found him in a small hotel, in typhoid fever I was told by the doctor, and *with a monk* near him."[7]

Knowing his great aversion to priests, Helena ordered this one out of the room. He refused to go. There was a row and, finally, she called the police and had the monk evicted.

She stayed on at the little hotel, nursing Metrovitch through "agony incessant and terrible." She was not sure whether he had been poisoned or was really suffering from typhoid. After ten days he died. This brought her an even bigger problem. "No Church would bury him, saying he was a *carbonari*. I appealed to some Free Masons, but they were afraid."[8]

There seemed nothing to do but bury him herself. With the help of an Abyssinian (a pupil of Hilarion) and a hotel servant, she dug a grave under a tree by the seashore. Then in the evening she hired men to carry his body down to the shore, and buried him there.

For this final brave act of friendship to the man who had helped *her* at a time of great need, she was severely reprimanded by the Russian Consul at Alexandria. "The Consul told me that I had no business to be friends with revolutioniers and Mazzinists and that people said he was my lover."[9]

A number of years later, in what came to be called the Coulomb conspiracy, an attempt was made by H.P.B.'s attackers to resurrect and make capital out of this incident in Egypt. At that time, her favorite aunt, Madame Nadyezhda Andreyevna de Fadeyev, writing to her from Odessa under date of November 23 (December 5, our calendar), 1884, commented:

". . . All this is absurd and I do not understand why you should pay any attention to it. I am writing this in French so that Colonel Olcott could read it, and you can show this letter to him. What can these vile Coulombs say, and who is going to believe them, when there are so many Russians you have known in Cairo and Alexandria—Madame de Pashkoff and the Russian Consul Elian Gregoire, and Mr. Lavison, and no one of them ever heard anything of the kind about you, though they lived in Cairo and saw you every day. Finally, if you consider it necessary, I am ready to write to Olcott and to deny these ridiculous gossips. I can tell him that Mr. Agardi Metrovitch whom we all have known as well at Tiflis and Odessa, and who was a friend to all of us, could have never been either your husband or your lover, as he adored his wife who died two years before his own death, poor man, at Cairo; that she is buried in the cemetery of Tiflis, and that your mutual friendship dates from the year when he married his wife. Moreover, everybody knows that it is we who had asked him to go and look for you at Cairo, in order to accompany you to Odessa (in the year 1871), and that he died without bringing you back, after which you returned on your own. The same applies to the absurd gossip which attempts to make of that poor child that you took charge of, a son of your own, when all that is required to prove *who he is* would be to show his papers. But it is your own fault; as I said to Colonel Olcott at Elberfeld, you have always scoffed too much at *what might be said.* Instead of contradicting the evil tongues, you took pleasure in adding a little more to it, laughing at the people. You are punished precisely where you sinned. . . ."

But at the time of the Russian Consul's reprimand, Helena was growing accustomed to the barbs of official bigotry and the shafts of malicious gossip. They meant little to her at this stage. She knew, however, that it was time for her to leave Egypt.

On her way back to Russia she visited Palestine, Syria, and Lebanon. Then she went on to Constantinople and took ship across the Black Sea to Odessa, reaching home about the middle of 1872—some "18 moons" after the mysterious letter.

She stayed in Russia for less than twelve months, however, on this, her last visit to her homeland. A letter from her Guru sent her to Paris in the spring of 1873. There she lived for several months at No. 11 rue de I'Université with her cousin, Nikolay Gustovovich von Hahn, son of her father's brother Gustav.

Helena Pavlovna de Fadeyev
1789-1860
H.P.B.'s maternal grandmother

Helena Andreyevna von Hahn
1814-1842
H.P.B.'s mother

Andrey Mihailovich de Fadeyev
1789-1867
H.P.B.'s maternal grandfather

Vera Petrovna de Zhelihovsky
1835-1896
H.P.B.'s sister

Birthplace of H. P. Blavatsky
Town of Ekaterinoslav, now Dnyepropetrovsk, from
a lithograph, first half of the nineteenth century.

The Eddy homestead, Chittenden, Vermont, in 1874 and
as it looks today. Here H. P. Blavatsky and Col. Olcott
met in October 1874.

Col. Olcott, about 1861
during military service.

Helena Petrovna Blavatsky. Sketch by
James Montgomery Flagg from an 1875
portrait.

W. Q. Judge, New York
attorney, first Counsel of The
Theosophical Society and first
president of American Section.

G. H. Felt, engineer and
architect, following whose
lecture the decision was made
to form a group, later to be
known as The Theosophical
Society.

"The Lamasary," home of H.P.B. on the second floor, 302 West 47th St., New York. Drawing by W. Q. Judge when *Isis Unveiled* was being written, and the same address as it looks today.

"The Crow's Nest," Bombay, first headquarters of The Theosophical Society

H. P. Blavatsky
Sketch by an unknown artist
probably around 1877-1878.

An early picture of The Theosophical headquarters building at Adyar, 1887.

A. P. Sinnett (1840-1921), Editor of the Allahabad *Pioneer* and prominent early member of The Theosophical Society.

Mohini Mohun Chatterjee (1858-1936), who traveled with the Founders and accompanied them to Europe in 1884.

Countess Constance Wachtmeister (1838-1910) who lived with H.P.B. during the writing of *The Secret Doctrine*.

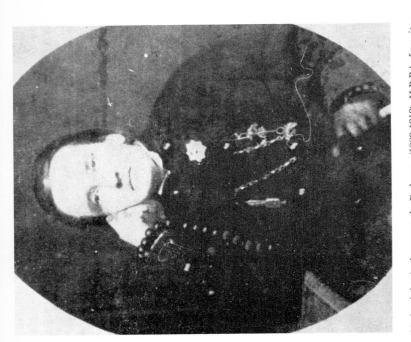

Nadyezhda Andreyevna de Fadeyev (1829-1919) H.P.B.'s favorite aunt, who visited her many times during her years abroad.

Portrait of H. P. Blavatsky by Herman Schmiechen
about 1884

Dr. Archibald Keightley (1859-1910) and his nephew Bertram Keightley (1860-1945), who helped H.P.B. get *The Secret Doctrine* into print.

Col. H. S. Olcott, first President of
The Theosophical Society, 1875-1907.

One of the best known portraits of H. P. Blavatsky
made by Enrico Resta, Jan. 8, 1889,
in his studio in London.

17 Lansdowne Road

19 Avenue Road

Two residences of H. P. Blavatsky in London

Annie Besant, who succeeded Col. Olcott as
President of The Theosophical Society.

Despite the fact that Helena was forty-one, stout and, at this time, with no claim to physical beauty, viperish tongues have accused her of being a member of the demi-monde, living a life of easy virtue in gay, inimitable Paris.

But a lady physician, Dr. L. M. Marquette, who knew her well during this short visit to Paris, wrote that Helena's behavior "was *unexceptionable* and such as to entitle her to every respect. She passed her time in painting and writing, seldom going out of her room. She had few acquaintances, but among the number were M. and Mme. Leymarie [leading spiritist who carried on the Allan Kardec movement after his death]. Mme. Blavatsky I esteem as one of the most estimable and interesting ladies I ever met, and since my return from France, our acquaintance and friendship has been renewed."[10]

Another letter came from the Master Morya. This asked her to embark without delay for America. A request from her Guru was always regarded by Helena as an order; she would never have dreamed of doing otherwise than obeying. Of course, she was aware that such an "order" was not an order in the military sense. She had freedom of choice. But she was also aware that if occult "orders" were not carried out, the *chela* (disciple) would be unlikely to receive any more. And that would be unthinkable to Helena Blavatsky.

It was June and hot in Paris. It would be even hotter in New York, but not a bad time for crossing the Atlantic. She went to Le Havre, and bought a first-class ticket on a ship due to sail the next day.[11] The ticket cost $125 in gold, and that left very little money in her purse. So she sent off a request to her father in Russia, asking him to forward a sum of money to her through the Russian Consul in New York. Colonel von Hahn always sent funds promptly when he knew where to send them.

Helena was not to know, of course, that at this time her father was very ill, and that before her request could reach him, the generous hearted old Colonel would be no more.

Several people who knew Helena personally have written of an incident—characteristic of her—that took place on the quay of Le Havre. She saw there, looking desolate and weeping, a poorly dressed woman with two small children. Going up to them, she asked gently:

"Whatever is the matter?"

Then the woman told her a pitiful story. Her husband was in America. He had saved and sent her enough money to make the crossing with her children, as steerage passengers. In Hamburg where she lived she had bought tickets from a supposed agent for emigrants. But he had swindled her, for now she was told by the shipping people that the tickets were bogus and worthless. She had not enough money to buy more, or even to return to Hamburg.

At this story Helena's wrath and indignation boiled over.

"Come with me," she said.

At the shipping office she repeated the poor woman's story. The people there were sorry, very sorry, but unless she had genuine tickets, they could not let her aboard.

"All right," Helena said, grimly. "Here's my first-class ticket. Take it back and give me a steerage ticket; with the balance provide passages for this lady and her children."

Everyone in the office looked at her in astonishment, as if she had taken leave of her senses. But she meant it, and finally, reluctantly, they agreed.

Steerage passages cost $30 each, and were robbery at the price. Helena had traveled enough to know what it would be like to spend ten days in the overcrowded steerage quarters of an emigrant ship—the filth, the bad smells, the rats! Ten days of horror, it was, except for the warm companionship of the grateful woman and her children.

Early in July, 1873, the ship docked in New York, and Helena said goodbye to the happy woman whose husband was there to meet her. As soon as possible, she herself hopefully took a hansom cab to the office of the Russian Consul. But no money had arrived from her father.

Helena was very nearly broke, but why worry, she thought. She had earned her living before, and would do so again, while she awaited her Master's directions.

CHAPTER 9

In the year 1873 no tall buildings scraped the New York sky, save the steeple of Trinity Church. On the rocks between what are now Second and Third Avenues, goats roamed among squatters' shanties.

Madison Street consisted mainly of small two-story houses whose resident owners kept their front and back gardens in good order. But among them was a tenement occupied by forty women. No. 222 Madison Street was a product of that era before women had invaded the business world. Those who *had* to work for a living could find only poorly paid jobs as telegraphers, teachers, or pliers of the sewing needle. Forty such had banded together to share this rented tenement. It was an experiment in cooperative living.

In a sitting room known as "the office" sat a woman seen by one of the young resident schoolteachers, Elizabeth Holt, as, "so broad, she had a broad face, and broad shoulders, her hair was a lightish brown and crinkled like that of some negroes. Her whole appearance conveyed the idea of power . . ."

This was in fact Madame Blavatsky, who had become a magnet to the working women of the place in their scant leisure hours. They gathered around her, watching her roll her cigarettes, while she told them marvelous tales of her travels or, if pressed hard enough, played the piano with the sensitive touch of a professional.

"She was considered to be a Spiritualist," wrote Elizabeth Holt later,[1] "although I never heard her say she was one, but the things she said which touched on those subjects, were Theosophical rather than Spiritualistic. Miss Parker [Elizabeth's close friend] had lost her mother, many years before, and when she asked Madame to put her into communication with her mother, Madame said it was impossible for her to do so, as her mother was absorbed in higher things, and had progressed beyond reach.

"In mental or physical dilemmas, you would instinctively appeal to her [Helena Blavatsky] for you felt her fearlessness, her unconventionality, her great wisdom and wide experience and hearty goodwill—her sympathy with the under-dog."

Helena had her own dilemma too. While frequent visits to the Russian Consul, accompanied by Miss Parker, proved to the latter that Helena was indeed a Russian aristocrat and not just an adventuress, it brought none of the badly needed funds she expected from her father. She wanted, she needed to work. But how to find it?

Mr. Rinaldo, the owner of the house, calling for his rents, had met the Russian lady; he became interested in her and learned about her predicament. Anxious to help her into the ranks of the workers, he brought two young Jewish friends along and introduced them. They owned a collar and shirt factory. Soon Helena, who had a gift for sketching, was designing advertising show-cards for them. "The card I remember best," says Miss Holt, was of little figures (*diaka* perhaps) dressed in the collars and shirts of their manufacture. I think these were the first picture advertising-cards used in New York."

Among the visitors to No. 222 who became fascinated by the world-traveled, strangely gifted Russian was one whom the girls called "the French Madame." She was a French Canadian widow named Madame Magnon who lived a short distance away in Henry Street, parallel to Madison. Mme. Magnon persuaded Helena to go and live with her until the expected money arrived from Russia.

This was a relief, both financially and linguistically; she was able to speak French again, instead of the still difficult English. But soon after this move a letter arrived from Russia. It was from her half-sister Elizabeth (Liza), and brought the sad news of the death of her father. He had, in fact, been dead since early July, but the family were unable to let Helena know until they received a letter from New York giving her address. Liza's letter was dated October 18, (o.s.) 1873.

It tells about the father's will and reads (in part):

". . . as you can see, according to the extracts of the testament, attested by the notary, your share amounts to 6,000 roubles in silver; 1,500 roubles will be paid to you presently; the rest, 4,500 roubles remain in my custody until you ask for them. Having your last letter, addressed to Daddy, I thought it appropriate to send you part of the money immediately, not waiting for you to ask for it, 1,500 roubles in 5% bank notes are already sent to you . . ."[2]

As soon as the money arrived Helena moved to a poorly-furnished room of her own at the corner of Fourteenth Street and Fourth Avenue. Young Elizabeth Holt used to feel excitingly guilty in visiting her there because the room was above a liquor saloon.

But Helena did not have enough money to choose luxurious quarters in a select area, especially as there were people needing help among her new friends. The housekeeper at No. 222 told a journalist: "One girl who had gone wrong and had a child, she [Madame Blavatsky] took and gave money enough to buy a little home in the farming part of the State, and she told her: 'Don't you ever say who gave you this money'."[3]

This may have taken place after she received the balance of her legacy from Russia. On the subject of money Elizabeth Holt quotes Madame Blavatsky as saying that when she needed money, "she had only to ask 'Them' for it, and she would find what she needed in one of the drawers of the little cabinet on her table." Elizabeth could not understand why Madame was ever short of cash. She did not understand, of course, the occult law that prevented Madame Blavatsky's using such powers for her own personal needs.

According to a story that Helena related to Colonel Olcott, who met her about a year later, she *did* have with her at this time, a large sum of money. The story does not tell how, or when, she received the sum (which the Colonel thought amounted to some 23,000 French francs) . It had, he says, been confided to her by her Master, to await orders. Meantime, she could not, of course, touch the money for her own daily needs.

Finally, he said, the order came. She had to travel to a certain address in Buffalo, in New York State, and hand the money to a certain man, giving no explanation, and immediately returning. When she arrived at the address, she found the man sitting with a loaded pistol on his desk while he wrote a farewell letter to his wife. He had got into financial difficulties, and intended to commit suicide that very hour. Helena's role was, apparently, to bring the money just in time to save him for "the sake of events that would subsequently happen as a consequence—events of importance to the world . . ." Helena told Olcott that she had—a year after the event—entirely forgotten the man's name, and his address in Buffalo.[4]

But in the ordinary way of life, as her friends pointed out, she had the Russian proclivity for shedding money as if it were a burden. In about the middle of 1874 she met an old acquaintance of Tiflis, a lady by the name of Clementine Gerebko, and was persuaded to join her in a farming venture. Helena entered into a legal partnership agreement, by which she paid one thousand dollars to Madame Gerebko to become a partner in a six-acre farm in Suffolk County, Long Island. The agreement stated that, "all proceeds for crops, poultry, produce, and other products raised on the said farm shall be divided equally, and all expenses" equally shared. The title of the land, however, was to remain in the name of Mme. Gerebko.

Helena no doubt thought that she had found a way to overcome her ever-recurring economic problems and enjoy material security. Joyfully, she left the heat of New York city in July—after a whole year of living there —and went to the Long Island farm.

But things soon went wrong. Here is Helena telling the story to the N.Y. *Sunday Mercury* in reply to an earlier article, published in that journal:

"The first month I spent nearly $500 for buildings and otherwise; at the expiration of which month she [Madame Gerebko] prayed to be released of the contract, as she was ready to pay me my money back. I consented, and gave her permission to sell at auction all we had except the farm land and buildings, and we both came to New York in view of the settlement. She was to give me a promissory note or a mortgage on the property to the amount of the sum due by her, and that immediately after our coming to New York. Alas! three days after we had taken lodging in common, on one fine afternoon, upon my returning home, I found that the fair countess [Mme. Gerebko] had left the place, neglecting to pay me back her little bill of $1,000."[5]

Friends in New York persuaded her to take legal action for the recovery of her money and introduced her to the Brooklyn law firm of Bergen, Jacobs and Ivins. There she met William M. Ivins, Attorney at Law, who was interested in Occultism, and became her good friend. But her case had to wait many months for its turn to be heard in the courts.

In the meantime Helena had found a new way to earn her bread. She worked at translating into Russian any articles on Spiritualism that appeared in the American press. She also finished off a Russian translation of the second part of *Edwin Drood,* the novel left unfinished by Charles Dickens at his death. A medium named James had completed it in English, declaring that the spirit of Dickens wrote through him.

"Whether the spirit of Dickens wrote it, or the medium James himself," wrote Helena to her fellow countryman, A. N. Aksakoff, "this second part is accepted by the American and European press (with a few exceptions) as a perfect fac-simile of Dickens's style and his inimitable humour."

At the same time she was making friends among people interested in Spiritualism, particularly those whose interests spread into the wider cultural currents of the day.

Fifteen years earlier, in 1859, Darwin's *Origin of Species* had been published, and its effects in America were growing in strength. The Evolutionary Theory was a live subject of dispute. Some accepted it readily and rejoiced at its blow to the old, moribund church theology. It provided a scientific basis for their atheism or agnosticism.

Other people rejected it savagely, holding to the traditional teaching that God had made the first man in His own image and placed him in the Garden of Eden, a certain calculable number of years earlier. They were completely revolted by the new theory that they had "descended from the apes," implying, as it did, that they had no souls, were nothing more than the body, and that the doctrine of a hereafter was a foolish, wish-fulfillment dream.

This was, indeed, a sad and painful philosophy to minds nurtured in the comfort of the Christian Faith. But offsetting it, and bringing new hope, Spiritualism was growing in strength and in exciting phenomena as the 1870s moved forward. "Let a few ungodly scientists say as they might," declared its enthusiastic devotees, "here is definite and factual proof that man does survive death."

Madame Blavatsky had by now a general concept of what her destined work for the world was to be. To begin, she had to use this new public interest in psychic phenomena to lead men to the deeper teaching beyond it. The current of intellectual thought must be led away from the false deductions of Darwinism. Spiritualism, though inadequate in itself, as it stood, could be used as a gateway to a deeper, satisfactory understanding of life's mysteries as revealed in the esoteric teachings of the Adepts.

Yes, she knew for *what* her Masters had trained her and had now sent her to this raw but free-thinking land. But she did not know *when* she was to begin, or exactly *where*.

It was important not to make another false start, as she had done impulsively in Egypt. She must wait for *their* word.

One day in the street, in early October, 1874, she paid a dollar for a copy of a New York newspaper called the *Daily Graphic*. She could not afford such a price; it was ridiculous, but quite impossible to buy one for less. The reason for the tremendous rush on the *Daily Graphic* was its sensational stories on "Spiritualistic materializations" taking place at an old farmhouse near the village of Chittenden in the State of Vermont. The journalist reporting the events from the spot was a man named Colonel Henry S. Olcott.

Helena read the reports with mild interest. She had seen phenomena just as remarkable—even more so—in other parts of the world. Yet this was certainly the most striking and powerful manifestation at present in America. Perhaps she should go up there, herself, and see what was really happening.

Then she received a message from her distant Guru, a distinct, unmistakable telepathic message, such as she had been able to receive since her training in Tibet. It was that she must definitely go to the old Vermont farmhouse where the "ghosts" were parading, for there she would meet the man selected to be her partner in the Great Work. The time had come for it to begin.

PART II

The Sun Climbs Slow, How Slowly.

To comprehend the principles of natural law . . . the reader must keep in mind the fundamental propositions of the Oriental philosophy . . .

1st. There is no miracle. Everything that happens is the result of law—eternal, immutable, ever active . . .

2nd. Nature is triune: there is a visible, objective nature; an invisible, indwelling, energizing nature, the exact model of the other, and its vital principle; and, above these two, *spirit,* source of all forces, alone eternal and indestructible . . .

3rd. Man is also triune: he has his objective, physical body; his vitalizing astral body (or soul), the real man; and these two are brooded over and illuminated by the third—the sovereign, the immortal spirit . . .

4th. Magic, as a science, is the knowledge of these principles, and of the way by which the omniscience and omnipotence of the spirit and its control over nature's forces may be acquired by the individual while still in the body. Magic, as an art, is the application of this knowledge in practice.

5th. Arcane knowledge misapplied, is sorcery; beneficently used, true magic or *wisdom.*

6th. Mediumship is the opposite of adeptship; the medium is the passive instrument of foreign influences, the adept actively controls himself and all inferior potencies.

7th. All things that ever were, that are, or that will be, having their record upon the astral light, or tablet of the unseen universe, the initiated adept, by using the vision of his own spirit, can know all that has been known or can be known.

8th. Races of men differ in spiritual gifts as in color, stature, or any external quality . . .

9th. One phase of magical skill is the voluntary and conscious withdrawal of the inner man (astral form) from the outer man (physical body) . . .

10th. The cornerstone of *magic* is in intimate practical knowledge of magnetism and electricity, their qualities, correlations, and potencies . . .

To sum up all in a few words, *magic* is spiritual *wisdom;* nature, the material ally, pupil and servant of the magician. One common vital principle pervades all things, and this is controllable by the perfected human will. . . ."

CHAPTER 10

Lunch was in progress at the Chittenden ghost-house. Helena sat with Mme. Magnon, the French-Canadian woman who had accompanied her from New York. They had just arrived, and this was the first meal.

Presently a man came and sat directly opposite to her, even though there were plenty of other empty places at the long table. Ignoring him, she continued her conversation in French with her companion. But she felt him studying her intently.

Glancing at him swiftly, she got an impression of a high nose with gold-rimmed spectacles perched on top of it, bushy side-whiskers, and a rather melancholy but intelligent face. He would be in his early forties, she guessed.

After lunch, as she and her friend walked from the dining-room, into the brilliant sunshine, she rolled herself a cigarette; then before she could light a match, the same man was in front of her, offering a light. Suddenly she knew that this self-assured man, with the strong profile and noble brow, was Colonel Olcott. She felt an impish urge to tease him.

In French, with a Yankee accent, he was making some polite remarks. She complained about having to pay a dollar for the *Daily Graphic* which had interested her in the Eddy Farm events.

"Even so, I hesitated about coming here," she told him.

"Why so?"

"Well, I was afraid that Colonel Olcott might drag me into one of his newspaper articles."

Momentarily his eyes turned away to the Green Mountains, then returned to look at her squarely.

"You need have no fear on that score, Madame," he said. "He won't do so unless you permit it. I can assure you of that because *I* am Colonel Olcott, at your service!"

Helena laughed, introduced herself, and shook his hand. She felt that this must be the man meant to become her partner. One could not be quite sure, of course, for even if the Masters had picked him out for the job, they would still test him for a time. But she felt that her geographical hunt, her interminable world-wandering, was over. Now she would go only where her Guru sent her. But though the outer search might be over, the inner one certainly was not.

But now it was October, 1874, and she was looking forward to some interesting evenings in what the profane called the "ghost shop," and some pleasant sunny days, talking to her new friend and, she thought, future partner.

Madame Blavatsky's presence in the seance room upstairs brought some new outlandish characters to the cast of materialized forms that had been parading nightly on the platform, while the medium William Eddy sat entranced in the little cabinet.[1]

Among the phantom visitors appearing specially for her was a Georgian boy who had been a servant in the household of her aunt, Katherine de Witte. At Helena's request, given in his native tongue, he played some national Circassian airs on a guitar he carried.

Another was an old Persian merchant, in perfect national costume, whom she and her family had known for many years in Tiflis. From Tiflis, also came a "nouker" (a man who runs either before or behind a person on horseback). When Helena pronounced his name wrongly, he corrected her. She repeated it, and he said, in guttural Tartar, "Tchoch yachtchi" (all right), bowed and went away.

One of the most startling of the ghosts was a gigantic warrior of Kurdistan, carrying a long spear ornamented with bright-colored feathers. This he shook and made other gestures of greeting and respect, typical of the tribes of Kurdistan. Helena recognized him immediately as Safar Ali Bek, the young chief who—on her husband's instructions—used to guard her on her rides in the country around Yerivan and Mount Ararat.

Seeing these and other picturesque characters from her past in a house in the farmlands of Vermont did not surprise Helena. But she felt quite faint at the moment a grey-haired gentleman came out attired in a conventional suit of black. She thought it was Colonel Peter von Hahn himself; at last she was seeing someone she loved and longed to speak with—her dear father! "Are you my father?" she asked, using English in her great excitement. He shook his head and answered in Russian: "No, I am your uncle." Everyone in the audience, she declared, must have heard clearly the word, "diadia," meaning "uncle." It was Gustav A. von Hahn, late President of the Criminal Court at Grodno, Russia. He was very like her father in appearance, she explained, though somewhat shorter.

Colonel Olcott, who was using all the tests his ingenuity could devise for his investigations, was delighted with these highly evidential manifestations. How could the most skeptical among the thirty or so sitters in the "circle room" credit any of the Eddy family with the knowledge of customs, folk-music, strange languages, and so on, that would be necessary for deliberate impersonations. Even if simple, poor Vermont farmers *did* somehow get the special knowledge, they would not have the costumes and props on hand, and to acquire them suddenly after Madame Blavatsky's arrival, would be a miracle in itself.

Helena felt that it was worth the trouble and expense of the long journey from New York to be able to strike such a stunning blow, through the pages of the *Daily Graphic,* against the smug skeptics and materialists, apart from the more important matter of meeting Colonel Olcott.

She learned, however, and was not surprised to learn, that there were some who came to the Eddy Farm quite determined to expose "the sham and fraud" that was being carried on there. Mostly these people's minds had been made up before they arrived. They stayed at the farm only a night, or perhaps two, and then dashed off home to denounce the Eddy family publicly.

One of the prejudiced "exposers" of the Eddies was a certain Doctor George Beard of New York. After a flying visit to the farm he wrote a scathing attack in the press, saying, "Three dollars worth of second-hand drapery would be enough for him to show how to materialize all the spirits that visit the Eddy Homestead."

He no doubt calculated—rightly—that this attack would have two good effects for him personally. It would start a controversy in the public media that would bring him publicity of value in his career, and it would establish him on the side of society's two protective, though warring, angels: the old Church and the new Science. Both were respectable; Spiritualism was *not*.

To Madame Blavatsky, Dr. George Beard represented the most dangerous of her enemies, those who would write off *all* supernormal phenomena as fraud, and thus, if possible, bind the nineteenth-century mind beyond rescue in the prison of materialism. Even though she did not agree with all the interpretations and explanations of modern Spiritualism, she knew that many of its phenomena were real enough. So, donning the mantle of Spiritualism for the time being, she took up her pen and wrote an article in English for the American press.[2]

The article, called *Marvellous Spirit Manifestation,* was published in the *Daily Graphic* of New York on October 30, 1874. It was polemical, as much of her future writing was to be, and was written in a lively, entertaining style. She addressed it from 124 East Sixteenth Street, New York.

It was a long article in which she told of what she had witnessed at the Eddy Farm (during some fourteen days there), took Dr. Beard apart with cutting irony, and finally challenged him "to the amount of $500 to produce before a public audience and under the same conditions the manifestations herein attested, or, failing this, to bear the ignominious consequences of his proposed *exposé*."

Beard never accepted the challenge, but he wrote more articles, and the press debate between Spiritualism and materialism continued. One promising result of her first article was a friendly appreciative letter from Elbridge

Gerry Brown, a young American who was Editor of the *Spiritual Scientist*. He thanked her for her service to Spiritualism, praised her "attractive style," and asked permission to call on her if she ever came to Boston (where his journal was being published).

Madame Blavatsky, who by this time had the journalistic bit well in her teeth, wrote an article for the *Spiritual Scientist* of December 3, 1874. In this she attacked the whole of the complacent Establishment, including the Church, as well as the "moral cowardice" of the so-called Spiritualists. As she wore publicly the Spiritualists' mantle—despite her criticism of certain sections of the movement—they still regarded her as theirs, their great and fearless champion.

Helena knew that it was her duty to keep alive a belief in the genuineness of Spiritualistic phenomena. Otherwise, with the exposure of the fraudulent practices of several well-known mediums, thousands of Spiritualists would lose faith and slip back into atheistic materialism.

So she let the public pin the Spiritualist label on her, and did not squirm too much. She found she could accept the position by regarding the term in its wider connotation. She was, indeed, a Spiritualist in the "ancient Alexandrian way," she explained in a letter to her Aunt Nadya, though *not* in the modern American way. Even with Colonel Olcott—now at last back from Vermont—she had to be careful how she talked. Through phenomena he had become convinced of the immortality of the soul, and was a very keen Spiritualist. But he *did* have an inquiring, doubting, philosophical mind and felt that there was something wrong somewhere about most Spiritualistic manifestations—or at least with the explanations he had so far found.

The Olcott soil was almost ready for the seeds of true occultism. But at the moment he was too identified with the Spiritualistic movement, and there was no doubt he was a loyal, staunch—not to say obstinate—type.

When won over, he would no doubt use these good qualities in the service of the vast experiment of the Great Ones. She began her campaign of winning and educating the Colonel by amazing him with phenomena created by her own trained will, making no use of dark rooms, tranced mediums, or the other trappings of Spiritualism.

At the same time certain Adepts of the Egyptian Lodge of the Great Brotherhood began writing letters to Olcott. Gently, they directed him toward certain goals, impressing him by their powers of conscious, directed telepathy and clairvoyance—and often by the magical transit of their letters to him.

Apart from the Colonel, it seemed to Helena that the Masters were planning to employ Mr. E. Gerry Brown and his paper, the *Spiritual Scientist,* the best of the Spiritualist publications. While the other journals exploited the movement for sensational stories, the *Spiritual Scientist* was much more serious and explanatory. It could, perhaps, become an organ for the spread of the esoteric philosophy that would bring true perspective and meaning to phenomena.

As soon as she saw this possibility, Helena worked hard toward it. She herself wrote many articles for the journal and tried to induce some of the intellectual, high minded Spiritualists of her acquaintance to do the same.

"By degrees the favour of such men as yourself," she wrote in a letter to Professor Hiram Corson of Cornell University, "Epes Sargent, General Lippitt, Colonel Olcott and others I might name, is being enlisted, and it is my desire that . . . a list of these eminent writers will be announced as . . . contributing exclusively to its columns. My idea is, by no means to depend on Mr. E. G. Brown alone for the direction of our campaign."

But Mr. Brown, unfortunately, soon began to show himself as a dyed-in-the-wool Spiritualist, not easy to dislodge on certain basic issues.

Besides these problems, Helena had an acute personal one. The Eddy Farm publicity had brought into her life a man from Georgia, Russia, who was now in Philadelphia struggling to establish an import-export business. He declared himself to be madly in love with Helena and proposed marriage.

This, in the first place, surprised her, for she regarded herself, though only 43, as an unattractive "hippopotamus of a woman." He was talking a lot of flapdoodle, she told him, bluntly. But he persisted. She grew angry. He threatened to commit suicide if she did not marry him. All he wanted, he told her was to watch over her and protect her against worldly wants and difficulties. His love was unselfish adoration of her intellectual grandeur. He asked nothing for himself. No conjugal rights. No marriage consummation. She could even keep her own name, and do just what she liked. He would not interfere and would ask no questions.

In the end he wore down her resistance. Perhaps she thought that such a marriage would bring her economic security, and she would be able to concentrate wholly on her mission. The lawsuit against Clementine Gerebko had not yet been heard, so she could not count on getting any of that money back. She was making a little from her articles and weird stories to the press but was by no means financially secure.

She may too have had sounder reasons for the marriage, occult and otherwise. Later she told Olcott that she was linked with the Georgian karmically, and the union was in the nature of a punishment "for her awful pride and combativeness which impeded her spiritual evolution."

On April 3, 1875, she went with Michael Betanelly to the First Unitarian Church of Philadelphia, where they were duly married by the Reverend William H. Furness. Helena had heard that her first husband was dead. But in fact he was *not,* so from a legal standpoint, the marriage was bigamous.

Colonel Olcott was in Philadelphia at the time of the wedding, but he did not attend. According to his view, the marriage should have taken place, if at all, two days earlier—on April Fools' Day. Betanelly was, he wrote, "inexpressibly her inferior in mental capacity; one, moreover who could never be even an agreeable companion to her, and with very little means—his mercantile business not being as yet established . . ."[3]

Shortly after her marriage, Madame Blavatsky went to

Riverhead, Long Island, where her lawsuit was to be heard. Staying with her at the country hotel were several lawyers, clerks, and others connected with the court. Her own attorney, William Ivins, was there, and a law student who was to act as interpreter (some of the evidence being in French). Both of these men proved to be keenly interested in Gnosticism, Kabalism, Alchemy, Neo-Platonism and other allied subjects. Lively and fascinating were the discussions within the walls of the dull country hotel. Ivins became an admirer of Madame Blavatsky and her friend for life. Through him she met several brilliant young Irish-American lawyers, who were to become loyal helpers in her work.

Before the trial her legal advisers went over the testimony with Madame Blavatsky, instructing her on the points she should emphasize. But when she stood in the witness box, they were greatly alarmed to hear her racing along lines of evidence quite opposite to their advice. What could the woman be thinking of? She would certainly lose the case, they felt.

When they later complained about her testimony, she answered, they said, that she was being prompted by "someone" who stood at her side, invisible to them. This someone she called "John King," and the lawyers thought of him as her "familiar" spirit.

Madame left Riverhead "after the court had taken the matter under advisement . . . but wrote several letters to Ivins asking about the progress of the suit, and finally astonished him by a letter giving an outline of an opinion which she said the court would render in the course of a few days in connection with a decision in her favor. In accordance with her prediction, the court handed down a decision sustaining her claim upon grounds similar to those which she had outlined in her letter."[4] She was awarded the sum of $1146 and costs of the action.

Helena's second marriage lasted less than four months. Betanelly was unable to sustain his side of the Platonic agreement, and she had no intention whatever of leading a normal married life with him, involving sexual relations and the loss of independence in her actions. Her nature

revolted against both and besides, her special work ruled
them out.

By the end of July she was back in New York, living
at 46 Irving Place in an apartment found for her by
Colonel Olcott. The two had a good deal of work to do
together. As he was still keenly interested in Spiritualistic
research, she assisted him in the investigation of several
outstanding mediums. This, she told herself, was also a
legitimate part of her own work because she wanted to
help establish firmly in the public mind the reality of
genuine psychic phenomena—even though many mediums
did cheat. Her battle was not yet so much with the Spiritualists; it was with the skeptics, the cynics, and the arro-
gant rank and file of the physical scientists.

Fortunately for the work, the Colonel had been divorced from his wife for some time; but with two sons
still being educated, he was not entirely free of family
ties. He worked hard at his law office in Beek Street,
and wrote a good deal for the press, mainly on psychic
subjects. His book on the same subject, *People from the
Other World,* published in March, 1875, had been well
received by leaders in psychic research on both sides of
the Atlantic, including some eminent scientists such as
Alfred Russell Wallace, F.R.S., in England, and the Russian author, philosopher, and Civil Councilor, Alexander
N. Aksakov.

, The latter wrote to Olcott and asked him if he would
procure, with Madame Blavatsky's help, a good and reliable medium who would be willing to travel to Russia
and submit to investigation by a committee of university
professors and scientists. Olcott and Helena agreed to try.

Apart from instructing the Colonel in higher occultism
—a job for which she felt inadequate, even though it had
been given to her by the Masters—Helena was becoming
extremely busy with her pen and in other ways. In the
daytime she wrote articles for publication in America
and translations for Russian journals. In the evenings
there were usually visitors who came to listen to her talk.
She was no good at giving public lectures—that was Olcott's side of the work—but at the *conversazione* she was

superb. Writes the Princess Helene von Racowitza:[5] "She possessed an irresistible charm in conversation, that comprised chiefly an intense comprehension of everything noble and great; and her really overflowing enthusiasm, joined to the most original and often coarse humour, was a mode of expression which was the comical despair of prudish Anglo-Saxons."

Many of the best intellects from the learned professions came to her *conversaziones;* some were brought by the Colonel; others came through her earlier contacts with William Ivins and with leading Spiritualists of the day.

Madame Blavatsky discoursed on all manner of things and ideas—mainly of an off-beat nature—often weaving them around her many travels and adventures. The deeper ideas of Occultism she introduced very tentatively and slowly. Some of her visitors agreed with her avant-garde thinking; others did not. But all found her stimulating. She was like a fresh breeze in the heavy atmosphere of 1875 American puritanism.

Sometimes she used paranormal phenomena such as the ringing of her "astral bells," which some said was done by an attendant sprite, named "Pou Dhi." Actually, whatever elementals she might employ, all her phenomena were beautifully under the control of her will. In reality, under the veil of appearances, people—including Olcott—were being interested, tested, selected, for the next big event— the event that would mark the official beginning of the work for which she had been training for so long.

In the big Scrapbook, where she had pasted cuttings of the press battles to date, she recorded her receipt of new instructions from the Brotherhood:

"*Orders* received from India direct to establish a philosophico-religious Society and choose a name for it—also to choose Olcott."

This meant that public teachings of true Occultism must begin. It meant, also, total war with the Spiritualists, many of whom—fine men such as Professor Corson, General Lippitt, Epes Sargent, Andrew Jackson Davis, and Robert Dale Owen—were her dear friends.

CHAPTER 11

People reclined on low divans, sat on chests covered with Indian hangings and cushions, or curled their legs under them on the soft oriental rugs spread on the floor. Smoke from incense rose in front of serene-faced Eastern statues and filled the room with its fragrance.

Colonel Olcott counted seventeen people present, including himself and Madame Blavatsky, and he recalled, with a strange feeling of the moment's pregnancy, that the date was September 7. Whenever there were "sevens" around, he felt an occult significance.

Though the meeting was at Madame Blavatsky's apartment in Irving Place, for once she was not tonight the center of attraction. The people had come to hear a talk by a Mr. George Felt, who was a geometer, engineer and —it was considered by many—a genius. At any rate the talk promised to be fascinating.

Showing a number of exquisite drawings, Felt discoursed on the lost Canon of Proportion, known to the ancient world and used for the creation of its masterpieces in architecture and art. He claimed to have rediscovered the lost Canon through clues found in the temple hieroglyphs of Egypt. He had discovered also, he said, that the ancient Egyptian priests were adepts in the magical science of evoking and employing the spirits of the elements. They had left formularies for this science on record in the hieroglyphs; he had tested them and found that they worked, he stated.

In the audience was a Dr. Seth Pancoast, an erudite Kabalist, who now cleared his throat, and asked the speaker:

"Can you prove in a practical way your knowledge of this occult science?"

"I can call into sight hundreds of shadowy forms resembling the human," Felt replied, "but as yet I have seen no signs of intelligence in these apparitions."

"Is this power of evocation demonstrable?" someone asked.

"Yes, I can exhibit the nature-spirits to spectators—but that would take time; it would require a *series* of lectures."

"But could *we* learn the formulas and test them ourselves?"

"*Some* of you, yes. It all depends on an individual's occult development."

At about this stage of proceedings an idea floated into someone's mind, Olcott's say some records; Madame Blavatsky's say others. Perhaps it was both, for the pair were in telepathic rapport with each other, and with powerful Adept minds outside. At any rate, a note passed between them, through the hands of their young friend and co-worker, William Quan Judge.

The note suggested the formation of a Society dedicated to this kind of occult study, and there was mutual agreement on the suggestion. Colonel Olcott then stood up and put the proposal to the audience. The idea met with enthusiastic general approval.

It was finally decided that all should meet again on the following evening to discuss the matter further, and to draw up a framework for such a Society. It was agreed, also, that Mr. Felt's offer to give a series of lectures and demonstrations be accepted, and that he be remunerated for this work.

The meeting, as proposed, did take place on the following evening; another one five days later (September 13), and a further one in the middle of October. As a result of these gatherings a Society was founded, with Colonel Henry Steel Olcott as President, Dr. Seth Pancoast and

Mr. George Felt as Vice-Presidents, and Mr. Henry J. Newton, a wealthy retired manufacturer, as Treasurer. Madame H.P. Blavatsky was to be the Corresponding Secretary, while the position of Recording Secretary was held by Mr. John Storer Cobb, an English barrister and Doctor of Laws. Legal Counselor for the Society was Mr. William Quan Judge.

The person credited with finding, after much discussion, an acceptable name for the Society was Mr. Charles Southeran, author, bibliographer, man of broad culture, a member of the Rosicrucian Society and a Mason of exalted rank. Some said he was acquainted with one, at least, of the Brotherhood of Adepts. The word "Theosophy," which was chosen, perhaps did not altogether suit the image of the new Society as then envisioned by sixteen out of the original seventeen. But it suited very well the concept of what it was to become—as planned by those behind the scenes and no doubt understood by Madame Blavatsky.

It was decided that the first official meeting of the new Theosophical Society would be held, and the President would give an inaugural address, in a New York public hall on November 17, 1875.

But before that important date, Helena, who knew what the Society's effects would be on her friends, the Spiritualists, decided to go on a trip to Ithaca, in New York State. There she would spend some time in the home of one of the leading intellects among the American Spiritualists of the day, Professor Hiram Corson.

She had been carrying on a correspondence with the professor for some time, and it was his great interest in her letters that resulted in her invitation to Ithaca. But she, herself, was rather worried about the effects on a small provincial town of what she called her inextinguishable cigarette, and "manners of a Prussian grenadier on furlough." Corson was an important figure with a growing reputation at Cornell University, where he was professor of Anglo-Saxon and English Literature. Helena knew something of the polite veneer of academic society and feared that she would not fit in. Still, the professor was intensely interested in questions of the spirits—an interest probably sparked, originally, by the death of his daughter. His wife, who was French, shared his interest in a more moderate way. Perhaps they could both be made good allies, not only in the war against the materialists, but also in spreading a deeper understanding of psychic phenomena.

So, a couple of days after the second meeting held to discuss the proposed Society, Helena set off on the 300-mile journey by boat (up the Hudson river) and rail to Ithaca. She arrived at the two-storied colonial house of the Corsons on September 17.

The visit was not an unmitigated success. The professor wrote to his son: "I had expected we should have some 'sittings' for raising spirits together; but she [Madame Blavatsky] is not only not disposed, but is decidedly opposed to anything of the kind . . . She is a great Russian bear."[1] And in another letter: "Never have I seen such an intense creature, intense in her purpose, intense in her endeavour; nothing around her mattered; though the heavens fall she would keep her way."[2]

Apparently her way was to "write from morning to midnight often, without stopping longer than to take dinner and make a cigarette." She was in fact, starting on her first, tentative draft of what was to become *Isis Unveiled*.

But though she would not humor the professor with a Spiritualist séance, she did show him that by the power of her conscious will she could produce psychic phenomena, such as raps on the furniture and body. He found some of her demonstrations quite startling. In one, for instance, she produced a striking portrait of the Corsons' dead daughter. When Mrs. Corson saw this, she burst into tears, exclaiming: "It's the work of the devil," and threw the portrait in the fire. But another piece of magic was more helpful to the French lady.

The Corsons' son, Eugene—who later in life published Madame Blavatsky's letters to his father and mother—describes this: "One evening a frost was predicted, and my mother was anxious to get in her potted plants from the porch, when H.P.B. told her not to worry, and she would get 'John' to bring them in. So they went to bed without any concern, and in the morning all the pot plants were found inside."[3]

Everyone who knew Helena at that time knew of "John King," the invisible, who seemed to be always at her beck and call, though he played up a little sometimes. "John" claimed to be the earth-wandering spirit of the notorious seventeenth-century buccaneer, Sir Henry Morgan. For some reason he had become the servant, or "familiar spirit" of Madame Blavatsky. She writes of many amusing anecdotes about him.[4] He also seemed to act at times as a messenger of one or another of the Adepts.

But "John King," whatever and whoever he was, did not confine his activities to one side of the Atlantic. He was well known to several eminent psychic researchers in Europe. Two of them, Professor Butleroff, the renowned Russian chemist, and A. N. Aksakoff, describing "sittings" in London during that summer of 1875, report that "Mr. Crookes [later Sir William Crookes] himself confirmed that the apparition of John King had appeared in his own house, whilst Mrs. Crookes had her hand on the shoulder of Williams [the medium], asleep behind the curtain."[5]

A quarter of a century later Arthur J. G. Fletcher wrote to Sir Oliver Lodge, describing a manifestation at a sitting: ". . . a kind of spiral column of cloud . . . seemed to shape itself until it assumed the full-length figure of a man, with a long black beard, a very fine forehead and noble appearance . . . He came straight to our table and stood on the far side opposite to me. He greeted us all very kindly, and after a while told us that his name was John King."[6]

The description is very like the "John King" who painted his own portrait for General Lippit in America in the 1870s. The portrait was later given to The Theosophical Society, and today hangs—as fresh as if just finished—at the Society's International Headquarters in Adyar, India.

Even in recent years a "being" with the same remarkable psychodynamism has manifested in psychic research circles in Europe and announced himself as "John King." Some theorists opine that a number of *different* entities (phantoms of the dead or the living, or beings that are neither) have, in Madame Blavatsky's time and later, used the same name. But all who have used it have had the same power to produce strong, often breathtaking, physical phenomena (PK) in the seance room. For Helena this robust, likeable character produced such phenomena anywhere, under whatever conditions prevailed.

Helena spent nearly four weeks with the Corsons. After she left, the professor wrote to his son: "Mme B. has gone. Though there were many things unpleasant in her stay with us, altogether we enjoyed her visit. She is a very remarkable woman . . . Beardsley [a photographer of Ithaca] has taken some magnificent pictures of her."[7]

But the important question for Helena was: had she sown the right seeds? Would the professor become a helper in the Great Work? Only time could tell that.

She was back in New York by about the middle of October, in time for the third meeting of the incubating Society, held this time at the home of a dynamic lecturer on Spiritualism, Mrs. Emma Hardinge-Britten.

Helena decided that the man the Adepts had evidently chosen as her main partner, Colonel Olcott, was a good complement to herself; he was a keen organizer and knew all about the proper legal basis for a Society that was to have a very long life. In fact, he was strong in the very points where she was quite helpless.

He was coming along well with his new studies, too, beginning to grasp the broad basis of Occultism and, most important, he had now been accepted as a *chela* by her own Guru, Master Morya.

Anyway, Olcott knew enough to give the inaugural address of the Society before the general public in Mott Memorial Hall, Madison Avenue, on November 17. She herself would not have cared to do so; the format of a set lecture given from a platform in a public place seemed to dry her up. So on that important night she sat in the audience. Scarcely listening to what her pupil Henry Olcott was saying, she studied the faces of the audience. What would be the public reaction, she wondered, to this birth of a "rebel"—a strange, foreign-featured rebel— among the set, conservative, respectable descendents of the stern Puritans.

Actually, the respectable, nonthinking public largely disregarded the birth, and the attacks on it came chiefly from the Spiritualists. Even her new hope, Professor Corson, wrote to her, criticizing some ideas in Olcott's inaugural address. "Et tu, Brute!" she replied. "Well, you have given me a nice blow and a very unexpected one."

But she was not at all surprised that the mass of the Spiritualists should dislike the new Society and all it stood for. The issue was largely an emotional one. Shorn by modern science of their hope of a life-after-death, they had found it again through Spiritualism. Found it not through dogma and doctrine this time, but empirically, by actually seeing and communicating—they believed— with those who had passed the portals of death. Here was something more than hope; here was certainty!

Then along came Madame Blavatsky, and her Theosophical Society, trying to tell then that what they had taken for fact was fallacy, that the shapes and voices and signs were not, as they had thought, from their dear departed dead, but from elementals, elementaries, astral shells—soulless denizens of other planes who, for some reason, were supposed to take delight in fooling human beings. According to this philosophy, if one escaped being cheated by the mediums, one was cheated by the "spirits." The idea was unacceptable to most Spiritualists.

Then, as the months moved on, and Olcott lectured in public places and Helena talked in her New York *salon,* and both wrote press articles and pamphlets defending the new teachings, the visible fortress of their hopes, The Theosophical Society, began, itself, to crumble away before their eyes.

CHAPTER 12

The experiment with Felt failed. He proved to be erratic, unreliable, and expensive. Opinions differed about whether or not he kept his crucial promise to give a practical, demonstration in raising the elemental spirits. Madame Blavatsky said that he did; Colonel Olcott, on the other hand, wrote that Felt failed to show so much as "the tip of a nature spirit's tail."

Felt, himself, maintained that when he began to produce the shadowy forms, an unpleasant feeling of dread was created in his audience. The reactions were such, he said, that Madame Blavatsky, "who had seen similar unpleasant effects follow somewhat similar phenomena in the East," requested him to stop, to turn the drawings over, and to speak on another subject. He had been able, he claimed, to convince some, but not all the members of the Society.

Whatever the truth, George Felt's series of demonstrations was terminated, and the *apparent* main purpose of forming the Society had failed. Helena knew, however, that magic and miracles were *not* the primary object of the Society, and Olcott was beginning to glimpse a broader purpose. But some members thought the organization had failed and drifted away from it.

The leading minds among the American Spiritualists wanted, of course, a satisfactory philosophy as a basis for the undoubted seance room phenomena, and some had shown interest in the new Society. But few of them were able, in fact, to accept and digest what Madame Blavatsky taught on the subject.

Several, indeed, believed, as medieval demonology maintained, that there were beings other than deceased humans in the invisible planes. The great "Poughkeepsie Seer," Andrew Jackson Davis, talked of mischievous, amoral imps who sometimes made their presence felt. He called them Diakki.

Supporting her ideas by quoting from various authorities, Helena wrote that "Prince Dolgoruky, the greatest mesmeriser now living except Dupotet, says, after thirty years experience with clairvoyants . . . that the gnomes and sylphs generally prevail if the medium is not pure . . ."[1]

American Spiritualists, however, balked at her assertion that practically all beings who came from the "other side" in the seances were imposters, masquerading as deceased friends and relatives; that only suicides, and those who had met with violent and untimely deaths, stayed in the vicinity of earth for any length of time, that attempts to bring genuine souls into communication were damaging to such souls as it tended to hold them back from onward progress. Further, Blavatsky's blunt declarations that Spiritualism in America was unconscious sorcery and necromancy, that it retarded the true spiritual progress of the "sitters" and often led to immoral and degrading relationships, were rejected with indignation.

Indeed, however, some of these unsavory aspects, such as "angel wives and husbands" (the demon lovers of old), were beginning to show their heads. Nevertheless Epes Sargent—Helena's favorite among the American Spiritualist authors—wrote to her: "I am not at all alarmed by all the abuses . . . The scum may come to the top for a time. But God reigns and I do not fear for the result." He admonished her for the harsh things she was writing about the Spiritualists and said that the natural reaction of the latter was to strike back, causing damaging conflict among the antimaterialists.

A. J. Davis wrote to her, with gentle humor: "We sympathise with your—enemies. They will need our aid and protection . . . Brigand Diakka are after going for you—we fear . . . and may the 'Lord have mercy on your soul' —which is the last word before 'hanging' a criminal. Mrs.

Davis sends her cordial best wishes . . ."

The pens and tongues of her enemies struck back all right, not only on questions of philosophy, but in calumnies on her character, calling her, she wrote to Mrs. Corson, "an immoral woman who has had her lovers in numbers. Whilst Dr. Bloede, of Brooklyn, tells secretly that I had a criminal liaison with the Pope and Bismark. Mr. Home, that immaculate medium, spread his venom over me in Europe. More then, that I . . . am accused in anonymous letters sent to my friends, who indignantly carry them to me, of frequenting houses of assignation."

Though, as a public figure in a new important movement, she was becoming more sensitive than of yore to this kind of slander, she still appeared to be as much amused as aggravated by it.

Need she have attacked Spiritualism uncompromisingly and gained so many enemies among its adherents? Some writers say not and think that she overstated the case against it, showing lack of subtlety, tact, and discretion. Mr. A. P. Sinnett wrote late in his life[2] "It unfortunately happened that Mme. Blavatsky's sweeping condemnation of all spiritualism as delusive and unwholesome alienated large numbers of people who ought to have been the most ardent sympathisers with the Theosophical Movement. All later students of occultism know now that the astral plane plays a much more important part in the future life of most people 'passing on' than the misleading old 'shell' theory led us to suppose at the beginning."

One who could not go all the way with her anti-Spiritualist teachings was E. Gerry Brown, editor of the *Spiritual Scientist*. Thus, the journal finally proved of no value in spreading theosophical ideas, and as it lacked appeal to the mass of Spiritualists, it had faded out of existence by 1877.

But before that Helena's pen was busy in various directions: she had become a full-time author, journalist, and pamphleteer. In America her articles were appearing in the daily press as well as in the *Spiritual Scientist* and other specialist journals. She wrote to Aksakoff that her articles of wide appeal were reprinted in the form of pamphlets, thousands of which would sell at ten cents a copy.

For the Russian papers she was not only doing translations but was writing original articles on many subjects, including feminism (her mother's favorite theme), suicides, crime, the power of money, the hypocrisy of clergymen, divorces, new discoveries (such as Edison's phonograph) and, of course, magic, sorcery, and Spiritualism. She was thus earning an adequate income from journalism.

From the beginning of 1876, however, her main writing project was the one she had begun tentatively in Ithaca. At the beginning she had no clear idea that she was launching on her first book—a book that would open windows on a secret world, an old yet ever new world, and lay strong foundations for the Theosophical Movement.

Picture a scene in Helena's writing room in her New York apartment. It is evening. Colonel Olcott, who occupies a suite of rooms on the floor above, has come down to help her with the production of the book, a chore that becomes for him a priceless occult education. Sitting opposite her at the long table, on which are spread pages of manuscript, he is sharpening a soft pencil. Helena is absently sketching a face on a sheet of paper. Suddenly she asks him for a loan of the sharpened soft pencil.

Henry Olcott has learned by bitter experience that she is what he calls a "stationery-annexer." If I lend her this, he thinks to himself, it will certainly go into her drawer with all the other pencils, erasers, and the rest, that I have "loaned" her in the past . . .

Looking up, he catches a mildly sarcastic expression in her eye. He glances quickly at the sketch before her; its quality confirms his sudden apprehension that not Helena herself, but a "certain artistic Somebody" is occupying her body, a Somebody who can easily read his thoughts. The beautiful Blavatsky hand now reaches out, lays the pencil it has been using in the tray between them, seems to roll it between the long fingers, and lo, a dozen pencils of identical make have materialized and are lying in the tray! Not a word is spoken, but the silent rebuke brings the blood to Henry's temples; he feels about the size of a pencil, himself.

Any conversation there is during the next hour or so is conducted in French, for Henry is well aware that the artistic Somebody dislikes talking in English.

Then, deeply absorbed in his work, Olcott is, later, only vaguely conscious of the fact that his companion leaves the room for a few minutes. Soon after her return he glances up and sees that she is deep in thought, while her fingers twirl an *imaginary* moustache, and beard. Presently, catching him watching her, she hastily removes her hand from her face and goes on with the work of writing. Henry knows now, with a warm joy in his heart, that he is in the presence of his own Guru, the moustached and bearded Rajput of great dignity and erudition, Master Morya himself.

In the first volume of his *Old Diary Leaves* Colonel Olcott gives a fascinating account of the *Alter Egos* who played their part in the writing of *Isis Unveiled,* of their different personalities, handwriting, and style.

As the psychophysical mechanism of Madame Blavatsky was the channel used, all the handwriting, of course, bore her stamp, but there was enough variation for him to know by a glance at the manuscript which *Alter Ego* had written it. All of them, save one, he said, were living men, with physical bodies which they left temporarily, to occupy, or overshadow, Helena Blavatsky's psychophysical vehicle.

The one *discarnate* entity was an old Platonist, whose name, Olcott says, is known in history.

Where was Helena's own self while this was going on? "It is as if I were asleep, or lying by not quite conscious— not in my own body but close by, held only by a thread which ties me to it. However, at times I see and hear everything quite clearly: I am perfectly conscious of what my body is saying and doing—or at least its new possessor."[3]

When the Adepts did not write *through* her, they often helped her in other wonderful ways: "Well, Vera," she says in a letter to her sister, "I am writing *Isis;* not writing, rather copying out and drawing that which *She personally* is showing me. Really, sometimes it seems to me that the ancient Goddess of Beauty in person leads me through all the lands of past centuries which I have to describe. I am sitting with my eyes open and, to all appearances, see and hear everything real and actual around me, and yet at the same time I see and hear *that which I write*. I feel short of breath; I am afraid to make the slightest movement for fear the spell might be broken. . . . Slowly century after century, image after image, float out of the distance and pass before me as if in a magic panorama. . . ."

When she needed a quotation from some rare, ancient book it would come before her eyes in the "astral light" and she would copy it down. In editing the copy, Henry found that sometimes she used quotation marks, and sometimes she forgot or was careless about them. He himself would put the marks in if, and where, he thought them necessary. But he did not have the time to check all passages carefully in the editing, and several other hands helped in the proofreading. This is probably the reason why the book has found criticism for using passages from other works without quotation marks or acknowledgements.

Beatrice Hastings writes about this criticism: "Verifying a list of 'plagiarisms' given by Emmette Coleman [an industrious bookworm who was H.P.B.'s worst critic], I found that, out of thirty-five names of authors, twenty-six were given by H.P.B. in the text of *Isis Unveiled*. Seeing that her one great concern was to pile up authorities in her own support, I conclude that she did not know where she had read certain matter, had perhaps made notes without setting down the author, or perhaps, had simply remembered the passages and recovered them from the famous subconscious: or, perhaps read them in the 'astral light'."[4]

Nobody knows how much of the book was actually written by Helena, herself, and how much by the co-operative society of Adepts working through her. Helena hated to be thought of as a *medium* (she had no great admiration for most of those she had met), and writers

on the occult point out some of the differences between
her and the ordinary spiritist medium. She had, for instance, been specially trained to cooperate as a mediator
or transmitter for—in the main—*incarnate* Adepts.

She did not lose normal consciousness during the transmitting process, being able, as she said herself, to know
all that was going on and to "remember it all so well that
afterwards I can repeat it."

Certainly it is true that some who are classed as *mediums*
do retain their personal awareness while other intelli-
gences work through them. Mrs. Curran, the American
housewife, for instance, was fully conscious while the discarnate entity known as "Patience Worth" wrote historical
novels—authentic novels, highly-praised by the critics—
through her hand. But she did not know who "Patience
Worth" was. Madame Blavatsky, on the other hand had
met her Adepts—or most of them—in the flesh.

As her mediator or Tulku work intensified, she became known among her friends as "H.P.B." While she
enjoyed the many nicknames Henry Olcott invented for
her—Jack, Mrs. Mulligan, Old Horse, Latchkey, and so
on—she really preferred to be addressed as H.P.B.; it was
a name that to her signified the cooperative group of
Great Ones who had, they said, waited a long time for
such a fine instrument as H.P.B. They were able to use
her, "an initiated *chela*," as a fulcrum, or a kind of receiving and transmitting aerial, while they, themselves,
were bodily in Tibet, or some other far-off place.

The production of *Isis Unveiled,* from its beginning at
the home of Professor Corson to the time it came off the
press, took two years. It was offered to the nineteenth-
century public as a master key to the mysteries of science
and theology, ancient and modern. In modern times the
two had become antagonistic, but in the ancient world
they were united and came closer to ultimate Truth, "for
the spiritual intuition was there to supply the limitations
of physical senses. Separated, exact science rejects the help
of the inner voice, while religion becomes merely dog-
matic theology—each is but a corpse without a soul.

"The esoteric doctrine, then, teaches, like Buddhism

and Brahmanism, and even the persecuted *Kabala,* that
the one infinite and unknown Essence exists from all eternity, and in regular and harmonious successions is either
passive or active. In the poetical phraseology of Manu
these conditions are called the 'day' and 'night' of Brahma."[5]

This concept of an eternal Essence, the Causeless Cause,
of which the spirit of man is a part, is the crux of the
esoteric doctrine. She introduces it in *Isis* and develops
it more fully in her later work, *The Secret Doctrine.*

The New York *Herald-Tribune* commented on the
audacity and versatility of *Isis Unveiled,* "and the pro-
digious variety of subjects which it notices and handles."
It was, the reviewer thought, "one of the remarkable pro-
ductions of the century." Several other newspapers gave
similar favorable reviews, while a few accused the author
of "spreading transcendental nonsense."

The thousand copies of the first impression sold out in
nine days. Fourteen other impressions were published
in H.P.B.'s lifetime. And, despite the fact that it was,
in a sense, superseded by *The Secret Doctrine,* it is still
being published and purchased.

There can be little doubt that *Isis* played a tremendous
role in the early spread of theosophical concepts, and
laid a foundation for the later international growth of
the Theosophical Movement. Letters of appreciation
came to H.P.B. from various parts of the world. The
Countess of Caithness, for instance, later to be a valued
friend of the Founders and of the Theosophical Society,
wrote to express to the author "earnest and sincere thanks
for the delightful hours I have passed with you while
reading your magnificent work, *Isis Unveiled,* and for
all the instruction and enjoyment I have derived from its
perusal."

The last year's work on *Isis* had been done at a flat on
the corner of 47th Street and Eighth Avenue. Officially,
this was the headquarters of The Theosophical Society,
but it was known unofficially to many friends and visitors
as the "Lamasery." It had a large sitting room and four
bedrooms. Colonel Olcott and Madame Blavatsky both

lived and worked there. These two, along with William Quan Judge, were about the only active members left in The Theosophical Society by the time *Isis* was published. Helena and the Colonel were very active indeed. He lectured at various centers. She gave fascinating discourses at her regular "at home" evenings and wrote most of the day. Both wrote on theosophical themes on free evenings, often until one or two in the morning.

But formal meetings of the Society had ceased for want of interest. Olcott says that the last meeting was held, as shown in the Minute Book, on November 15, 1876. Because they were standing almost alone in the cold winds of hostile criticism, they called themselves the "Theosophical Twins."

The American soil seemed, indeed, too thin and barren for the theosophical plant. Those behind the scenes of the movement had apparently come to this conclusion. The Masters concerned—in constant communication by various occult means—let Helena know that the only solution was to take the headquarters of the Society to India. Both Founders should go there.

The idea made a strong appeal to Helena for herself. She loved India and was tired of America—tired of the bitter battles with her critics, of the fruitless attempts to pierce the country's apathy and materialism. But how could she persuade the Colonel to make such a big move? Certainly, the image he held of India was a rosy one. Theoretically, the notion of going there piqued his romantic, adventurous nature, but practically it was another matter.

He was a man in the prime of life, about 45 years of age, doing very well in the legal profession which he had entered some dozen years earlier, just after the close of the Civil War.

During that war, as a Special Commissioner investigating corruption among companies supplying the fighting services, he had proved himself, in the words of one writer, as "a slashing crusader against graft." Near the end of the war he had become so respected for his efficiency and integrity that he was chosen as a member of the elite committee of three colonels whose purpose it was to investigate the conspiracy behind the assassination of President Abraham Lincoln.

The Colonel's success as special investigator earned him great praise and glowing testimonials from his chiefs in the services. It may have been also one of the reasons why the Adepts, with a vision of things to come, had selected him as Helena Blavatsky's partner.

Further reasons, no doubt, lay in his other activities and character traits. Experience in New York journalism had trained him as a popular, lucid writer. Years as a practical teacher of scientific farming had proved his initiative and developed his latent talent as a lecturer. In many ways, during his legal career, he had shown himself to be an energetic organizer and reliable administrator.

His personal life, however, was in a rather unsettled state. In 1860 he had married the daughter of a Congregational minister. The union had not been happy. His wife seems to have been a narrow Puritan, who took strong exception to Henry's interest in Spiritualism and the Eastern ideas that were beginning to penetrate, in a vague and limited way, the mental world of America. Even though the Colonel was divorced before he met Madame Blavatsky, Mrs. Olcott still wrote long moral essays to him, lecturing him on his sins and telling him how he should live.

The point, with regard to the hoped-for move, was that he still supported his ex-wife and his two sons, who were at college.

His life style was changing rapidly, not through Mrs. Olcott's moral essays, but through the training in high Occultism to which he was now being exposed, to his delight, by Madame Blavatsky. His old tastes for worldly pleasures, and the pursuits of self-glory, fame, and power, were slowly evaporating. Helena noted this and was pleased. But even so, she did not think the time yet ripe for urging him to leave all and follow wherever his Master beckoned. Yet step by step things seemed to be moving in that direction.

CHAPTER 13

Talk at the dinner table had drifted to the subject of precipitations, that is, the projection onto paper of a mental image of handwriting, art-work, or something of that nature. As this was one of the occult powers that H.P.B. had developed, her three companions at the table were very keen to learn more about it. William Quan Judge, being something of an artist himself, was particularly interested in this occult art. He longed for a demonstration.

"Would you precipitate someone's portrait for us tonight?"

H.P.B. smiled and rose from the table. As the party moved along the passage toward the writing-room, she asked:

"Whose portrait would you like?"

Judge thought for a moment, then replied: "That of Tiravalla."

This was an Indian yogi of whom H.P.B. had often spoken—one held in great esteem by the Masters, she said. Colonel Olcott, writing later in *Old Diary Leaves,* opines that the name "Tiravalla" was an abbreviation of "Tiruvalluvar," the "revered philosopher of ancient Mylapur, the friend and teacher of the poor Pariahs. . . . He is classed in Southern India as one of the Siddhas, and like the other seventeen, is said to be still living in the Tirupati and Nilgiri Hills, keeping watch and ward over the Hindu religion."

In the writing-room H.P.B. went over to Olcott's table and took a sheet of crested note paper from a packet which the Colonel had brought home from the Lotos Club that evening, just as the other three were starting dinner. H.P.B.'s selection was no doubt to assure her watchers

(Judge, Olcott, and Dr. L. M. Marquette, the lady doctor she had known in Paris) that she had had no opportuntiy to tamper with the paper. She tore the sheet in half, kept the lower part and placed it on her blotting paper. She scraped onto it about a grain of plumbago from a lead pencil. Then with the palm of her right hand she began to rub the surface of the note paper in a circular motion. After about a minute of this, the desired portrait appeared on the upper surface of the note paper, under her hand.

"The yogi is depicted in Samadhi. . . . There is a beard and hair of moderate length, the latter drawn with such skill that one sees through the upstanding locks, as it were—an effect obtained in good photographs, but hard to imitate with pencil or crayon.

"Le Clear, the noted American portrait painter, declared it [the portrait] unique, distinctly an 'individual' in the technical sense; one that no living artist within his knowledge could have produced."[1]

Attorney Judge was so impressed with this phenomenal production, and the conditions under which it was brought about, that he set forth the details in sworn testimonies.

Writing some years later in praise of the quality of H.P.B.'s phenomena, Mahatma K.H. says: "She can and did produce phenomena, owing to her natural powers combined with several long years of regular training, and her phenomena are sometimes better, more wonderful and far more perfect than those of some high, initiated chelas, whom she surpasses in artistic taste and purely Western appreciation of art—as for instance in the instantaneous production of pictures: witness—her portrait of the 'fakir' Tiravalla. . . ."[2]

Helena lost no opportunity of intensifying the Colonel's interest in India, and leading him toward a firm conviction that their only hope of getting the Theosophical Movement "off the ground" was to transport its headquarters to the land of the Rishis.

She was helped in this by an unexpected chance event. At least it *seemed* to be chance, but perhaps, like many other happenings out of the blue, it had been engineered by those behind the facade.

In a conversation with an old Spiritualist friend (a Dr. Peebles) who had just returned from India and Ceylon, it was found, to the surprise of both, that Peebles had met in Bombay an old acquaintance of Henry's. Peebles had the current address of the man, whose name was Moolji Thackersey, and the Colonel promptly wrote to his old acquaintance, telling him of The Theosophical Society.

In his reply Moolji Thackersey spoke of a "great Hindu pandit and reformer who had begun a powerful movement for the resuscitation of pure Vedic religion." This movement, known as the *Arya Samaj*, had a following of many thousands throughout India. The name of the "great pandit and reformer" was Swami Dayanand Sarasvati.

Moolji put Olcott in touch with the President of the Bombay branch of the *Arya Samaj*, a man named Hurrychund Chintamon. A subsequent exchange of letters between New York and Bombay convinced the Colonel that the *Arya Samaj* and The Theosophical Society had almost identical aims, outlook, and philosophy.

Hurrychund Chintamon suggested an amalgamation of the two organizations. The "Theosophical Twins" thought this a good idea, and the necessary steps were taken. The New York body, which apart from the "Twins" existed mainly on paper, changed its name to, "The Theosophical Society of the Arya Samaj." A collection-box now appeared on a shelf at the Lamasery for contribution to the funds of the great Indian organization. In fact, all subscriptions and donations received by the Society in New York from that time went to the *Arya Samaj* through its Bombay branch. And Helena, who loved large figures, was able to write to her friends abroad that her Society had thousands of members.

Some big disappointments were to come later from the great *Arya Samaj*, but for a time it had its function. At this stage it built a mental bridge to India, offering a rosy image of thousands of Indian co-workers in spreading the light of the Ancient Wisdom. Henry Olcott's grass-roots in America showed greater signs of weakening but were not yet quite ready to be plucked away.

Though The Theosophical Society was moribund in New York, there were signs of a growing interest in England. An English visitor had been personally present at the founding of the Society in America. This was Mr. Charles C. Massey, a barrister who gave up law practice to devote himself to the study of philosophy and psychology, especially the new avenues that were opening up in parapsychology. Massey was the son of a British Cabinet Minister.

Another learned friend across the Atlantic was the Reverend William Stainton Moses, known to the Founders and to the Spiritualists of his day by his pseudonym, M.A. Oxon. He was a brilliant writer and a high-class medium, with interests extending into the deeper doctrines of Occultism. Until his health broke down, M. A. Oxon was a professor of Classics and English at University College, London.

A lively correspondence was carried on between the "Twins" and this lovable high-minded scholar, preacher and Spiritualist.

Two other English citizens who made early contact with the movement in America were Miss Emily Kislingbury, Secretary of the British National Association of Spiritualists, and Dr. H. J. Billing whose wife was a well-known English Spiritualist medium. Both of these Londoners had paid visits to the Lamasery in New York. In fact, Miss Kislingbury, who had a tremendous admiration and affection for H.P.B., had been there during the latter part of the *Isis* period, and had sketched out the Table of Contents for Volume II of that work.

Eventually, in London, after many months of preliminary discussions, a group of those interested in Theosophy met at 38 Great Russell Street, Bloomsbury, on June 27, 1878, and formed the "British Theosophical Society." C. C. Massey was chosen as President of this London Branch of the mother Society, and Miss Kislingbury was appointed its first Secretary.

The "Twins" were overjoyed that a seed of international brotherhood, for which The Theosophical Society stood four square, had sent up a tender shoot in the leading center of nineteenth-century imperialism, the land from which Britannia ruled the "lesser breeds without the law." It was a happy omen of a great change to come in the world. And H.P.B. decided that she and the Colonel must visit this, the first-born of their international family, when—and, indeed, *if*—she managed to get Henry away from America.

Still, she knew that eventually all obstacles must be overcome, and they *must* go, no matter what the material and personal sacrifice to her partner, pupil, and fellow disciple of Master Morya. Knowing this, and that she would be leaving America, perhaps forever, she did a very strange thing.

On July 8, 1878, accompanied by Dr. Marquette as a witness, she went to City Hall in New York and became naturalized as a citizen of the United States of America. In the ceremony she had to forswear all allegiance to the Emperor of the land of her birth, a land she could not help loving, though she did not like living in it. Russia to her was the family for whom she had an undying affection.

Why did she want to become a citizen of a country she was planning to leave as soon as possible, a country which, though ghost-crazy at the time, had proved itself spiritually barren for her work? Perhaps some intuition told her, or she knew from past experience, that a Russian living in British India, without any officially recognizable function, would always be suspect, and perhaps she thought that to hold American papers would in some degree mitigate such imperial suspicion.

Colonel Olcott obviously had a tremendous love for his Guru, or spiritual father, the Rajput prince, who had once talked with Helena in Hyde Park, London, had helped her write *Isis Unveiled,* and now in these crucial days of the Society's infancy often made his subtle, but unmistakable, presence felt at the Lamasery. Henry, with his easygoing Yankee ways and love of the informal, often referred to the Master Morya half-jokingly as "Father." H.P.B. understood that this touch of Olcott humor was really a sign of devotion too deep for words. The Master had the power to inspire such devotion; this she knew well enough, from a lifetime of personal experience.

Despite his devotion, poor Olcott had not yet even received a vision of his Master in his subtle body, the kind she herself used to have long before she actually met him in the flesh. But Henry did have his portrait hanging in his bedroom. This crayon sketch was a good likeness, even though done entirely by telepathic influence working through the brain and hand of the French artist, M. Harrisse, who had never actually seen the Master Morya.

One night, after reading until very late as was her custom, H.P.B. seemed hardly to have fallen asleep when a loud banging on her door made her start up in bed. Who the deuce could it be at such an hour? Olcott was the only one sleeping in the apartment that night, and he would never waken her like this, unless. . . . The knocking continued insistently.

"All right. I'm coming," she called.

She opened the door to find Henry standing there, fully dressed, holding a candle. His eyes were shining and he was smiling blissfully, like a child who has just seen Santa Claus loading his stocking. Then he held up somethig in his other hand, a turban of amber striped fabric, embroidered in yellow floss silk. Even without seeing the embroidered "M" on it, she would have recognized the Master Morya's turban.

In silence she came through the door, and they sat down in the writing room while Henry told her—his voice often unsteady with emotion—how Master Morya had suddenly appeared in his room, looking as real and solid as if he were there in the flesh. Henry had been sitting, reading, when he first caught the flash of a brilliant white robe in the corner of his eye.

Looking up and seeing the tall, benign figure, he had dropped his book in amazement, and then fallen on his knees at the Master's feet. A gentle hand had touched his head and a sweet voice bade him be seated.

He had sat for—well, he did not know how long—while the Master sat opposite him on the other side of the little bedroom table. Henry did not tell H.P.B. all that their

Guru had said to him, but she gathered that he had talked about the great work to be done for humanity, and Olcott's right to share in that work if he would make the necessary sacrifices. Though the New York lawyer was a lay *chela* of the Great Lodge, he had not been *"ordered,"* but *invited* to go.

The invitation, however, with its vision of great things to be done, had been so inspiring, so elevating, that for Olcott it made all worldly activities seem utterly lacking in point or importance.

Finally, as Master Morya stood up to leave, he unwound the turban from his long, raven locks and, with a smile, placed it on the table. This was no doubt his reply to Henry's unspoken thought that the whole scene might be some kind of hypnotic illusion brought about by the uncanny power of H.P.B.

By the way in which the Master had come (through locked doors), and now left, Olcott realized that he must have been traveling in a subtle, nonphysical body, which he had solidified temporarily and sufficiently to be seen as normal by the ordinary human eye. The turban, Henry hoped, was permanently and completely materialized, and would remain through the years as a proof to himself that the Master's visit and talk had been an actual reality.[3]

"Very gracious of Master to be concerned about your silly doubts and suspicions," H.P.B. said. "Did you find him much like his portrait?"

"Yes, but no artist could do him justice."

"Well, Henry, it's not many hours till you leave for your office, and you've had no sleep yet."

He laughed. "What a poor thing is sleep compared to what I've had!"

He returned to his sparse, soldier-like sleeping quarters beyond the writing room, facing Eighth Avenue. But H.P.B. guessed it was not to sleep, but to think and plan and try to resolve the many problems connected with leaving America. Now it would not be "Shall I go?" but "How? and how soon?"

Master M. had achieved in one night what she herself could not have done in a year, or perhaps even a decade.

CHAPTER 14

The *Daily Graphic* of New York, December 10, 1878, reported:

Helena P. Blavatsky . . . is about leaving America, as she says, forever. A very damp reporter found his way to the pleasant French flat at Eighth Avenue and Forty-seventh Street, this morning, and his ring was answered by a colored servant, who expressed serious doubts as to whether his mistress would see anyone at so early an hour. The interviewer was, however, ushered into a breakfast room which was in a very disordered condition, and invited to a seat on a vacant stool. The disorder was a necessary result of yesterday's auction sale, and the only semblances of occupancy left were an uncleared breakfast table— and three human occupants.

Colonel Olcott, the new hierophant of the Arya Samaj, sat at the table busily making memoranda in a note-book, and burning his handsome moustache with a half-finished cigar that struggled ineffectually to reach beyond the outskirts of his beard. A male companion sat Eastern fashion on a bench under a window and read a morning paper which he held with one hand while he twisted one end of his moustache with the other.

When the reporter was finally ushered into Madame Blavatsky's own room, he found that lady seated at the end of a letter and tobacco laden table, twisting a fragrant cigarette from a quantity of loose tobacco of a famous Turkish brand. The inner room was the inner temple of the Lamasery, which has become so widely known in recent years. . . .

The reporter said, "And so you are going to leave America?"

"Yes, and the Lamasery where I have spent so many happy, happy hours. I am sorry to leave these rooms, although there is little to regret about them now," glancing about at the bare floors and walls, "but I am glad to get away from your country. You have liberty, but that is all."

"When shall you leave?"

"I know neither the time nor the vessel, but it will be very soon and very secretly. No one shall know when I go. I am going to Liverpool and London, where we have branch Theosophical Societies, to whom I must take their charters, and with whom I must arrange other matters. . . ."

H.P.B. did not mention that the Colonel was going too, because she was afraid his dependent ex-wife might attempt to prevent it. In the diary that the "Twins" kept mutually at this time, she wrote: "Kali [her nickname for Mrs. Olcott] suspects departure and thinks of arresting H.S.O. He received his regular nomination from the Govt. and was appointed commissioner with special passport."

The diary shows that many visitors were coming to the apartment in these last days. Some, hearing of the departure, were now anxious to be initiated into the Society before the Founders left.

Several newspapers described the last Sunday gathering at the Lamasery. The New York *Sun* said:

The usual refreshments were provided in the usual plenty. Tea was served in rotation, only three teacups being left from the sale. . . . The long series of "Sunday Nights At Home" was ending . . .

There was much talk of the probable future of The Theosophical Society which, now that it is in coalition with the Arya Samaj, is expected to become a powerful factor in the development of the mental and religious freedom of the world. . . .

Presently a man came in with a phonograph [not long ago invented by Thomas Edison, who was a member of The Theosophical Society]. A tall sculptor [Edward Wimbridge who was secretly slipping away from New York with the Founders] was dislodged from a barrel on which he sat, and the phonograph was put in position, after which greetings were shouted into the paper funnel, and a song in pidgin Hindustanee was sung into it by a jolly English artist. Charles, the huge Theosophical cat, was then induced to purr at the machine . . .

On December 19, the New York *Star* reports them aboard:

"Ho! for the heathen lands," said Mme. Blavatsky to her companion as she stood on the deck of the steamer *Canada* outward bound. She looked glad as she spoke, and she seemed to see far out beyond the somewhat unpleasant surroundings of luggage, machinery and busy sailors, into the limitless jungles of India. . . .

The *Sun,* of the same date, said:

The Hierophant [Olcott] wrote dozens of last despatches on the cabin table, sending messenger after messenger away on various errands, and giving all sorts of instructions as to the future management of the Society to the newly-chosen officers. . . .

Charles [the cat] had been sent to a good Theosophist's house, but had disappeared from the basket in transit, and has not been seen since.

"I don't know where he is," said the Hierophant, "but I presume we shall find him in Bombay when we get there."

The *Daily Graphic* reporter concluded *his* description of the great departure with a remark of H.P.B.'s:

"I love a fair-minded atheist better than a Christian, for he is at least in search of the truth and it is possible to convince him."

And so saying, H.P.B. shook the reporter by the hand, and bade him and the others an "eternal farewell." As the steamer put out into the stream, she vied with the smokestack and seemed unmoved.

It was 3 p.m. on December 18, 1878 when the *Canada* left the wharf, but H.P.B., Olcott, and Wimbridge had been aboard since late on the night of the 17th.

Extract from the London *Spiritualist* of January 24, 1879:

It may interest some of your readers to learn that Mme. H. P. Blavatsky and Col. Olcott have been paying a visit to this country on their way from the United States to India. They arrived on the 3rd. instant and were the guests of Dr. and Mrs. Billing, at Norwood [London] until Friday last, the 17th, when they left for India, direct from Liverpool. . . .

The Brotherhood of Humanity is with her [H.P.B.] and Col. Olcott no mere sentimental phrase or visionary aspiration. To break down all the barriers of race and religion between man and man by the eradication of prejudice, and to emancipate the mind from its theological and materialistic trammels are the main objects of the great Indian Society, of which she has been so active and efficient an agent in the West. No greater undertaking and none with more hard fighting before it has ever been attempted. . . .

One of Mme. Blavatsky's objects in visiting London was to consult certain books and manuscripts at the British museum, where most of the time she could spare from Norwood was passed. Two other members of the New York Society accompany them to India. . . .

Colonel Olcott goes as a Commissioner from the Government of the United States, to report upon the state of commerce and means of promoting intercourse for trade purposes between the two countries. Mme. Blavatsky will be the Indian correspondent of one of the leading Russian Journals.

The fourth person mentioned in the theosophical party leaving for India was Miss Rosa Bates, an English schoolteacher who had been living in New York, and had traveled to England a few weeks ahead of the others.

George Wyld, M.D., in the *Spiritualist* of the same date, wrote a description of H.P.B. for the benefit of the many who had heard of her, but had not had a chance to see her personally during her short stay in England:

> Swarthy and of Tartar aspect, she is tall, strong, vigorous. . . . Her jaws are large and furnished with perfectly regular and strong teeth; and her eyes, though almost without colour, yet can read without glasses the smallest print, and can look you through and through, and can read your character and thoughts at will. She is highly accomplished in languages and music. . . . She is possessed of a form and bearing of queenly dignity, if she only condescended to assume the garments and the mien. With irresistible powers of fascination, she seems only to despise the use of these powers. Enjoying enormous fits of laughter, yet she is forever restless and sad. . . .
>
> She declaims on all subjects, rapidly passing from one to another, yet ever returning to her central idea: the spiritual wisdom and power of the East, from which must appear the coming man to rule the spiritual world.
>
> Of truly a great nature, but with, to my mind, one extravagant defect, shown in her book and in her talk, an unreasoning and intolerant hatred of the doctrines and works of all Christian teachers. . . .

He concludes:

> Beyond all doubt she is a magician controlling the movements of matter and counteracting the action of poisons, as I experienced in my own person. She is wonderful and unique, and to have known her as I have, is always to remember her with affection, admiration and respect.

Several people took up the cudgels against Dr. Wyld's statement that H.P.B. showed "unreasoning and intolerant hatred" of the Christian churches. Wrote one: "He . . . who wishes to show to men the way to appreciate their own spiritual capacities, must needs combat all systems so far as they are despotisms; and he may do this with courage, for he need never fear but that the gold will survive, whatever the force of the flame which he may turn upon the alloy."

Another writer said: "It is true that her task in life being combative, she has the combative characteristics which can only be replaced by contemplative calm when the work of life is over."

The debate on the mysterious Madame frothed and bubbled for a while, like the foam in the wake of the steamer *Speke Hall,* chugging its way across the seas to deliver the Theosophists in Bombay.

But, whereas in England Madame Blavatsky was, at this juncture, of interest to only a small section of the public, in India she made news for all the English speaking papers. Most of them dealt with her arrival in far from friendly terms, attacking her and the theosophical party as enemies of Christianity, and spicing their press letters with insulting innuendos about Madame's character. All such cowardly shots came from behind the protective wall of pseudonyms.

Madame Blavatsky replied over her own name through the columns of the *Indian Spectator,* a friendly journal. She had by this time developed a powerful journalistic style for polemical writing, and she turned its withering fire on the "swarms of pseudonymous wasps," as she called them. They were, in the main, she thought, missionaries and their minions, who were doing their best to bury under mounds of contempt the great Hindu religio-philosophy. So she trained her metaphorical guns on them with as much zest and satisfaction as she had used real guns against the reactionary enemies of the great Garibaldi.

But she was very careful not to criticize the British government in India. On the contrary, she often praised it, and told the Indians that they would, in fact, be much worse off if they were under Russian rule—which did not, of course, help her popularity in certain quarters in Russia.

Though H.P.B. was often assailed as being anti-Christian, she has made it clear in her letters and writings that she had nothing against the immortal teachings of Jesus of Nazareth, but a great deal against the way the churches were interpreting his teachings. In the way that Jesus had, himself, attacked the official, corrupt priesthood—

the hypocrites and false teachers—of his time, she too waged open war on all those she regarded as enemies of truth. No other consideration weighed with her. Under her white banner of truth she now lived, fought, bled and would have been happy to die.

H.P.B. realized that the situation in India was loaded against her in a particular way. Though not generally Christian in the true sense of the term, the British Raj had to uphold the superiority of his official Christian religion. It stood as one of the symbols of his overall superiority, cultural and spiritual as well as secular. Once let the natives feel sure that their spiritual grass roots were as sound as those of their overlords, and the floodgates would begin to open.

It came as a pleasant surprise to H.P.B., therefore, when soon after their arrival in Bombay, the Founders received a letter from Alfred Percy Sinnett, Editor of *The Pioneer*, considered the most influential newspaper in India at the time. He wrote that, from having had a number of chances in London to investigate modern spiritualistic phenomena, he had a genuine interest in occult questions, particularly in the philosophy behind the phenomena. He would be happy, he said, to publish any interesting facts about the theosophic mission to India, and should the Founders be coming up-country to Allahabad, where he lived, he would be delighted to meet them.

Thus began a correspondence which led to a friendship resulting in important developments. But before that, many new experiences and personalities came crowding into the Founders' first twelve months of India.

Hurrychund Chintamon, to whom they had sent the donations for the Arya Samaj from New York, proved to be a cheat who had pocketed all the funds for himself. He was expelled from the *Arya Samaj* and went off to England, there to spread whatever poison he could as an enemy of the Theosophical Movement in general and of H.P.B. in particular.

Early in April, 1879, the two Founders, with their Muslim servant Babula and their Bombay friend, Moolji Thackersey, set off on a journey to the north. This seems to have been a kind of reconnaisance over country in which they hoped later to form branches of the Society. They met some interesting yogis; they heard many stories of wonderworkers, but actually saw none. They passed, with great delight, through Rajputana, the native land of their Guru, Master Morya.

Train travel was suffocatingly hot and dusty, even though the zenith of the hot season had not yet been reached. All the way their footsteps were dogged by a man with a red face and drooping moustache. Very soon they realized that he was a police spy of the British government in India. But what kind of a spy was this who revealed his role in the first few days? The "Twins" were irritated and angered, but were also half-amused; if they had *really* been political agents, they would have been put wholly on their guard by such clumsy methods.

At Saharanpore they met at last Swami Dayanand Sarasvati, the famous leader of the *Arya Samaj*. In a long conversation "he defined his views on Nirvana, Moksha and God in terms to which we could take no exception. . . . he fully approved of our scheme of having sections composed of sectarians such as Buddhists, Parsis, Mohammedans, Hindus, etc."[1] Later the Founders were to discover that this show of "altruistic eclecticism" had apparently not been sincere.

But for the moment the close ties between the two societies were confirmed, and the *Arya Samaj* provided the Colonel with his first big audience in the north. He enjoyed talking to the sea of dark, eager Indian faces around the painted poles that held up a great canvas canopy. But his pleasure was somewhat spoiled by the sight of the familiar red face—with the moustache now shaved off, apparently for purposes of disguise! Moolji Thackersey interpreted Olcott's address, which was on the benefits of a cultural exchange between East and West.

One day early in May the Founders were back on the station platform in Bombay where H.P.B. broke the silence with their police shadow, congratulating him on his wardrobe, his props, and his ability to spend government funds on first-class travel. Then she and the Colonel drove to the American Consulate and lodged a protest against the offensive treatment of two American citizens. But this did not stop the aggravating signs of official surveillance.

A pile of written inquiries awaited them in Bombay and, as Corresponding Secretary of the Society, H.P.B. found more than enough to do, answering all the questions about the theosophical organization, its aims, teachings on various topics, and future plans. Soon she realized that she was wasting a great deal of time and effort in writing the same answers, more or less, to many different people throughout India.

To overcome this problem the Founders conceived the idea of starting a monthly magazine. Because they had no working capital for the project, they adopted the, for then, revolutionary idea of asking for subscriptions in advance. The Indian members shook their heads in doubt, but were persuaded to set about canvassing for subscribers. And while the heavy rains of the monsoon beat against their Bombay windows, the Founders prepared material for the first issue of *The Theosophist* to appear in October 1879.

The monsoon season also brought a person who was to play an important part in the lives of the Founders and the early affairs of the Society. He came one night out of the drenching rain, wrapped in a white rubber waterproof, a lantern in his hand, and water streaming from his long nose. His face was sombre and gaunt, but an intense fire burned in his eyes.

The visitor proved to be a young Brahmin named Damodar K. Mavalankar. His one desire was to find his true Guru, become a chela, and train for Adeptship. It did not take him long to realize that H.P.B. was his gateway to this and that work for the Society was the necessary probation. He very soon took the step that many young Indians have taken. He renounced the life of a householder, which had been planned for him by his family, and became a *sannyasi,* an ascetic. But instead of going to an ashram, as was the custom, he joined The Theosophical Society, becoming its first Recording Secretary and living at its headquarters in Bombay.

Among the many letters received was one from Madame Emma Coulomb in Ceylon. The letter told of great press publicity there and excitement among the Buddhists concerning a promised visit to the island of the Founders. It enclosed a paragraph from the *Ceylon Times* (June 5, 1879), written by Emma Coulomb, herself, defending H.P.B. against an ill-natured attack in one of the papers. Mme. Coulomb stated in the paragraph that, having known Mme. Blavatsky well in Cairo, she could testify that the latter was a lady of high character.

Her letter went on to tell H.P.B. a doleful tale of the financial straits to which she and her husband, Alexis, had been reduced since leaving Egypt. She would like, she said, to come to Bombay and find some sort of situation for herself and her husband.

H.P.B. told the Colonel that this was a woman who had been very kind to her and had loaned her money when she was broke in Egypt following a shipwreck. The Colonel agreed that they should help the destitute couple as much as was in their power. So H.P.B. wrote a kind letter to Emma Coulomb offering help if they should come to Bombay.

Toward the end of March the next year (1880) the couple suddenly appeared on the doorstep of the humble theosophical residence. They had, they said, obtained steamer passages to Bombay through the help of the French Consul in Ceylon (Alexis Coulomb was French). So here they were, with all their bags.

Alexis had a pale face, black beard, and a glass eye; Emma is described by Dr. Franz Hartmann as, "wrinkled and witch-like." Without hesitation the Founders took them in and made them welcome, hiring extra furniture for their use.

Thus the cat's-paw of the main antagonists made entry on the theosophical stage.

CHAPTER 15

Madame Blavatsky rolled a cigarette nervously with one hand while she frowned over a letter held in the other. It was from Major Henderson of Military Security. He was the man, she understood, who was actually responsible for having them followed by the bungling detective, still popping up embarrassingly in unlikely places. The letter was a blunt resignation from The Theosophical Society, which Henderson had joined only a few days earlier under circumstances that were to become matters of speculation and debate, not only in the social circles of Simla, but in the faraway drawing rooms of London.

She threw the letter on the table and rested her eyes on the snowy Himalayan peaks that blessed the windows of "Brightlands," Mr. Sinnett's house in Simla. The affair had begun innocently enough, she reflected. Six of them—including Major Henderson—had gone on a picnic. A seventh person had joined them just as they left the house, and so there had been one teacup short at the picnic. They had challenged her to put her powers to practical use and materialize another teacup. With the help of a "Brother" (invisible to them) she had done so, producing one to match Mrs. Sinnett's rare English set, brought for the outing.

In spite of himself, Major Henderson was impressed but still suspicious of some trickery somewhere. To test her, he said that he would even join The Theosophical Society if she could produce, then and there, a diploma of membership already made out in his name and fully completed with the date and the President's signature. This she did, further stunning the party, and even making the well seasoned Colonel's eyes pop, for he knew he had never signed the diploma. And Henderson—temporarily humbled—could do nothing but accept the diploma of membership.

But later he demanded yet another test of the genuineness of H.P.B.'s powers. The strained thread of her patience snapped, and she lost her temper. This was unfortunate, for he then proceeded to give her some bad publicity, and now here was his written resignation. Instead of a useful friend, another enemy had been made.

Was she wrong, she wondered, in expending so much of her vital energy in phenomena for the Philistines? Reactions on the whole in Simla had been most unfavorable. The British overlords could not believe in the possibility of yogic powers, so if she performed what to them looked like miracles, they decided that she must be cheating, or else she was an agent of the devil.

Why did she do it then? Well, it *did* capture public attention, create interest among many, and—among a few —the desire to learn more of the occult. These things were necessary in the early stages of a great, new revolution of the mind and heart. Had not the Nazarene used startling phenomena? Yet, perhaps, she *was* overdoing it. It was certainly draining her vitality and having a bad effect on her health.

Behind her chair she heard her host, Mr. Alfred P. Sinnett come into the room and go to his writing-desk. What would he want today? she wondered. Like Olcott, he had an insatiable thirst for phenomena. And he was one whom she found it hard to refuse. There was no doubt that the Masters expected Sinnett to play an important role in the Theosophical Movement. Signs had told her that much.

Now the sound of shuffling papers had stopped, and he was clearing his throat as if he wanted to attract her attention. He came and stood in front of her, with his back to the window.

She gave him an encouraging smile.

"I hesitate to ask this, H.P.B." he began, "but I am intensely interested in those great Beings you talk about— the Mahatmas of the trans-Himalayan Brotherhood. Could I be put in touch with them *directly?* Would such a thing be possible?"

H.P.B. gazed beyond him to the gleaming white peaks.

After a while she replied: "I can't say. It might be very difficult. But, if you like, I'll *try*."

"Will you? I am most grateful."

The eager excitement of his voice broke through his usual British restraint.

"Write a letter," she told him. "I will send it and see what happens."

He hastened back to his desk, and Helena left the room to talk to his wife, Patience, a well-read, highly intelligent, sincere woman whom she liked very much indeed.

Later in the day Mr. Sinnett handed H.P.B. a letter which he had written to the Brotherhood, but not to any particular member. She would have to work through her own Master, of course, but whether he or another, or anyone at all, would respond to Sinnett was something else.

There was no postal service to Shigatze, and anyway Master Morya might well be somewhere else. But she had her own psychic post—something they had perfected for her in Tibet. She could use any one of several methods, the simplest being to hold the sealed envelope against her forehead, then: "warning the Master to be ready for a communication, have the contents, reflected by my brain, carried off to His perception by the *current formed by Him*."[1]

Several days later Mr. Sinnett unlocked a drawer of his writing-desk and found lying on top of his papers a letter from the great Lodge. It was not from Master Morya, as he had half-expected (if there was to be any reply at all), but from Master Kuthumi Lal Singh.

It was in fact the beginning of Sinnett's famous four-year correspondence with the great Brotherhood. Most of the letters received were from Master K.H., with a few from Master Morya. Based on what he learned through the letters, Sinnett wrote his book, *Esoteric Buddhism,* published in 1883.

"It took the theological and scientific world by storm," wrote Francesca Arundale of London.

A collection of the epistles, entitled, *The Mahatma Letters to A.P. Sinnett,* was published in England some forty years later, in 1923, and the originals of the letters are now in the British Museum.

Simla had been shocked by the previous Viceroy, Lord Lytton, because he smoked between courses at dinner; but now its respectable foundations were cracking under the onslaughts of the Russian aristocrat who rolled her own cigarettes, produced articles out of nowhere like some huge cosmic conjuror, and talked brilliantly but shockingly on all manner of off-beat subjects. She created quite a diversion from prattle about servants, politics, polo, and pig-sticking.

While almost all were interested in her as a social curiosity and something of a mystery, there were a few who took her more seriously and wanted to plumb the depths of this strange, tempestuous woman and her mysterious Mahatmas, who were said to hold the keys to the ultimate wisdom of life.

The most important of these few was Mr. A. O. Hume of Rothney Castle, Simla. Hume had for nine years, until 1879, been Secretary to the Government of India. Then, through a collision with his superiors, he was demoted to a position on the Board of Revenue. He had a brilliant brain, but seems to have been inordinately proud of it. His inbuilt feeling of superiority toward the natives included, in a sense, the Mahatmas.

The latter apparently had hopes of his playing an important part of the renascence of the *sanatana dharma,* the timeless wisdom. He became the recipient of several letters from the Mahatmas, particularly from Master K.H. He helped to organize the theosophical branch called the "Simla Eclectic Society." He took the initiative in forming the Indian National Congress, though he did not contemplate the eventual fruits of this, the separation of India from the British Empire.

While, through his intellectual arrogance and lack of spiritual perception, Hume soon disappointed the Founders and fell away from the Theosophical Movement, he did, unbeknown to himself, play a useful part in the work. By fathering the National Congress, he helped materially in the emancipation of India, a necessary step for the world spread of the ancient wisdom with its spiritualizing and civilizing effects. So the Founders' first visit to Simla, in 1880, initiated something worthwhile.

On the political side there was an achievement, too. Armed with his special diplomatic passport from the American Secretary of State, his letter of recommendation from the President of the United States, and other official documents, the Colonel seems to have been able to make some slight impression on the top-brass at the summer seat of the government, Simla. So, despite the *faux pas* of the magical picnic—or perhaps even helped by it—Major Henderson was ordered by his superiors to call off his infuriating, comic opera detective.

But relations with Russia were still highly sensitive at this time (1880). During the seventies "the steady advance of Russia in central Asia again aroused alarm. The coincidence of this movement with the Balkan crisis of 1875-78 induced Disraeli and Salisbury . . . to seek safety in Asia by using the Afghans as a buttress against Russia. Their agent, Lord Lytton [in India] had dreams of marching into Turkistan, and plunged into the second Afghan War (1878-80)."[2]

The *status quo,* satisfactory to the British, was restored within the buffer state of Afghanistan, but suspicion of Russia's ambitions toward India remained strong. If we can judge from Kipling's writings, the Secret Service in India would take no chances. It seems likely, therefore, that after the removal of the over-obvious detective, a less obtrusive official eye may have been kept on the activities of Helena Blavatsky.

On October 21, 1880, Madame Blavatsky and Olcott left Simla for Amritsar. Knowing that even Sinnett harbored some lurking doubt about the genuineness of the remarkable psychic forces behind Madame Blavatsky, Master K.H. gave him a proof.

Sinnett had written a letter to the Master addressing it to H.P.B. at Amritsar for forwarding in the usual way. Helena received it on October 27. It certainly came to her hand some time *after* 2 p.m. that day because the Amritsar postmark on the envelope showed receipt there at 2 p.m.

Master K.H. was at Jhelum, some eight hours by train north of Amritsar. Yet he received there the contents of the Sinnett letter—evidently through H.P.B.—in time to telegraph a reply to Sinnett at 4 p.m. that same day. The fastest means of sending a letter in those days was by rail, and there was no known physical way in which H.P.B. could have sent the Sinnett letter over the distance involved in less than two hours. Yet post office marks at Amritsar and Jhelum were evidence that, between 2 and 4 on the afternoon of October 27, H.P.B. had received the letter at Amritsar, conveyed its message to Master K.H., who had decided on his reply and made it in the form of a telegram at 4 p.m. at Jhelum.

So that no reasonable doubt could remain, Master K.H. told Sinnett to apply to see the original telegram form lodged at Jhelum post office. Sinnett did so, and found that it was in the handwriting of K.H., which by this time he knew from previous correspondence.

The two Founders, after leaving Amritsar, began a tour of centers in the great plain of the Ganges, with Allahabad as their ultimate destination. The Sinnetts had returned there and the plan was that the four should spend Christmas together.

The theosophical work was actually progressing quite well. Previous to their 1880 journey to Simla and the north, they had traveled southward from their Bombay headquarters to Ceylon. There, in a Buddhist temple in Galle, they had formally and publicly accepted the five chief precepts of the Buddha, thus becoming official members of the Buddhist faith.

Then, in what looked like a triumphal procession, they moved across the island through seas of smiling brown faces and yellow-robed priests, in the bright shimmering air. They were feted as the great white Buddhists who had come to emancipate the islanders from the religious oppression of the British government and the Christian missionaries.

Neither Olcott nor H.P.B. found any strain to their consciences in joining officially the Buddhist religion. They felt that the original teachings of the Lord Buddha were practically identical with the Wisdom-religion, the Theosophy, which they were striving to spread in the world. Any impurities and misconceptions that had crept into temple practice they hoped, through Theosophy, to remove. They were swept on such a wave of popular and priestly acclaim that, during this two-months visit, seven branches of The Theosophical Society were formed in Ceylon.

Later on, Colonel Olcott made many trips to the island, compiled his officially accepted *Buddhist Catechism,* and agreed to put the Buddhist grievances about religions oppression and injustices to the Colonial Office on his first trip to England.

Back in Bombay again after their Ceylon triumphs, they found a storm brewing on the domestic front. Madame Coulomb, whom they had appointed as housekeeper, was at daggers drawn—or was it kitchen knives drawn?—with ex-schoolteacher Rosa Bates. Petty female rivalries and wild accusations brought matters to a climax. The judgment of the Founders went in Emma Coulomb's favor. Rosa Bates left the household and architect Wimbridge went with her.

The fate of this pair who, it seems, had come to India with the Founders mainly for personal, and not theosophical, reasons was that Wimbridge went into an art-furniture business in Bombay, with some help from the Colonel, and did well; Miss Bates, bitter and disillusioned, refused any help and vanished from the records of the Society.

So while the Founders were visiting Simla and centers of the north in 1880, the crafty Emma Coulomb and her one-eyed quick-tempered husband were reigning supreme in Bombay. They had been asked to find a new house for the residential headquarters of The Theosophical Society and this they had achieved. It was an old bungalow, they reported, that had been unoccupied for some time, mainly because of a rumor that it was haunted by a powerful ghost.

Returning by train from Allahabad, where they had just enjoyed an English Christmas with the Sinnetts, the Founders were driven by carriage to the new residence,

called "Crow's Nest." It was perched on a peak at Breach
Candy, commanding fine views of the sea. They liked
it immediately.

But the Colonel found some substance in the rumor of
the powerful ghost. "One night I had gone to bed and
was dropping asleep, when I felt one corner of my *charpai*
being lifted, as if by someone standing in the thickness
of the wall, which it was touching. Instantly recovering
my full consciousness, I pronounced a certain Arabic word
of power, that H.P.B. had taught me in New York, and
the cot was replaced on its legs and the meddlesome spook
decamped and never troubled me more."[3] Mr. Sinnett,
who spent some time on a visit to Crow's Nest in 1881,
described H.P.B.'s life there:

> She would generally be up at an early hour writing
> at her Russian articles and translations [she was
> then writing *From the Caves and Jungles of Hindu-
> stan*, serially for Russian papers] . . . or at articles
> for *The Theosophist;* then during the day she would
> spend a large part of her time talking with native
> visitors in her verandah room, or hunting them away
> and getting back to her work with wild protests
> against the constant interruptions . . . and in the
> same breath calling for her faithful "Babula", her
> servant, in a voice that rang all over the house, and
> sending for someone or other of the visitors she knew
> to be waiting about below and wanting to see her.
> Then in the midst of some fiery arguments with a
> pundit about a point of modern Hindu belief . . .,
> she would perhaps suddenly 'hear the voice they did
> not hear'—the astral call of her distant Master, or
> one of the other 'Brothers' . . . and forgetting every-
> thing else in an instant, she would hurry off to the
> seclusion of any room where she could be alone for
> a few moments, and hear whatever message or orders
> she had to receive.[4]

Entries in the Colonel's diary, which he kept faithfully
through the years, tell of frequent contacts with the Masters. This was achieved by telepathic messages to H.P.B.,
or by the Masters actually appearing in the *Mayavi-rupas*
or thought-bodies (a higher astral-mental form). On

rarer occasions one or another would come in his physical
body. Once, for instance, Master Morya rode up to their
residence on a horse, his favorite mode of transport. At
another time Hilarion (a Greek Adept) called physically
to see them on his way through to Tibet.

These were certainly wonderful days, with the Masters
giving close guidance on the general lines of the work to
be done. They directed the editorial policy of *The
Theosophist,* and sometimes one of them would even dic-
tate an article for it. When A.O. Hume wrote his criticism
of the Mahatmas for *The Theosophist,* H.P.B. as Editor,
refused to publish it. But she was ordered to do so by
the Maha Chohan, himself, who was Morya's and K.H.'s
superior. Personal opinions and criticisms, however unfavorable, must not be suppressed.

It was while they were still at "Crow's Nest," in the
year 1882, that H.P.B. wrote in a letter to Prince Dondukoff-Korsakoff that she had found the "Stone" (philosopher's stone). Early in 1879 she was still in search of it,
but by March 1882, when she wrote the letter, she had
found it.[5] She says not how nor where, and her words are
an enigma. One can only assume that in the constant contact with the Great Ones, and the selfless service of the
theosophical cause, she had reached some inner vision,
some new scale of values by which she could live.

Certainly the discovery of the "Stone" had not trans-
muted all the lead of her own nature into gold. The years
ahead were to bring many struggles with her tempestuous
emotions. But there was a difference. She had become the
witness of herself playing a part in life's drama, and so
was able to forgive swiftly, and love altruistically, even
those who flayed her, while she railed loudly against their
persecutions.

But the Founders could not linger forever enjoying the
lotus breezes of Breach Candy. Apostles, not of a new
religion but of a new spiritual understanding of the old
religions, they must be ever on the move to wherever the
work took them. Travel in the great subcontinent of India held strange mysteries, unexpected adventures, and
punishing discomforts.

CHAPTER 16

All around was a great silence, punctuated by the lap-lap of water against the side of the boat, the low murmur of coolies' voices, and the occasional yelp of a jackal. The stars in the velvet-black sky seemed to hang over them like lamps as they sat on deck, watching the banks slide by in the odor of wet paddy fields.

Save for the faithful Babula, the Founders were alone on the houseboat, heading northward from Madras along the Buckingham Canal toward Nellore. It was May 1882 and the breeze of the monsoon filled their sail and carried them along through the silent light.

"At an early hour," writes the Colonel, 'we tied up at the bank, for the coolies to build their fire and cook their curry and rice; our people in the other boat joined us, I went for a swim, and Babula cooked us a capital breakfast, which our colleagues, because of their cast prohibitions, could not share. Then on once more, the boats as noiseless as spectres."[1]

It was a chance for rest after the excitements of Madras where their welcome had been tumultuous but wearing. It was a chance to review the progress they had made in their work and talk over future plans for the "coloring of modern thought with Theosophical ideas," which at this time occupied their minds more than any hope of extending the Society throughout the world.

Above all it was a chance to enjoy the quiet of true companionship. "Dear, lamented friend," wrote Olcott in later years, "companion, colleague, teacher, chum: none could be more exasperating at her worst times, none more lovable and admirable at her best. . . . This open page of my Diary, with its but few fragmentary notes, brings back to memory one of the most delightful episodes of the Theosophical movement, and I see a picture of H.P.B. in her shabby wrapper, sitting on her locker opposite me, smoking cigarettes, her huge head with its brown crinkled hair bent over the page she was writing on, her forehead full of wrinkles, a look of introverted thought in her light blue eyes, her aristocratic hand driving the pen swiftly over the lines . . ."[2]

After two days of this peaceful life, their round of bustle recommenced. At Nellore they lectured, answered questions, discussed, and formed a theosophical lodge. Then they went further north on the Canal. When that ended they were transferred to palanquins and swayed through the jungle on the shoulders of coolies. By this means they forded rivers, and when the water came up to the coolies' arm-pits, the palanquins were raised and carried precariously on the bearers' heads.

The temperature was near 100 degrees Fahrenheit by day, and almost as bad at night. In the dark the coolies carried large torches of cotton twist saturated with cocoanut oil, choking their passengers with black evil-smelling smoke. But one night they saw why the torches were necessary; the head coolie killed a big cobra right in their path.

Palanquin travel was not as painful as the bullock-carts in which the intrepid pair journeyed scores of miles (78 miles on this particular trip). But for a 51-year-old lady who turned the scales at some 237 pounds, and whose health was already beginning to break, it was certainly painful enough.

At sunset one evening they reached their northern destination, Guntur, and all the discomforts seemed worthwhile. The whole population—thousands—had come outside the town to meet them. At a snail's pace they moved on through a wall of human flesh into the town, where limelights and Bengal colored fires blazed at every step, while a continuous roar of cheering flowed along with them like a river of sound.

"Guntur," writes the Colonel, "was as light as by day. Two triumphal arches spanned the principal streets. Arrived at the house, we had to receive, and reply to, two addresses in English and two in Telegu . . ." The next day he gave a public lecture, while the Rev. L. L. Uhl, of the Lutheran Mission, sat among the Indians and energetically took notes. The reverend gentleman gave notice that he would answer Olcott's criticisms of church theology at his chapel on the next morning.

Guntur's reception typified the attitude of the missionaries and the welcoming hearts of the Indians. The latter loved metaphysics to a man (as Indians do), and were curious and enthusiastic about these two Westerners who had come, it appeared, for an amazingly pure and selfless purpose—to restore the prestige of the long neglected spiritual wisdom of the immortal *Rishis*.

Following her strenuous travel program, H.P.B.'s health was not improved by the Bombay humidity and heat when she returned there. In fact, she became seriously ill. She wrote to the Sinnetts in mid-September 1882, telling them of her sufferings with "Bright's disease of the kidneys" and how her doctor had said she might "kick the bucket at any time in consequence of *an emotion*. Ye lords of creation! Of such emotions I have twenty a day. . . . Boss [her Guru] wants me to prepare and go somewhere for a month or so towards the end of September. He sent a chela here Gargya Deva from the Nilgerri Hills, and he is to take me off, where I don't know, but of course somewhere in the Himalayas."[3]

The Master K.H. refers to this same matter in a letter to A.P. Sinnett, undated but probably written before September 1882:

"I am not at home at present, but quite near to Darjeeling, in the Lamasery, the object of poor H.P.B.'s longings. I thought of leaving by the end of September but find it rather difficult on account of Nobin's boy. Most probably, also I will have to interview in my own skin the Old Lady [H.P.B.] if M. [Master Morya] brings her here. And—he has to bring her—or lose her forever—at least as far as the physical triad is concerned."[4]

Master Morya, himself, in a letter received in September, told Sinnett of his intention to heal his lay chela, H.P.B., who was "so sick that as in 1877 I am again forced to carry her away—when she is so needed where she now is, at Headquarters—for fear she will fall all to pieces."[5]

H.P.B., borne up by joyful anticipation, headed for Calcutta, from where she would strike out toward Sikkim and Tibet. Word spread among her followers that she was going to see the two great Mahatmas in person, and more than a dozen Calcutta Theosophists grimly determined to accompany her. They became a great nuisance to her, but she said little, knowing that they would never get near the Masters unless the latter willed it so.

One Theosophist, S. Ramaswamier, took leave from his office in Tinnevelly in southern India, and went north in search of H.P.B., hoping through her to reach the feet of his Guru, Master Morya.

Ramaswamier made contact first with a number of Theosophists dashing about the countryside like mad March hares, looking for H.P.B. Finally they—and he—found her at Chandernagore. With her was a Tibetan chela who had been apparently sent to guide her beyond the borders to where the Masters were waiting.

She went to the Chandernagore railway station to catch a train. Ramaswamier and the others went too. The train pulled into the platform; H.P.B. and her Tibetan guide stepped aboard, and immediately the train pulled out—not waiting, as expected, for the bell to be rung. A few of her followers managed to scramble aboard as the train moved, but most were left behind on the platform.

Further along on the journey there was another unaccountable "accident" Ramaswamier related, by means of which he and the others who had jumped aboard at Chandernagore were shaken off the trail.

From inquiries Ramaswamier had "learned for a certainty," he said, that two of the Mahatmas were in the neighborhood of British territory. Now, left behind by H.P.B., and absolutely determined to find his Guru or die in the attempt, he decided to try to cross the border into Sikkim alone.

Meantime Madame Blavatsky went on to Cooch Bihar where the Rajah was a Theosophist. There she stayed for three days, sick with a fever brought on, she thought, by the sudden change from the terrible heat of the plains to the cold, rain, and fog of the mountains.

She knew that she was supposed to have a pass from the British for crossing into Sikkim, "a nearly independent state of robbers," or into Bhutan, "where the devil can break his legs." She had tried to get a pass but the authorities had refused, so she was traveling without one.

She felt sure that the power of her Master would get her, unseen, across the border and protect her from danger, while the Tibetan chela would guide her footsteps to the secret place where her beloved Sadguru and Master K.H. had established their temporary residence. Her heart quickened at the thought. Like the time at Shigatze, it would be a taste of sweet heaven, a balm, and a renewal for her work in the mad and terrible world.

CHAPTER 17

H.P.B. had not described her journey into Sikkim or her meeting with her Guru, but in a letter to Sinnett, written from Darjeeling after her return, she states that there, with Master M., whom she often referred to as "my boss," Master K.H. and a party of their chelas, she spent two wonderful, blessed days. It brought back all the sweetness of other times in the physical presence of the Great Ones, the memory of which ever nourished her spirit and resolve in her Herculean task. She gives a brief but vivid picture of the scene on this occasion.

"It was like old times when the bear paid me a visit. The same kind of wooden hut, a box divided into three compartments for rooms, and standing in a jungle on four pelicans legs, the same yellow chelas gliding noiselessly; the same eternal 'gul-gul-gul' sound of my Boss's inextinguishable chelum pipe; the old familiar sweet voice of your K.H. (whose voice is still sweeter and face still thinner and more transparent) the same *entourage* for furniture—skins and yak-tail stuffed pillows and dishes for salt tea etc."[1]

As on previous occasions the balm of her Master's aura seemed to heal her sick, depleted body—or perhaps he consciously exercised some positive healing power. At any rate the symptoms of her Bright's disease and other ailments vanished. She was cured, but for how long would depend on herself and her emotional reactions to the hostile world down there beyond the stillness and sanctuary of her Master's presence.

Two days only—must she really go back!

"Yes, I'm afraid you must; the chelas may fall in love with your beauty; so we must put you out of their reach," Master M. joked.

So she was escorted to Darjeeling. But Master M. stayed in the area for about ten days and visited her several times. "I saw him last night at the Lama's house," she wrote to Sinnett on October 9.

Of the hopeful Theosophists who had earlier been clinging to H.P.B.'s skirts, only one, the do-or-die S. Ramaswamier, had managed to get across the border into Sikkim. There, dressed in the yellow garb of a monk, and armed only with a pilgrim's staff and a rolled umbrella, he walked all day along a narrow footpath through the impenetrable jungle. The only signs of habitation he saw were solitary huts at very long intervals.

At dusk he found an empty hut by the roadside. The door was locked but a small window had been left open. Through this he climbed and lay down to rest. In the middle of the night he heard footsteps and voices in the adjoining room. He held his breath, but, miraculously, the people did not come into the room where he lay. At the first streak of dawn he climbed out through the window to the accompaniment of heavy snoring beyond the thin partition.

The gathering light found him walking through hills and dales, toward the city of Sikkim. Ramaswamier felt that his Guru, Master Morya, was guiding and protecting him, and was, himself, not too far away. He did not know that H.P.B. had been returned to Darjeeling and that the Master was actually only a few miles from where this yellow-garbed pilgrim from southern India was trudging alone and single-mindedly through a dangerous countryside. He passed an occasional pedestrian; then about midmorning a solitary horseman came galloping down the path toward him. "A military officer of the Sikkim

Rajah, now I am caught," he thought, apprehensively. The horseman reined in his steed and stopped a few yards from the yellow-robed pilgrim. With a leap of his heart, Ramaswamier recognized the tall, stately rider.

He writes: "I was in the awful presence of . . . my own reverend *Guru* whom I had seen before in his astral body, on the balcony of the Theosophical Society Headquarters. . . . The very same instant saw me prostrated on the ground at his feet. I arose at his command and, leisurely looking into his face, I forgot myself entirely in the contemplation of the image I knew so well . . ."[2]

The excess of happiness at seeing his Master in the flesh rendered him dumb. But the Mahatma speaking in Ramaswamier's own mother tongue, Tamil, told him important things about his probation as a chela, spoke of other matters close to the pilgrim's heart, and ordered him to return to India before he came to grief.

"Before he left me, two more men came on horseback, his attendants I suppose, probably *Chelas,* for they were dressed like *lama-gelungs,* and both, like himself, with long hair streaming down their backs. They followed the Mahatma as he left, at a gentle trot."[3]

After an hour or more of gazing at the spot where his Master had been, Ramaswamier left and, in a kind of dream, made his way back to India.

After the heightened reality of being close to the two Masters, the profane world seemed to H.P.B. nothing more than a poor stage performance in which the actors had forgotten their true identities and thought they were the characters they played. But she enjoyed a month with the Sinnetts at Allahabad. She was very fond of Alfred Percy, who was beginning to have trouble with the owners of *The Pioneer* because of his interest in occultism or, as he called it, esoteric Buddhism.

Before December of that year 1882 Madame Blavatsky was back at Headquarters in Bombay. On the 7th of the month all celebrated the 7th Anniversary of the Theosophical Society at Framji Cowasji Hall, where they hoisted a banner showing that 39 branches had by then been formed.

The Founders were not dissatisfied with this sign of progress made in seven years.

Ten days later, on December 17, the Theosophical Headquarters pulled up its stakes at "Crow's Nest," Bombay. The Founders and their staff—gaunt, spindle-legged Damodar, staunch Babula, the two Coulombs and two faithful four-legged friends, the dogs Djin and Pudhi—entrained for Madras.

There on the outskirts of the city they moved into a palatial, pillared house on a 25-acre estate by the Adyar River. This estate, then known as Huddlestone's Gardens, was to be their permanent home and Society Headquarters. They had bought it for the proverbial song (9,000 rupees, or about 600 pounds sterling) .

But even such a "song" was too difficult for the poor Founders who eked out their living by free lance journalism and small profits from the publication of *The Theosophist*. So one wealthy Madras Theosophist advanced about a third of the sum as a deposit, and another—an Indian Judge—secured a mortgage for the rest on easy terms.

But the chance for a home of their own was not the only reason for the move to Madras. On the earlier visit, when they had done the houseboat trip along the Buckingham Canal, they had found a large number of keen would-be Theosophists in Madras. The eagerness of many to help promote the ideals of the Society had been very encouraging indeed.

One of the most promising of the Madras members was a brilliant young lawyer named T. Subba Row. His interest in Theosophy had induced him to write to H.P.B. at Bombay soon after her arrival, and when he met her, it was, he said, as if a curtain had been raised, revealing suddenly a store of occult knowledge that he must have acquired in former lives.

Both H.P.B. and the Colonel developed a great admiration and affection for the young man. He became a chela of Master Morya; he sometimes acted as adviser to the Founders on Hindu questions; and he seemed to be making great strides forward in raja yoga.

Nevertheless this young Brahmin, like Damodar, had a different outlook from the Westerners on basic approaches to the occult, as was to be seen later in the great testing time.

Psychic conditions at Adyar were evidently good for the invisible work of the Mahatmas. According to the Diary entries of President-Founder Olcott, Master Morya came there in his subtle form almost every day in the early part of 1883. And in order to facilitate the vital work of liaison with inner planes H.P.B. decided to establish a special shrine-room where power might be more easily focused. Whether this was suggested by her Guru or not, he certainly must have agreed with the idea.

So the shrine room, or occult room, as it was sometimes called, was constructed in the little penthouse on the roof overlooking the river where it languidly joins the Bay of Bengal. Madame Blavatsky had her own quarters up there adjacent to the new shrine room.

Now began strange psychic events in which members of the Society were able to participate, and press reports brought a good deal of publicity to the movement. The *Indian Mirror* quotes this, for instance, from the *Philosophic Inquirer* of April 22, 1883:

> A correspondent who has just been visiting the Headquarters of the Theosophical Society at Madras sends us particulars of some wonderful phenomena that are occurring there almost every day. It appears that, under special instructions from the higher authorities who preside over the destinies of the Society, a special room has been constructed on the house-roof, to which few visitors are admitted. In it is a small splendidly carved cabinet or almirah, standing upon a pedestal. In it are two portraits of Adepts and a figure of the Buddha. If letters, addressed to the Mahatmas, be placed in here and the doors closed for a few moments, the letters will be found to have disappeared, and replies written upon Chinese or Tibetan paper to have come mysteriously from the addressed Adepts. . . .

Sometimes the letters received were replies to unwritten questions in the minds of the inquirers, and other objects, besides letters, appeared in the cabinet, many of them demonstrating some telepathic understanding as well as the power of *apporting* solid articles through walls and closed doors.

Among both the Indian and Western students of the occult the shrine room greatly strengthened faith in the reality and yogic powers of the Mahatmas, and their close association with The Theosophical Society. But later when echoes reached the general public of the West, H.P.B. had to pay a heavy price.

Her health was beginning to go down again by the middle of the year when the breathless summer heat stole over Madras, and even the sea breezes failed. Fortunately, however, she had made friends with General Rhodes E. Morgan, of the British army, and his wife. This couple were among the first settlers at Ootacamund in the Nilgiri mountains, which was fast becoming a summer resort for European residents of Madras. Early in July H.P.B. accepted their invitation to stay with them at "Ooty."

"I am at the Morgans," she wrote to Sinnett, who had by this time lost his job on *The Pioneer,* and gone back to London, "General and Generaless, six daughters and two sons with four sons-in-law constitute the family of the most terrible atheists and the most flapdoodlish or the most kind Spiritualists. Such care, such kindness and regards for my venerable self that I feel ashamed . . ."[4]

The Morgans became active members of the Society and staunch friends of H.P.B. when her time of troubles came.

During her three months with them in the summer of 1883 she wrote *The Enigmatical Tribes of the Blue Hills* for the Russian paper, *The Russkiy Vestnik.* It was later published as a book in English. At the same time she was doing a lengthy series of articles for *The Theosophist* called "Replies to an English F.T.S." The English Fellow of the Theosophical Society who had sent the questions was Frederick Myers, one of the Cambridge dons who had recently formed the British Society for Psychical Research in London. But these *Replies* were, H.P.B. said, dictated to her by Adepts and their chelas—mainly Master M, however.

"Holy shadow!! and who is Mr. Myers that my big Boss should waste a bucket full of his red ink to satisfy *him?* . . . For Mr. Myers will *not* be satisfied . . .," she wrote to Sinnett.

Colonel Olcott, with "beard to the seventh rib and hair floating in silvery locks like a Patriarch," was back from a tour of his much loved Ceylon by the middle of September, 1883. He came to "Ooty"; together the Founders visited Pondicherry and then returned to Adyar.

At Headquarters the trying summer months had not improved the disposition of Emma Coulomb. As housekeeper she was able to make a little for her own pocket by pilfering, but money was a scarce commodity around the Theosophical precincts, and the Coulombs' dream of putting away enough to start their own hotel again seemed a long way from fulfillment.

Madame Blavatsky had proved a great disappointment to Emma Coulomb. There were Indians with plenty of money in the Society, and Madame B. had enough opportunity to enrich herself and her fellow workers, such as the Coulombs, by the use of her "magical powers." That these powers were actually, in the main, nothing but clever conjuring tricks Emma had no doubt. Anything that she could not figure out as such she attributed to the work of the devil. Whatever lay behind the show, sleight-of-hand or satanic powers, it convinced and impressed a lot of wealthy people, and could have made enough money for all of them.

But for some reason the old Russian witch let her opportunities slip by. Worse still, she blocked all Emma's attempts to extract money on her own initiative from rich members.

One of the wealthy in whom she had great hopes was that easy, soft fellow, Prince Harisinghji. More money than Queen Victoria, by all reports! When she had approached him for a loan of two thousand rupees, he seemed willing and made a kind of half-promise. Unfortunately he had left next day before she could do more work on him. Still he would no doubt be visiting Adyar again and, providing Blavatsky did not hear about it and spike her guns, there was a good chance of getting the money. The sum would be nothing to him, but a lot to her.

Correspondence between H.P.B. and A. P. Sinnett shows that during 1883 trouble was brewing at the London center of Theosophy. The conflict revolved around strong, clashing personalities and their basic beliefs.

One of the personalities was Anna Kingsford, M.D., who had married an English Vicar in 1867, three years later entered the Roman Church, and thirteen years after that (in 1883) became the President of the London Lodge of Theosophy. H.P.B. described her as yellow haired and jingling with jewels.

The "divine Anna,"[5] as she was sometimes called in jest, had strong ideas on Theosophy, or rather the kind of Theosophy she thought would be acceptable to the British public. She wanted The Theosophical Society to be understood as a "Philosophical School, constituted on the ancient Hermetic basis, following scientific methods and exact processes of reasoning independent of any absolute authority. . . ." It is probable that she did not really believe in the existence of the Mahatmas, although she claimed that she did. At all events, she thought that the policy of teaching doctrines as emanating from mysterious, inaccessible Adepts was wrong.

Anna's close friend and Vice-President of the Lodge, Edward Maitland, strongly supported her ideas and policy. The opposing personality to them both in London was the recently arrived A.P. Sinnett. In actual correspondence with the Mahatmas for some years, he had given out, with the approval of the Brotherhood, fragments of their teachings in his book *Esoteric Buddhism*. Many London members were keen to hear more from him about the Great Ones, about their esoteric philosophy, and the yoga training required to become their pupils. This placed

Sinnett in a strong position.

His home meetings soon became a counterattraction to Anna's gatherings, Stresses and strains developed and the London Lodge began to divide in two.

Madame Blavatsky did not agree with Anna's outlook and was indignant at what she considered her disrespectful attitude toward the Mahatmas who were the real founders of the Theosophical Movement. She would have liked to dethrone Mrs. Kingsford forthwith, but the Masters thought otherwise. H.P.B. had just finished an eight-page letter, expressing her indignation to Anna when the hand of Master M. appeared before her nose and tore up the letter. Later she told Sinnett:

"They (the Bosses) have put their heads together and decided that the 'divine Anna' should be humoured. *She is necessary* to them; she is a wonderful *palliative* (whatever on earth the word means in the present case!) and they mean *to use her*."[6]

But it was decided that President-Founder Olcott should go to London and try to calm the turbulent waters there. His diplomacy and organizing ability would be used to put affairs in London on an amicable working basis. Olcott had another reason for going. The Buddhists of Ceylon had appointed him as their representative to intercede with the Colonial Office in London for the removal of the many injustices they felt they were suffering through the religious intolerance of their "Christian" overlords.

At first the plan was for H.P.B. to remain in India, but her health had gone down again. "It appears that I am *mortally sick* and, as the Masters have cured me repeatedly and have no time to bother with me, and that besides what I want is constant air charged with something (some scientific flapdoodle word) that cannot be got here in India— my Boss ordered Olcott to take me to Southern France . . ."[7]

But she added that she had no intention of going anywhere near London. The very thought of it, and some of the characters there, gave her "a feeling of horror, of inexpressible *magnetic disgust*." Sinnett must understand, she wrote, that it would be a great suffering for her to be there and "see how the Masters and their philosophy are both misunderstood."

Helena needed a servant more than ever now that she was so sick. She was fond of Babula and it was decided to include him in the party to go to Europe. Mohini Chatterji, a handsome young Calcutta lawyer, was to go for two purposes: as secretary to the Colonel and as a lecturer. His brilliant discourses would back up Sinnett's teachings on the true esoteric philosophy. The fifth of the party due to sail on the fateful trip was a highly intelligent Parsi graduate of Bombay University, Mr. B. J. Padshah.

On the way to Bombay to embark, H.P.B. intended to visit Prince Harisinghji, and in her big-hearted, generous way she granted Emma's request to be taken as far as Bombay. She realized that life at Adyar was dull for her housekeeper, who did not understand the Theosophical Movement, and a change of air would do her good.

At the Prince's mansion Emma seized her opportunity, and reminded him of his "promise" to lend her 2,000 rupees. But Harisinghji thought it would be correct to ask Madame Blavatsky's approval before lending money to her housekeeper. He did so.

H.P.B., knowing that a loan meant a gift in this case, let him know that she did not approve, and instead of getting the expected money, Emma got the rough edge of Madame Blavatsky's tongue for trying to make money out of theosophical contacts.

For the Lebanese Emma this was the very last straw. Not only was she a slave at Adyar—working for no wages— but she was frustrated at every opportunity and lectured like a school-girl into the bargain.

Well, she thought grimly, the nest will be empty back at Adyar, except for a couple of European newcomers, who know nothing, and a few stupid natives. I will have a free hand to take whatever chances come and get my revenge on this high-and-mighty Russian. If I can wreck her evil, anti-Christian Society, that will be a good turn to the missionaries, and maybe at the same time I can raise enough money so that Alex and I can get back to a decent life in the hotel business.

Aboard the *S.S. Chandernagore,* on February 20, 1884, Emma enacted a tearful farewell, embracing her mistress tenderly, with assurances that she would take special care of Madame's rooms and personal property. There was no need to worry about anything; Madame should have a good long holiday in Europe, she said, and get completely well before returning.

But later, on another part of the deck, Emma showed the other side of her face to Babula. She had found him in a black mood, as often happened, over some temperamental outburst, with "unjust demands" from his mistress. She expressed great sympathy for the harsh treatment he had suffered. Then with hate darkening the granite of her eyes, she hissed:

"As for me, I'll never forgive her for poking her potato nose into my affairs. But she'll pay for it. You see if she doesn't!"

Babula was startled by the venom in her voice and was to remember it later.

CHAPTER 18

Marie, Countess of Caithness and Duchess de Pomar, always made a remarkably handsome, if eccentric, figure when, dressed in crimson velvet with a long chain of huge diamonds about her neck, she stood receiving guests in the elegant salons of her mansion, the Palais Tiranty, in Nice.

Lord Caithness had been dead since 1881, and his widow lived alone with the son of her deceased first husband, a Spanish grandee, the Duc de Pomar.

Marie, who had first made contact with H.P.B. after the publication of *Isis Unveiled,* was a keen Theosophist, who still kept an interest in Spiritualism. At Holyrood, her magnificent home in Paris, there was a chapel used for direct communication with the spirit of Mary Stuart, Queen of Scots. Marie had steeped herself in the lore of the dead queen and was surrounded with "Mary relics." She often dressed after the fashion of the unfortunate monarch.

It was often said, indeed, that Lady Caithness believed herself to be a reincarnation of Mary Stuart, but this seems hardly compatible with her belief that the Queen was still on the other side and could be contacted mediumistically in the seance chapel. Moreover, a woman who knew the Countess intimately for many years—the Scottish authoress Violet Tweedale—writes that she had never heard

Marie even hint at the belief that she was the reincarnation of Mary Stuart.

Among the guests received by the Countess at Palais Tiranty during the season were members of the Russian nobility who flocked to the Côte d'Azur by the hundreds, bringing their retinues of servants. No people ever spent money so freely or so capriciously. Prince Cherkassky, a story goes, rented a villa with vast grounds and insisted on seeing a new gardenscape each morning. Every night four dozen gardeners toiled to shift old plants and set in new ones.

At Monte Carlo the Czarist Russians brought a note of glamor and excitement. There never were such gamblers. With gargantuan indifference and nonchalance they staked their entire fortunes, their estates, even their wives, it is said, on the turn of a card.

It was inevitable that Helena should meet some family friends among the Russian visitors, but their interests were not hers. She constantly refused their invitations to social gatherings, to join parties for the theater or the casino, mostly using her poor state of health as an excuse. Sometimes she found herself at home completely alone, even the Colonel having gone off to enjoy the theater or observe the strange antics of the wealthy international set. Then she would settle down happily to a few hours of quiet writing—some of her long letters, perhaps, or an important article for *The Theosophist,* which T. Subba Row was now editing in Madras.

H.P.B. did not stay long in the south of France, or go to any other health resort as planned. After twelve days she left for Paris with the Colonel and Babula. Mohini and Padshah had gone there directly from Marseilles where they had all disembarked from S.S. *Chandernagore.*

H.P.B. states that she had received orders from her Master to go to London, but she evidently did not mention this fact to Olcott who was preparing to handle the London Lodge situation alone.

When they stepped off the train at Paris, they were overjoyed to see standing on the platform the small figure of William Q. Judge. H.P.B. embraced him and the Colonel shook his hand warmly. Then they all drove together in a cab to 46 Rue Notre Dame des Champs, where the generous Lady Caithness had rented an apartment for the Founders and their friends.

It had been more than five years since H.P.B. or the Colonel had seen William Q. Judge. During that time he had often been away from New York on business trips, and the theosophical branch there had remained a sleeping nucleus. Now, however, it was becoming active again.

Its awakening had come at a meeting called by a visiting Hindu during the previous December. The New York *Herald* of December 4, 1883, reported that General Abner Doubleday, the "originator of the grip and cable system," and inventor, it is said, of baseball, "introduced the Hindu, not by name, but as the messenger of the Society. . . . He was attired with Oriental magnificence, strangely contrasting with the business suits of the others. On his breast gleamed a jewel wrought with the mystic sign OM. He spoke very little, but after announcing that the time had come for active work of the New York branch of the Theosophists, he read in Hindustani a short passage from the *Mahabharata* and gave the Acting President (Gen. Abner Doubleday) a copy of the Bhagavad Gita. . . . After delivering his message and the book, the Hindu disappeared. No one followed him or asked a question. . . . The Society immediately organized under the rules of the Theosophical Society, now of Madras, elected officers and appointed a meeting for next Monday night."[1]

Judge who, like Olcott, had studied Occultism under H.P.B. in the early days in New York, was to become the main force in reviving and spreading Theosophy in America. Now in Paris in the spring of 1884, he was full of the joys of reunion and anticipation. Master Morya had at long last given him the green light to visit India. He was on the first leg of that exciting journey, but he planned to stay in Paris for a while with his friend and teacher, H.P.B.

The Colonel and Mohini soon went on to London. On April 7 a meeting of the London Lodge was in progress. On the platform sat the portly Founder-President, venerable beard down to his seventh rib, as H.P.B. described it, and a worried look on his noble brow. Beside him was Mohini, slight, with long black hair under his small white Indian cap. He had the dark soulful eyes of his race. Also on the platform were the key figures in the great dispute, Anna Kingsford, Edward Maitland, and Alfred P. Sinnett.

The debate was waxing warm. The Colonel was doing his diplomatic best to adjust the differences and create an atmosphere of calmness. Then he planned to put forward his positive proposals for a compromise that would, he hoped, create harmony within the theosophic body of London. He was not having much success.

A stout lady was seen by a few to walk into the meeting and unobtrusively take a seat at the rear of the long darkened room, unrecognized by those who saw her. Soon afterward one of the speakers in the dispute (which was growing more heated and emotion-charged every minute) referred to some previous action of Madame Blavatsky's.

"That's so," remarked the stout lady, loudly.

People looked around in curious silence, those on the platform strained to see to the rear. Suddenly the meeting broke up in confusion. Angry emotions changed to joy and excitement. The crowd gathered around her, all talking at once, and Mohini arrived on his knees at the feet of his adored teacher, H.P.B.

Asked how she had known the meeting was at chambers in Lincoln's Inn and had found her way from the railway station, H.P.B. answered simply: "I followed my occult nose."

Her dramatic appearance at the right moment caused the dissolution of the stormy meeting. Later the Colonel relieved the London tensions quietly and in the best way by acknowledging the two factions and establishing a separate group, known as the Hermetic Lodge, with Anna Kingsford at its head. Sinnett, who had the larger following, became the Leader of the old London Lodge.

After a week with the Sinnetts in England, H.P.B. returned to Paris where there was some reorganizing to be done in the Theosophical Branch of which Lady Caithness was the head. And she had plenty of work ahead on a new project ordered by her Master.

A little later she went to a Chateau at Enghien, a few miles from Paris, as guest of the Count and Countess Gaston d'Adhémar. But as usual, even when a house guest, Helena spent most of her time writing—at this period on the beginning of the new project, *The Secret Doctrine*. In its early stages she regarded this as an expanded version of her *Isis Unveiled,* and asked Judge, who was also at the Chateau, to go carefully through the latter book, noting in the margins what subjects were treated.

One day the Swedish Countess Constance Wachtmeister called at the Chateau to see Madame Blavatsky. She was told that H.P.B. was occupied and could not receive her.

"I'm perfectly willing to wait," said the Countess, who had come from England specially to see the controversial leader of the Society of which she was, herself, a humble member. She had no intention of leaving Enghien until she had achieved her purpose.

Her determination was rewarded; she met H.P.B. and was invited by the Countess d'Adhémar to take up her quarters at the Chateau. Madame was, however, shut up in her room working all day, and Constance Wachtmeister had to be satisfied with meeting her at table and in the evenings when she was "surrounded by a *coterie.*"

At last through the good offices of William Q. Judge, the Countess obtained a private interview with "the Old Lady," as many friends were now calling the 53-year old Helena Blavatsky.[2]

"She told me," writes Constance, "many things that I thought were known only to myself, and ended by saying that, before two years had passed, I should devote my life wholly to Theosophy."

"That I'm afraid is an utter impossibility," replied the Countess Wachtmeister, frankly.

H.P.B. smiled. "Master says so, and therefore I know it to be true," she said.

Echoes from London reaching Enghien and Paris during May and June indicated that Theosophy was having a great success there. Under the influence of Sinnett, the benign Colonel and the picturesque Mohini, it was on the verge of becoming the fashion in social circles. More to the point, some leading intellectuals, scientists, and literary men were taking a serious interest in the new, broadening concepts from the East: Robert Browning, Matthew Arnold, Sir William Crookes, Sir Edwin Arnold, Sir William Barrett, Frederick W. H. Myers.

The last, a poet and distinguished classical scholar, had been a Fellow of the Theosophical Society for some time, and was the F.T.S. for whom the long *Replies* had been crowding the columns of *The Theosophist,* much to H.P.B.'s annoyance.

Myers had a particular interest in supraphysical phenomena connected with The Theosophical Society, because he and some friends, all learned men, had recently formed a Society of their own specifically for the investigation of such phenomena. This new organization was called the Society for Psychical Research, and its members hoped to apply the objective techniques of modern science to the elusive areas of the psychic, which scientists —with a few exceptions, such as Sir William Crookes— were scornfully avoiding.

Sinnett had written his *Occult World,* and now both he and Colonel Olcott were amazing the drawing rooms of London with talk of incredible things. If, said Myers, these things were factually true, the old maxim about "Light from the East," must indeed be a reality, and not just a dream! But first the alleged phenomena must be investigated by the strict, impersonal methods of the new psychical research. The question was, would the Theosophists cooperate?[3]

Hindus, in general, preferred to restrict knowledge of the esoteric doctrines to the initiated few, but Mohini was prepared to do what the Founders wished. Sinnett, who thought that Theosophy was not for the masses, but for the intellectuals, was happy enough to cooperate with the scholars and scientists of the Society for Psychical Research (S.P.R). The open-hearted American Colonel was always ready to share with everyone the good things he had found. In fact he regarded the investigation as a golden opportunity. The S.P.R. was aiming to maintain the high standards of a "learned body," and if this body, after investigation, declared the genuineness of the theosophical phenomena—as it must, thought the Colonel—it would bring a complete revolution to the materialistic thought patterns of the western world. He was eager to cooperate.

Too eager, in the opinion of H.P.B. who considered that he was pressing his experiences of miraculous events overmuch on the skeptical, cautious minds of the investigators. She had misgivings about the whole investigation. These proud British intellectuals knew nothing of the deep Vedic concepts of man that lay behind the phenomena, nothing of the yoga of renunciation and self-surrender that changed one's whole set of values. To them the reasoning mind was the highest deity. Their minds might be highly trained, but they were limited and puny against the supramental world they were tackling—tackling from the wrong angle and without the essential humility!

Still, as acknowledged leader and much publicized wonderworker of the Society, she felt she could not refuse to cooperate with the S.P.R. That would look suspicious. She would have to agree and hope for the best.

Olcott, Sinnett, Mohini, and Padshah met several times with a Committee of Investigation for question-and-answer sessions while H.P.B. was in Paris. When she came over to London at the end of June, she went, with the Colonel and the Sinnetts, to a meeting of the S.P.R. and, early in August, sat with Mohini before the investigators at Cambridge. It was a lot of flapdoodle, she thought. Without training under an enlightened guru how could anyone understand the reality and rationale of the *siddhis* (superhuman powers)?

During this second visit to England from Paris (for a period of about six weeks), she stayed in the home of the Arundale ladies at Notting Hill, London. To Mrs. and Miss Francesca Arundale she once wrote in a letter: "If I had two dozen like *you two* and a dozen like Sinnett—Masters would be with you and the Society long ago. I *mean* what I say and what is more—*I know it.*"

George Arundale, the nephew and adopted son of Francesca, was later to become President of the Theosophical Society.

While Theosophy in Europe seemed to be flourishing, back in India it had acquired enemies enough. For some time its old ally, the Arya Samaj had been working against the Society. Swami Dayanand had turned against the Founders because, says Colonel Olcott in *Old Diary Leaves,* they would not "consent to hold aloof from the Buddhists or Parsis." The eclecticism of the Society did not suit the Swami's worship of the Vedas as he interpreted them. He began to vilify Theosophy in general and H.P.B.'s phenomena in particular.

The missionaries, with a few individual exceptions, were strongly opposed to the theosophical teachings. The churches' efforts to draw the natives away from their own heathen Hindu and Buddhist beliefs were not being helped by this new gnostic movement. The Colonel and other theosophical speakers, were declaring that Christian church theology made a poor showing against the ancient verities drawn from the heart of Hinduism; their arguments fanned to life the smoldering embers of the old faith.

H.P.B.'s much publicized phenomena made matters worse, and her actions did nothing to appease the churchmen. When at Ootacamund in 1883, for instance, she had held meetings at the home of the Morgans during the hour of church services. Large numbers of churchgoers came to her gatherings, hoping perhaps to see miracles, and the church pews were empty on these Sundays.

Now letters from India to the Founders in Europe indicated that some sinister plot was afoot between Madras missionaries and the Coulomb couple.

Mr. Lane-Fox, a wealthy English electrical engineer on the Board of Control at Adyar, wrote that Emma Coulomb was spreading abroad rumors about "trap-doors" in the Shrine Room. She was also saying that the Society's secret but real purpose was to overthrow British rule in India. Letters from Damodar told the same story: "She, Madame Coulomb, tells me, and has been saying to everyone, that you [H.P.B.] are a fraud—performing phenomena by means of secret spring trap-doors."

Master K.H., in a letter to the Colonel, delivered phenomenally in a train while Olcott and Mohini were on their way from Paris to England, wrote: "You have harboured a traitor and an enemy under your roof for years, and the missionary party are more than ready to avail of any help she may be induced to give."[4]

T. Subba Row, hearing some of the rumors, wrote to ask H.P.B. if there could possibly be any compromising letters of which she needed to "beware"; it would be better, if there were, to buy them at any price. It is significant, in view of what happened later, that H.P.B. replied that she had not written any compromising letters.

The Founders wondered if they should return immediately to India. But as there was still important work to be done in Europe, they decided to try to mend matters by correspondence with the Coulombs. After all, they argued, Emma had for quite a time been against the Society and had spread unfavorable gossip. Perhaps now, as earlier, it was just a storm in a teacup and would pass. They both wrote long letters, trying to persuade her to desist from spreading false and malicious stories about H.P.B. and the Society. She could not, they said, overthrow the Society for it was founded on the rock of Truth.

"All the evil proved," wrote H.P.B., "will be that you have never wished to believe that there were *true* Mahatmas behind the curtain, that you do not believe the phenomena real, and that is why you see tricks in everything."[5]

But events in Madras were moving ahead faster than the Founders could learn, or handle, by slow correspondence—letters that took weeks in transit. Emma and Alexis Coulomb had the run of the roof at the Adyar Headquarters bungalow. Alexis, as official handyman, was busy, ostensibly, carrying out some new construction work up there ordered by the President before leaving. Emma had the keys of H.P.B.'s rooms and would let no one else enter them, saying that *she* alone was responsible for Madame's property there. In vain did another leading member of the Board of Control, Dr. Franz Hartman, tell her that Madame Blavatsky had given him permission to use her desk when he needed somewhere quiet for writing.

Emma's innuendos about trapdoors and secret panels made members of the Board begin to suspect something. Could it be that Alexis's hammer and saw were employed in preparing such contrivances to support his wife's stories? The members' concern was increasing, too, about the slanderous Coulomb tales that were coming to their ears from various sources.

Finally, they decided to impeach the couple. They obtained affidavits from a number of responsible people stating that Madame Coulomb was guilty of attempts to extort money from members, of wasting the Society's funds, of slandering Madame Blavatsky and spreading false stories about the objects and operations of the Society.

Spurred on by a strongly-worded letter from Master Morya, the Board cabled the Founders in Europe for permission to expel the Coulombs from the Society's premises. The permission was given.

But before the Coulomb couple left, they tried to blackmail the Society leaders at Adyar. For their silence about "things they could tell" they demanded three thousand rupees. This, they insinuated, was a big sacrifice on their part, for they had been offered ten thousand rupees to ruin the Society.

But the blackmail attempts failed and, with much difficulty, the Coulombs were expelled from the premises on May 25, 1884. They went to lodge with a member of the Reverend Patterson's church. There they set to work preparing the documents which would, they hoped, spell the ruin of the Society, avenge the "injustices" Emma felt she had suffered at the hands of Madame Blavatsky, and earn—from certain "Christian" missionaries—approbation, gratitude, and something much more substantial.

Apparently unaware of the deadly brew that was being cooked in the witches' cauldron, the Founders lingered on in Europe.

CHAPTER 19

Stories of "miraculous" happenings told by those who lived with Helena Blavatsky, or saw a great deal of her, would fill a large volume in themselves. Even blown-in-the-glass skeptics should feel that beneath such a lot of smoke there might perhaps be just a little fire. But many of her own day would not concede the possibility of the tiniest flame. And her character assassins today are as unreasonable, even though some of the powers her followers claimed for her have since been demonstrated in modern parapsychological research.

In the following incident H.P.B. gave one of her numerous demonstrations of a particular ESP and of psychokinesis in the form of what was called "precipitation." The feat was attested by several witnesses on the spot, including one of her most savage critics.

On a June morning of 1884 in Paris, half-a-dozen people sat in the reception room at H.P.B.'s apartment on the Rue Notre Dame des Champs. Present were: H.P.B.'s sister Vera who had been in Paris about a month, Colonel Olcott, William Q. Judge, Madame Emile de Morsier, and the Russian writer Vsevolod Soloviov, who later became H.P.B.'s bitter enemy for unfathomable reasons of his own.

It was about 10 a.m. and the reception room door to the hall was open. A ring came on the front door bell. They saw the servant go to the front door, open it and take some letters from the postman. The servant then came straight into the reception room and put the mail on a table. One of the letters was from Odessa, and both

H.P.B. and Vera recognized the handwriting on the envelope as that of a relative. It was addressed to their Aunt Nadyezhda who had come to Paris with Vera, and was at that moment in another room of the apartment.

H.P.B. expressed some curiosity about what the relative in Odessa had written in the letter, and Vera, always ready to challenge her sister on such matters said:

"Since you profess to have the power, why don't you find out by reading it before it's opened? I defy you to do so."

Helena, who was in high spirits that morning took the envelope and held it against her forehead. For a few moments her face was a mask of intense concentration. Then she began to read aloud.

Someone provided paper and pencil, and she wrote down what she thought were the contents of the enclosed letter. When she had finished, Vera expressed her doubts about the reading, saying that some of the idioms Helena had used were not characteristic of the person who had written the letter.

Helena was irritated with her. "You will find it correct," she snapped. "But I will do still more."

Taking the page on which she had written her version of the letter's contents, she underlined a word with red crayon and, with the same crayon, drew an interlaced double triangle beneath another word.

"Now," she said, "I will cause these two red marks to appear in the corresponding places within the letter itself."

Placing the page and the letter together, and putting her hand over them, she appeared to go again into a state of one-pointed concentration.

After a few moments she relaxed, and tossed the closed letter across the table to her sister, declaring, *"Tiens! C'est fait."*

When Nadyezhda joined the company and opened the letter, it was found that H.P.B. had accurately probed its contents and, even more astounding, had "precipitated" the two red marks under the correct words in the letter. Of exceptional significance was the fact that a slight defect in the drawing of the interlaced triangles had been faithfully reproduced within the closed letter.

A statement describing the phenomenon was drawn up and attested by those present, and V. Solvoviov wrote an account of it for the St. Petersburg *Rebus*, a journal devoted to psychological sciences. He noted as important the fact that the postage stamp was on the back flap of the letter, "glued on the place where the seal is habitually placed," a strong indication that it had not been tampered with in transit. He concluded his article with these words:

"The circumstances under which the phenomenon occurred in its smallest details, carefully checked by myself, do not leave in me the smallest doubt as to its *genuineness* and reality. Deception or fraud in this particular case *are entirely out of the question.*"

In the middle of August that year, H.P.B. went to Germany as the guest of Mr. and Mrs. Gebhard who occupied a large house at Elberfeld in the Ruhr. With her went a number of Theosophists, including Mohini, Mr. Bertram Keightley, and the Arundales. The Colonel had already been there for about three weeks, busy organizing the German Theosophists into an active branch.

The Gebhard home was the magnetic center of Theosophy in that part of Europe, Mrs. Gebhard (Mary) having been one of the few pupils of the late occultist, Éliphas Lévi. Her husband, though a successful and wealthy manufacturer, banker and consul, was also interested in the deeper questions of life.

Even the Gebhard mansion must have been full to capacity that autumn, for apart from those with H.P.B., a number of other visitors came later, among them Frederick Myers of the S.P.R. and his brother. All visitors stayed a few days or more. They came, they said, to confer with H.P.B., but no doubt most hoped for something to prove she could do more than talk brilliantly. Some, at least, were testing her.

Judging by what he wrote afterwards, and the decisive action he took against H.P.B., Frederick Myers failed to get his ration of the signs and wonders which his generation, like that of the Nazarene, demanded. But others found at Elberfeld, as they had hoped, some miraculous events taking place within the mansion walls. A well witnessed and attested case is described fully by Rudolph Gebhard, one of the four adult sons.

Rudolph prefaces his account by explaining that he was a trained amateur conjurer, having met, and been instructed by, some of the leading "wizards" of the day. For this reason he had an expert's eye for detecting any sleight-of-hand tricks.

It was about nine o'clock one night, he says, when Madame Blavatsky made the remark that she felt the presence of one of the Masters, and that she thought he had the intention of doing something unusual for the company. Most of the people in the drawing-room at the time were members of the newly formed theosophical branch, but one was a visiting Major-General of the U.S. army. Madame Blavatsky, herself, still not in the best of health, was reclining on a couch.

"Think and decide what you would like to take place," she invited the company.

There was a little discussion and then all agreed that they would ask for a letter addressed to the host, Mr. G. Gebhard, on any subject he himself cared to nominate.

Mr. Gebhard decided that he would like advice from the Master in connection with one of his sons who was then in America. The subject was, in fact, suggested to him by Rudolph.

H.P.B. called their attention to a large oil painting hanging over the piano. Several clairvoyant people saw bright lights around the painting, and H.P.B. said to one of them, Mrs. Laura Holloway: "See, and describe, what is going on there."

"Something is forming over the picture, but I can't quite make out what it is," replied Mrs. Holloway.

"Well that is certainly where the phenomenon will take place." said H.P.B.

Now conjurer Rudolph left his chair and climbed onto the piano in order to look behind the painting which hung from a hook in the wall. The room was well lighted, particularly the area around the painting where there were two wall gas brackets.

Rudolph lifted the bottom of the picture away from the wall by some six inches, shook it, and looked thoroughly behind it. But there was nothing whatever to be seen. He returned to his seat and the company waited, watching the picture intently.

After a while Rudolph was induced to try again to see if anything had yet developed. This time he not only held the painting out and looked behind it, but ran his hand carefully along the back of the frame twice. Convinced that nothing was there, he turned to Madame Blavatsky and asked:

"What is to be done now?"

She was silent for a while, her eyes concentrated on the painting; then she exclaimed:

"I see it! Look, there it is!"

Rudolph who had been watching her, turned quickly around in time to see an envelope dropping from behind the painting. It fluttered onto the piano. Picking it up, he saw it was addressed to 'Herrn Consul G. Gebhard'.

"I must have had rather a perplexed face," Rudolph writes, "for the company laughed merrily at the 'family Juggler'."

But Rudolph felt sure he had witnessed something that none of the world's leading sleight-of-hand wizards could have done under identical conditions. He was further convinced of this, and so were the others present, when the contents of the letter were found to be on the subject requested by Mr. Gebhard a few minutes earlier.

Rudolph sent a report of this Elberfeld letter phenomenon to the S.P.R. in London. The S.P.R. Committee of Investigation was unable to find a rational explanation of this "trick," and one of them suggested that H.P.B., or a confederate, might have thrown the letter behind the picture.

With so many people in the room, eagerly on the alert, this seemed to Rudolph a very lame theory. But he decided to test it anyway. He found it impossible to throw the letter—the one his father had received—from anywhere on the floor to fall accurately behind the picture. Such an achievement would be a lucky shot indeed. But supposing someone had managed to do so, unseen by all the watching eyes, what then? He climbed on the piano and from that position was able to toss the letter behind the painting. It held securely between the frame and the wall. Pulling the picture out to make sure it was not stuck to the wall, he tried again and again, several times. Finally he was quite convinced that the bottom of this heavy frame held too firmly against the wall for a letter to fall from behind it by its own weight alone. Some other force must have been at work.

One morning a copy of the London *Times* was brought to H.P.B.'s room. Opening it, she read an article that pierced her heart with a cold, sharp blade of horror. It was a story that had appeared first in the September issue of the Madras *Christian College Magazine,* had then been cabled from India by the *Times* correspondent there, and printed in London on September 20, 1884. It gave extracts of letters which she (H.P.B.) was supposed to have written, at various dates and from various parts of India, to Emma Coulomb at the headquarters of The Theosophical Society.

If the extracts had been genuine, they would have proved that Madame Blavatsky, co-Founder and Corresponding Secretary of the Society, had been for years producing bogus phenomena. The conclusion to be drawn from the article was that the Mahatmas were H.P.B.'s own invention, and that she had fooled everyone, including her partner, ex-sleuth and lawyer Colonel Olcott. The only ones not hoodwinked were the self-confessed unscrupulous Coulombs who were confederates in the roguery.

And who would not believe the diabolical story? People were only too ready to believe the worst, especially about things so far outside their everyday experience as Mahatmas and miracles. The trouble was that the extracts seemed so plausbile. She recognized her own words and phrases, but inserted among them were interpolations that were certainly not hers. And it was these insertions, put in cleverly by someone, that were so damning.

Who was the someone? The press story appeared some three months after Emma and Alexis Coulomb were expelled from the headquarters. They had evidently spent the time doctoring H.P.B.'s letters which Emma had kept with evil, Iago-like intent. Alexis was an expert counterfeiter; he had once even fooled Damodar with a note forged in H.P.B.'s handwriting. He had most likely done the job. Then they had taken the letters to one of H.P.B.'s worst enemies among the missionaries, the Reverend Patterson, editor of the *Christian College Magazine*. Did Emma get her "thirty pieces of silver?" She would get all she could. But what a hatred this woman must have harbored!

The Masters had hinted at a plot but had not ordered H.P.B. back to India. If they had, she might have been back in time to prevent this horrible outcome. But now it was too late. She evidently had to bear this karma of her impetuosity, unwise liberality, and lack of proper caution in the exercise of occult powers. It was her Garden of Gethsemane, and she would sweat blood, for she had not yet conquered her sensitive nature.

But for the sake of the Society she would certainly not sit back and do nothing. In fact she would do all in her power to prevent the ruthless, spiteful Coulomb witch from wrecking the movement to which she and the Colonel had given their all. Olcott and others who knew her well, and had even met some of the Masters, could scarcely believe her a fraud. They must help her in the fight.

Her partner, the old Civil War veteran, left almost immediately for the field of battle—Madras. She, herself, planned to go via England and Egypt. In the latter country she would collect dossiers on the rascally Coulombs, for she intended to sue them for defamation of character in the courts of Madras.

Before leaving her friends at Elberfeld, she wrote to Francesca Arundale, who had returned to London: "I have resigned my corresponding secretaryship in the Society; I have disconnected myself with it publicly; for I think that so long as I am in and at the head of the Society, I will be the target shot at, and that the Society will be affected by it. . . . My heart—if I have any left—is broken by this step."[1]

Early in October she left for London, accompanied by Rudolph Gebhard and the clairvoyant Laura Holloway.

From Elgin Crescent, Notting Hill, the home of the Arundales, she sent a letter to the London *Times,* denying authorship of the scandalous passages attributed to her by the Coulombs.

"Sentences here and there I recognise, taken from old notes of mine on different matters, but they are mingled with interpolations that entirely pervert their meaning," she wrote.

The letter was published on October 9, 1884, along with a letter from Mr. St. George Lane-Fox who was just back from India. As a member of the T.S. Board of Control during the Founders' absence, he denounced the Coulombs, stating that they had been constructing "all sorts of trap-doors and sliding panels in the private rooms of Madame Blavatsky who had very indiscreetly given over these rooms to their charge. As to the letters purporting to have been written by Madame Blavatsky . . . I, in common with all who are acquainted with the circumstances of the case, have no doubt whatever, that, whoever wrote them, they are not written by Madame Blavatsky."

But the shining theosophical balloon of hope, which had begun to rise over London, was effectively pricked. Among the most alarmed observers of the scene were the investigating members of the Society for Psychical Research, who had cautiously formed a favorable opinion on the theosophical phenomena. Now they decided that they could well be wrong, and that the matter must be looked into with what they considered their high standard of scientific thoroughness.

H.P.B. had scarcely left the country when an S.P.R. investigator set sail for India. He was a young graduate of Melbourne and Cambridge universities, keen, but utterly ignorant of India and her ancient wisdom.

One of the S.P.R. Committee, Frederick Myers, felt some interest in what might lie behind the stories of Indian wonders. He for one was anxious to determine if there was truly a mind-illuminating Light from Eastern windows. Were there, in fact, Mahatmas, Supermen? Were conscious, volitional supramental powers a reality? Theosophical phenomena might be the key to the mystery. The Committee would probe it thoroughly with a man on the spot.

So, unaware of the immensity of his responsibilities, a brash, inexperienced youth named Richard Hodgson set foot on the land of the Rishis for the first time. All his investigations had to be done in one visit, and because available funds were limited, it must be a short visit.

CHAPTER 20

One day late in November, 1884, Helena Blavatsky sat on the deck of the S. S. *Navarine*, trying to catch a breath of air over the stifling Red Sea. It was the first day out from Port Suez and she had not yet made the acquaintance of any of her fellow passengers, some of whom were now reclining on deck chairs near at hand, drinking their various alcoholic beverages and talking in the loud voices the English seemed to adopt when abroad.

Suddenly she realized that one of them was reading aloud from a pamphlet issued by the missionaries in Madras. It was about the Coulomb letters and Madame Blavatsky. There were guffaws, titters, and some cruel remarks, obviously intended for her ears. A hot flush of indignation passed over Helena, almost choking her.

Then she felt a hand on her shoulder and looking up saw Isabel Cooper-Oakley, one of the two friends who had accompanied her from England. Isabel began to say something, but stopped as her ears caught one of the insulting comments from the nearby group. For a moment she seemed petrified with angry shame for her countrymen; her cheeks turning scarlet. She started to move toward the offending group, but H.P.B. took her hand and held her back. Isabel snorted her disgust as she helped the Old Lady out of her chair. Together they went further forward and leaned over the rail where there was a little breeze and clouds of flying fish skimmed the water. After a while they were joined by the other friend from England, the Reverend Charles W. Leadbeater.

Thirty-seven-year-old Mr. Leadbeater was a Curate of the High Church of England, but a most unusual one. As a child he had met the famous occultist, Bulwer Lytton,

and witnessed phenomena in Lytton's presence. Coming
to Theosophy through Spiritualism and Sinnett's writings,
he had met Madame Blavatsky in London and decided to
go to India with her, leaving the Church to devote his
life to the cause of the Masters.

Isabel Cooper-Oakley was an independent thinker with
a deep interest in the esoteric and mystical—an unusual
trait, perhaps, to find in a scholar of one of England's
leading colleges for ladies of the upper classes, Girton.
Undeterred—in fact, spurred on—by the Coulomb frame-
up, she was launching on a life's work for Theosophy.

Her husband, Mr. A. J. Cooper-Oakley, a Cambridge
graduate and deep student of Indian philosophy and San-
skrit literature, had given up a promising career as an
educationist to work for Theosophy. He and Isabel had
shared accommodations with H.P.B. in England and then
set sail with her from Liverpool. Mr. Cooper-Oakley was
now spending some time in Cairo to collect documents in
support of H.P.B.'s case against the Coulombs.

Colonel Olcott came down to Colombo to meet his old
chum and accompany her on the last leg of her journey
back to India. She had much to tell him, and their plan
of action was not settled when their ship docked in Madras and they met with a great surprise.

The pier was crowded with students from the college
whose professors had been damning H.P.B. and her Society in papers and pamphlets. They had come to meet
the great "charlatan"—not to denounce, but to cheer her
to the echo. Yoga philosophy, and the consequent belief in
the existence of Mahatmas, belonged to their age-old
tradition; it was in the nation's spiritual bones and blood.
The missionaries and Coulombs had conspired to throw
aspersions on the great traditional beliefs. Madame Blavatsky was its great champion.

A large Committee garlanded her and escorted her
through the cheering crowd to the Pachiappah Hall. As
she entered, holding onto the arm of the Colonel, the
crowd in the hall rose to its feet and the rafters shook
with a mighty roar of applause. The grip on the Colonel's
arm tightened, and H.P.B.'s mouth set like iron to hold

back her powerful emotions, but her "eyes were full of a glad light and almost swimming in tears of joy."

The Old Lady's spirits were lifted to such a supreme level that she made what Olcott believed to be her first and last public address. Speeches were also made by the Colonel, Mr. Leadbeater, and Mrs. Cooper-Oakley. Tumultuous applause, more garlands and bouquets to Madame Blavatsky and to the rest of her party terminated this wonderful welcome home.

The leader of the defiant students' demonstration, N.P. Subramania Iyar, came, he wrote later, "very near being dismissed by Dr. Miller, the Principal of the College." But, more important, the event brought him close to H.P.B., for whom he had great reverence and affection, often doing errands for her.

One day Babula informed his mistress that Subramania, who had been on a shopping errand, was waiting below to see her. She thought her servant meant the Honorable S. Subramania Aiyyer, a member of the Madras Legislative Council. Hastily donning the formal black gown she kept for meeting distinguished guests, she ordered Babula to bring the waiting visitor straight upstairs. Babula did so, and when H.P.B. saw the young student instead of the Honorable Councillor, she cried:

"What, you! You dishonorable!"

After that he was always known affectionately as "the dishonorable."

H.P.B. was delighted with the evidence she and her helpers had collected while in Cairo. Witnesses stated that Emma had been sacked from a position as a French governess in that city for showing filthy pictures to her young charges. Also she had obtained money from several gullible people under the false pretences that her clairvoyance could detect hidden treasure. Following her advice, her husband had been ruined in business, had become a fraudulent bankrupt and had stolen 25,000 francs. And so on, and so on.

Helena urged the Colonel to take her to a barrister in Madras where she could file her suit for slander against the Coulombs. But Olcott hesitated; he did not think the documents were in a suitable form for production in court. The annual convention, he reminded her, was only a few days off, and during that time, a Committee of legal advisers would advise on the best course for her to adopt. But H.P.B. was too impatient to wait. Angrily she told him:

"If you don't take me to a barrister today, I'll go by myself."

"Then I'll resign my office and let the Convention decide between us," he threatened.

She knew he meant it, so perhaps there was some force in his argument. She decided to wait.

While the world Theosophical Convention of 1884 was on, Richard Hodgson of the S.P.R. was also at Adyar carrying out his investigations. The Founders treated him as a guest and friend, and the President, an old investigator himself, gave the Australian-born young man every cooperation.

But everyone was very busy, and the Indian members, in particular, were not helpful to Hodgson. They did not feel that occult and yogic truths were subjects for his style of investigation. Damodar took pleasure in bamboozling him; T. Subba Row was like a clam; Judge N. D. Khandalvala, a leading member, entirely distrusted Hodgson, considering him ignorant, unfair, and clumsy in his methods.

After a short time at Adyar, Hodgson moved to the enemy camp, among the missionaries and Coulombs, to take up their side of the story.

At the Convention, the Indian members, and the Committee of legal men in particular, advised strongly against H.P.B.'s suing her slanderers. A number of reasons were given. For one thing, they said, it would be very difficult to prove the Coulomb letters a forgery in court, especially as the Madras Bench was known to be hostile to The Theosophical Society and strongly biased in favor of the missionaries. Moreover, why give the world the spectacle of a spiteful cross-examination, in which the existence of the Mahatmas would be brought into debate and public ridicule! A Court of Law was no place to decide such deep questions. Besides, even in the unlikely event of

H.P.B.'s obtaining a favorable verdict, the opinion of the sceptics would not be changed.

Helena herself writhed and fretted under the reins of such restricting advice. She was eager for the open fight, eager to wipe the stain from the reputation of the founder of a great Society. But the weight of opinion was too strong for her. And she finally saw that a victory would indeed be hollow if, to gain it, the names of the Great Ones must be trampled further into the mud of public prejudice.

But the inner conflict, the frustration of being prevented from revealing the truth to the world, took toll of her ever-precarious health.

None of this was helped by revelations about the attitude of Richard Hodgson. If he *had* begun the investigations with an unbiased mind, it would not have been easy for him to retain it. As Isabel Cooper-Oakley put it: "A continuous round of dinner parties did not tend to clear his views, for he had incessantly poured into his ears a stream of calumny against her [H.P.B.]. . . . From hearing everyone say Madame Blavatsky was an impostor he began to believe it: after a few interviews with Madame Coulomb and the missionaries, we saw that his views were turning against the minority [the Theosophists]." His report, she goes on to say: "omitted some very valuable evidence of phenomena given to him by Mr. Oakley and myself."[1]

H.P.B.'s first intimation that Hodgson was against her came in a psychic vision of his mind and thoughts. This was soon confirmed by a number of things. Despite her repeated requests, he would never show her any originals of the incriminating letters published over her name, letters in which she knew there were forged interpolations.

Furthermore, Hodgson's unfavorable view of the evidence had been communicated in conversation to the Cooper-Oakleys, and to one or two other leading Theosophists, who relayed it to Madame Blavatsky. His talk in public was not, indeed, what should be expected of a just and unbiased investigator preparing a confidential report for a Society of scholars and scientists. It came to

H.P.B.'s ears that at social gatherings he spoke of her open-
ly as "a Russian spy," a "consummate fraud," and even
"a woman capable of every and any crime."

During January, 1885, Colonel Olcott had gone off
to revive Buddhism in Burma, at the invitation of King
Theebaw III. H.P.B. was trying to make a start on a new
plan, given her by Master Morya, for her work, *The
Secret Doctrine*. But the atmosphere of suspicion, rumor,
tension, and downright calumny around her was more
conducive to illness than constructive work.

"I carry two mortal diseases in me which are not
cured—heart and kidneys," she wrote to Sinnett. "At any
moment the former can have a rupture, and the latter
carry me away in a few days . . . All this is due to five
years of constant anguish, worry and repressed emotion.
A Gladstone may be called a 'fraud' and laugh at it. I
can't, say what you may."[2]

Several accounts have been given of the grave illness
that fell on Helena at this time.

Isabel Cooper-Oakley, who was on the spot acting as
nurse, wrote:

"Very anxious were the hours and days of nursing that
I went through those weeks, as she grew worse and worse,
and was finally given up in a state of coma by the doctors
. . . who said that nothing could be done, it was impossible
. . . The doctors said that she would pass away in that
condition, and I knew, humanly speaking, that night's
watch must be the last. I cannot here go into what happened, an experience I can never forget; but towards 8
a.m. H.P.B. suddenly opened her eyes and asked for her
breakfast, the first time she had spoken naturally for two
days.

"I went to meet the doctor, whose amazement at the
change was very great.

"H.P.B. said: 'Ah! doctor, you do not believe in our
great Masters.' "[3]

Colonel Olcott returned to Adyar following a cable
from Damodar that H.P.B. was dangerously ill. But after
a few days he left again to complete his tour of Burma
because, as he said, her Master by coming one night and

laying his hand on her had snatched her back from death, just as he had done several times in her life before, to the Colonel's personal knowledge.

On February 23—twelve days after Olcott had left Adyar for the second time—Damodar set sail for Calcutta. But H.P.B. and T. Subba Row knew that, in fact, he planned to go far beyond Calcutta into Tibet. He hoped to reach the ashrama of his Guru, Master K.H., and be allowed to remain there indefinitely for development toward Adeptship.

If Hodgson had known this, it might have shaken his conclusion that the Mahatmas were an invention of H.P.B., aided and abetted by Damodar. A man would be mad, indeed, to go seeking the flimsy figment of imagination in a dangerous land like Tibet. But Damodar's intention at the time was known only to a close few.

Helena Blavatsky was glad for Damodar's sake that he had been provisionally accepted to live at the ashrama of the Master. He represented, in a way, the first fruits of the Theosophical Movement, the inner object of which was to raise men to the superhuman level of the Great Brotherhood.

But his going left an emptiness at Adyar. His place as Recording Secretary could be filled, but he was one of the very few who understood what it was all about, esoterically. Now at Headquarters she had only the relative newcomers—Dr. Franz Hartmann, the Cooper-Oakleys, and Mr. Lane-Fox who had returned from London. Mr. C. W. Leadbeater, a loyal and promising man, was away in Burma with the Colonel.

As well as the feeling of emptiness at Adyar, there was something hostile in the air. The missionaries were busy with more pamphlets; there were constant bizarre rumors that a further plot against H.P.B. was being hatched; a well founded report said that Madame Coulomb was bringing suit against General Morgan, who had publicly denounced her in a courageous defense of H.P.B.: some Society branches in India were threatening to dissolve if H.P.B.'s case was not made good against the padris and Coulombs. Worst of all, loyalty for the Founders was disintegrating at Adyar itself.

Even though what her attending physicians, Dr. Franz Hartmann and Dr. Mary Scharlieb (wife of one of the magistrates of Madras Presidency), called a "miracle" had saved H.P.B.'s life, she still carried the mortal diseases in her body. Those around her felt that at any moment she might drop dead. Then what? The European gentlemen at Adyar were convinced that they themselves could run the Society better, more efficiently and more democratically than had the now-absent Colonel. He should be made to step aside, they decided, while theosophical affairs were run by a Council of Westerners at Headquarters. To this end they plotted.

But before the plan could be put into effect, H.P.B. had a dangerous relapse. Greatly alarmed by her condition, her doctors cabled Olcott to return to India without delay.

On March 19 he walked into the stately bungalow by the Adyar river to find, as he writes in *Old Diary Leaves*: ". . . . that the very moral atmosphere was dark and heavy; H.P.B. was struggling for life and as vehement as an enmeshed lioness. . . . The wonder is that she did not die before I could get there and fight for the *status quo ante*."

The President-Founder had no doubt that he could soon put to rout those plotting for power, and get the reins of government back into his own experienced and dedicated hands. It was *his* job, as given to him by his Master, and he would hold on to it against all opposition until the Master himself told him to let go.

But he was worried about the life of his old chum. It was not right to be forever calling on the psychic power of their Guru to keep her on the mortal coil. Hartmann and Mary Scharlieb warned him repeatedly that at any moment his chum might shuffle off it. Not only was there the constant worry and excitement from the enemy camp to be considered, but also the ferocious heat of the Madras summer, which was already beginning to show its 1885 claws. Could she survive it all?

"The condition of her heart renders perfect quiet and a suitable climate essential. I therefore recommend that she should at once proceed to Europe, and remain in a temperate climate—in some quiet spot,"[4] wrote Dr. Mary Scharlieb.

Other medical advisers entirely agreed with the verdict: to save her life and recover her health she would be wise to leave India, for a while at least. H.P.B. did not actually take a great deal of persuading. It was not that she valued her life very highly, but her Master had given her to understand that she still had some important work to do on the physical plane. And she knew she could not bear much more of the psychic atmosphere—to say nothing of the heat—of Madras.

It was thought by her friends that a quiet spot near Naples, Italy, would be a good place for her to summer. The French ship *Tibre,* leaving Madras in a few days, would call there. Dr. Hartmann agreed to accompany her on the journey. Mary Flynn, at whose parents' Bombay home Madame Blavatsky had sometimes been a guest, decided to go too, and stay with H.P.B. as long as needed. Another for the journey to help take care of the Old Lady was a young Hindu named Bawaji (sometimes this was spelled 'Bowaji' or changed to 'Babaji'). He had been on the Headquarters staff for a long time and, according to an entry in the Colonel's Diary, his Guru had ordered him to go with H.P.B.

On March 29 Hartmann and Olcott drove to town in the carriage and secured the necessary tickets for the *Tibre,* sailing only two days later. Babula packed H.P.B.'s trunks—his last office for his often exasperating, but well-loved, mistress. He had to stay behind at Adyar with the Colonel.

H.P.B., though now strong enough to travel, was not able to walk aboard the ship. So Mary Scharlieb's husband procured a hospital chair for her. On this she sat while the ship's hoisting-tackle lifted her aboard.

Thus on March 31, 1885, she made her last departure from her beloved India. She knew that her friends really had her interests at heart, but she suspected that they were glad to be rid of the embarrassment of her presence in the stirred-up cauldron of Madras.

CHAPTER 21

On the journey from Bombay to Naples, Helena felt defeated, unwanted, depressed. Mary Flynn and Bawaji, who were traveling third-class, were not permitted to come to her second-class cabin to give her the assistance she needed. Dr. Hartmann, more interested in magic than in medicine, does not seem to have been a great deal of help.

In a long letter from Aden to her "Dear Old Chum" she wrote:

"I have either to die of thirst, or climb up and down myself the steepest ladders, performing the ceremony on all fours. . . . I climbed so much that here I am sick again with cold and fever, and I tremble lest it should bring back rheumatism and gout or a fit of kidney disease."[1]

Further on in the letter she complains that she was turned out of India so fast that half of her things had been forgotten: "Say to Babula: my spectacle *case* is here but the spectacles are at Madras. My sponge, nailbrush, etc., forgotten. I cannot find my *duster,* with the green velvet collar and trimmings."

But though her outer mind was aggravated by suffering, discomforts, and resentment, she knew in her calm moments that her mission for the Masters had not failed, but was moving into a new phase. During the last serious illness, when Master M. had come and restored her, he had given her a vision of that phase, and she had pledged her word to dedicate to it the few disease-ridden years that were left.

An important—perhaps the most important—part of the work before her was writing *The Secret Doctrine*. And even during this painful shipboard journey she was engaged with that task. "On the sea," writes Dr. Hartmann, "she very frequently received in some occult manner many pages of manuscript referring to *The Secret Doctrine*, the material of which she was collecting at the time."

On April 23, 1885, their ship arrived in the bay of Naples. After a few days in that city, H.P.B., Mary, and Bawaji found a quiet place for the summer a few miles away— Torre del Greco. There they took rooms at the Hotel del Vesuvio, while Dr. Hartmann continued on his way to Bavaria.

Apparently it was not a warm summer; the hotel was damp and had no heating; H.P.B. suffered a good deal from rheumatism. Nevertheless, as the bright, cool, days passed, and Vesuvius smoked enigmatically outside her window, she stayed glued to her desk, writing, writing, writing. . . .

After three months H.P.B. had had enough of southern Italy, and Mary Flynn had had enough of Madame Blavatsky. So Mary deserted for England, while H.P.B. took Bawaji with her to Würzburg in Germany. About the middle of August, 1885, the pair arrived there and rented a ground floor apartment at No. 6 Ludwigstrasse. It was small but comfortable, with good-sized, lofty rooms. Also, unlike the rooms at Torre del Greco, it was warm and dry.

In an earlier letter to Mrs. Sinnett, H.P.B. had given the reasons why Würzburg was chosen. It was "only about 4 or 5 hours from Munich . . . near Heidelberg and Nurenberg, and all the centres one of the Masters lived in, and it is He [K.H.] who advised my Master to send me there. Fortunately I have received from Russia a few thousand francs [from her writings], and some benefactors sent me Rs. 500 and 400 from India. I feel rich and wealthy enough to live in a quiet German place, and my poor old aunt is coming to see me there."[2]

Early in September came Aunt Nadyezhda, and two others Helena loved and trusted: Francesca Arundale and Mohini. A fourth visitor at Würzburg was the Russian writer Solovyov, still seemingly a friend. Although the full S.P.R. Report on Hodgson's investigations and the Committee's conclusions had not yet been published, preliminary reports and rumors indicated that the verdict would be quite adverse. Solovyov knew this and was, at this time, fighting for her cause among important people.

After leaving Würzburg, he wrote to her in a letter from Paris. "Today I passed the morning with Richet, and again talked a great deal about you, in connection with Myers and the Psychical Society. I can say positively that I convinced Richet of the reality of your personal power and of the phenomena which proceed from you."[3]

The Sinnetts, too, were standing staunchly behind the Old Lady. "Even if I were convinced tomorrow that you had written those wretched letters, I would love you still," wrote Patience Sinnett. *"I hope you would not,"* was H.P.B.'s reply. "Had I been guilty *once only*—of a deliberate, purposely concocted fraud . . . no 'love' for such a one as I! At best *pity* or eternal contempt. Pity if proved that I was an irresponsible lunatic, hallucinated *medium* made to trick by my 'guides' . . .; contempt—*if* a conscious fraud—but then where would be *the Masters*?"

Mr. Sinnett was writing her Memoirs[4] hoping by this to vindicate her in the eyes of the public. He was also keeping her informed—and agitated—about the contents of the Report being prepared for publication in the *Proceedings of the S.P.R.* When he and his wife came to Würzburg, late in September, to consult Helena on her Memoirs, and other matters, he gave her more deails about the conclusions of her self-appointed judges in London. Thus the poor woman, struggling to get on with the serious writing of *The Secret Doctrine,* was kept constantly on the rack of anticipated injustice.

Late the same autumn the Countess Constance Wachtmeister was packing her bags at her home in Sweden, getting ready for a trip to join friends in Italy for the winter.

As she was making a heap of the articles she intended to lock away in cupboards at home during her absence, she heard a voice within her say: "Take that book."

The book which she had just placed among the things to be left—was a manuscript volume compiled by a friend. It was, in fact, a collection of notes on the Tarot and passages from the *Kabalah,* and seemed very inappropriate reading for a holiday. But the Countess had rather strongly developed clairaudience, as well as clairvoyance, and felt sure the voice had not been just her imagination. She put the book in the bottom of one of her traveling trunks.

On her way to Italy she called for a short stay at the home of Madame Gebhard in Elberfeld. The latter persuaded her that she should spend some time at Würzburg with H.P.B. who was "lonely, ill in body and depressed in mind." After some resistance in a letter from H.P.B., herself, the matter was finally arranged, and the Countess arrived at No. 6 Ludwigstrasse one day in late November.

H.P.B. gave her a warm and affectionate welcome, explaining that her earlier reluctance to have the Countess as a guest was simply that she felt her apartment was too small. She had only one bedroom, and thought that such a fine lady might not be prepared to share it, and also to put up with the many other discomforts. But Master M. had then told her to let the Countess come, so she had obeyed.

As they were having tea in the dining room on that first day. H.P.B. announced abruptly:

"Master says you have a book for me of which I am much in need."

"No, indeed, I have no books with me."

"Think again. Master says you were told in Sweden to bring a book on the Tarot and the *Kabalah.*"

Then the Countess remembered about the voice, hurried to the bedroom, rummaged in her trunk, and brought the book out to Madame Blavatsky. The latter made a gesture and said:

"Stay! Do not open it yet."

The Countess waited, and presently H.P.B. continued:
"Now open and turn to page ten. On the sixth line you
will find the words. . . ." and she quoted a passage.

The Countess did as instructed. As it was only a manuscript album, with no copy that H.P.B. could have seen
before, Constance was quite thrilled to find the precise
words in the stated position on page ten.

"But why did you want the book?" she asked, handing
it to the Old Lady.

"Oh, for *The Secret Doctrine*. Master knew that you
had it, and told you to bring it so that it would be on
hand for reference."

The Swedish Countess and the Russian occultist shared
the large bedroom with a curtain between them. On the
first morning Constance was awakened at six o'clock by
a Swiss maid arriving with cups of coffee. Then Helena
dressed and by seven was at her desk in the sitting room.

Breakfast was served at eight, after which H.P.B. returned to her writing desk. She had a short break again
for dinner at one o'clock, and then continued her work
until seven in the evening. After supper she settled in
her big armchair, chatting to the Countess while laying
out her cards for a game of Patience. This, she said, rested
her mind, freeing it from the pressure of the day's concentrated labor.

At nine o'clock she went to bed, surrounding herself
with Russian newspapers and journals which she read
until a late hour.

This, Constance found, was a typical day, though often
enough H.P.B. did not come when the small hand-bell
was rung for dinner, remaining at her desk hour after
hour, until the dinner was dried up or cold and utterly
spoiled. The maid would be in tears; then either another
dinner was cooked, or the Countess would send to the
hotel for some nourishing food for the exhausted writer.

Yet, when the trees were "etched like iron in the silent
park" and sleet-laden winds lashed the Ludwigstrasse, life
was still far from boring in the little apartment. Many
strange, moving phenomena happened there. And it did

not take the Countess long to discover—as Henry Olcott
had discovered at the time *Isis Unveiled* was being written—that H.P.B. was not writing *The Secret Doctrine*
alone.

But Constance had the advantage over the Colonel of
being clairvoyant. Often she was able to see the Master
there in his subtle body and sometimes even hear what he
was saying. This was very thrilling and a wonderful occult
education. She discovered, for instance, that being the
mouthpiece of a great Seer was no sinecure.

One day the Countess came into the writing room to
find the floor strewn with sheets of discarded manuscript.

"Whatever does this mean?" she asked.

"I have tried twelve times to write one page correctly,
and each time Master says it is wrong. I think I'll go mad
writing it so often. But I won't pause until I've conquered
it—even if I go on all night. Leave me alone."

Constance brought her a cup of coffee and left her to
her weary task. An hour later she heard H.P.B.'s voice
calling her. The passage had been completed to satisfaction.

The Countess gives a sincere and charming account of
those days and of the writing of H.P.B.'s *magnum opus*
in her slim volume, *Reminiscences of H.P.B.* "How often
. . . did I grieve over reams of manuscript, carefully prepared and copied, and, at a word, an intimation from the
Masters, consigned to the flames. . . ." She spent much of
her time making fair copies of the manuscript and nursing
the sick Old Lady.

Unlike Olcott and others who lived close to Helena,
she does not seem to have suffered from the well-known
Blavatsky emotional outbursts and biting tongue. Either
she was a very understanding and tolerant woman, or
H.P.B. treated her with unwonted gentleness. The
Countess certainly understood that she was enjoying a
rare experience.

Once, and once only, she made the grave mistake that
Olcott and others had sometimes made. It happened at
one o'clock in the morning. The familiar rustling of

papers beyond the screen had ceased, H.P.B. was breathing in a deep rhythm of sleep; there was no sound even of the usual nightly, regular raps—the "psychic telegraph" —on the bedside table. Yet H.P.B.'s oil-lamp still burned brightly by her bed, reflecting on the walls and keeping the Countess awake. She arose, went around the screen and turned the lamp out. But before she had got back to bed, it flamed up again. Something must be wrong with the spring, she thought, and returning, turned the wick down again, until every vestige of flame was extinct. Yet before she had moved away, the lamp was burning as brightly as ever again. A third time she tried, and a third time the wick and flame came up of their own volition. She felt determined to continue all night, if necessary, until she found the cause of this weird oddity.

As the lamp flame flickered up again next time her clairvoyant faculty flickered into use, and she saw a brown hand turning the knob of the lamp. Concluding that it was a chela watching by the bedside, she returned to her blankets. But some spirit of perversity took possession of her—and a crazy curiosity.

"Madame Blavatsky!" she called. Then louder, again and again: "Madame Blavatsky!"

Suddenly came an answering cry: "Oh, my heart! My heart! Countess you have nearly killed me. Oh, my heart!"

She dashed to H.P.B.'s bedside and felt her heart. It was fluttering and palpitating wildly. She brought a dose of digitalis and sat beside the bed until the Old Lady grew calmer.

"I was with Master. Why ever did you call me back?" she asked weakly.

The Countess could not answer, so full was she of grief and contrition. She knew well enough that the shock of calling H.P.B.'s astral body back so suddenly into her frail physical form made her suffer and could have killed her.

Soon after the Countess arrived at Würzburg, Bawaji, whom she described as "a little man, of nervous temperament, with bright beady eyes" had an invitation to visit the Gebhards at Elberfeld. Persuaded by Constance, Madame Blavatsky agreed to let him go. There was an effusive scene of leave-taking, during which he declared that H.P.B. had been more than a mother to him and that his time with her, at Adyar and in Europe, had been the happiest days of his life.

The Countess knew, however, that he had been quite miserable at Würzburg and was even contemplating running away or committing suicide. She felt that he was jealous of Mohini who was then enjoying much acclaim and adulation in London, while Bawaji himself was doing nothing but look after a sick old woman who frequently insulted him and wounded his vanity. Constance thought he really needed a change.

But it was not long before rude, cheeky letters began to arrive from the little Hindu for H.P.B. He obviously felt he was safely ensconced at Elberfeld, with the Germans listening reverently to the Tamil tales and "gems of Eastern Wisdom" that flowed from his lips. Both ladies at Würzburg deduced from his letters that he was doing as much mischief as he could in the German Section. Adulation, vanity, personal ambition had evidently gone to his head.

H.P.B., knowing personally what terrible temptations are brought to a probationary chela of the Adepts—which Bawaji was—felt great sorrow for him. Yet she could not let him bring harm to the already much shaken Theosophical Society; so something must be done. However, before she could take any steps to neutralize the evil effects of this latest defector, another blow, the worst blow of all, fell on her. It was not entirely unexpected, yet much worse than expected. It came on New Year's Eve, December 31, 1885.

"By the early post, without a word of warning," writes the Countess, "H.P.B. received a copy of the . . . *Report of the Society for Psychical Research.* . . . I shall never forget that day nor the look of blank and stony despair that she cast on me when I entered her sitting-room and found her with the book open in her hands. 'Now that I am dubbed the greatest imposter of the age, and a Russian spy into the bargain, who will listen to me, or read The Secret Doctrine?' she wailed."

The Countess went to her and read the section of the report to which her finger was pointing. The Committee of Investigation, after studying and deliberating on Richard Hodgson's report, had come to the cruel, cold, publicly-stated conclusion that: "For our part we regard her [H.P.B.] neither as a mouthpiece of hidden seers, nor as a mere vulgar adventuress; we think that she had achieved a title to permanent remembrance as one of the most accomplished, ingenious and interesting imposters in history."

Glancing through the Report, Constance saw that the S.P.R. men considered the Mahatmas as purely a Blavatsky invention, aided and abetted by various confederates, such as Damodar and the Coulombs. Likewise, all her supernormal phenomena, they decided, were trickery, the result of sleight-of-hand, or some other form of deception, helped by the credulity and mal-observation of the dupes around her, Olcott, Sinnett, and such.

As to her motive, the Committee could not accept Hodgson's theory that her theosophical activity and conjuring tricks were a cover for her real work as a Russian spy. Nor could they determine any other adequate motive to fit the crime, so they left that problem unsolved.

The Countess, with her recent experiences of psychic phenomena—sometimes taking place outside the house and well away from H.P.B.—to say nothing of actually seeing and hearing Master Morya, herself, could have laughed at the ignorance and arrogance of these self-important Englishmen. But it was really no laughing matter. Tragedy was written on her friend's broad expressive face, and behind the great eyes a volcano of emotions swirled.

"O, cursed phenomena, which I only produced to please private friends and instruct those around me! What an awful karma to bear!"

The Countess tried to soothe her, but she would not listen.

"Why don't *you* leave me, too?" she cried. "You are a Countess; you cannot stop here with a ruined woman, with one held up to scorn before the whole world, one who will be pointed at everywhere as an impostor. Go before you are defiled by my shame."

The Countess looked at her, holding her in a clear, steady gaze, as she replied:

"H.P.B., since I know now, as well as you, that our Master lives, that he founded the Society, that therefore it cannot perish, how can you suppose that I could desert you and the Cause we both are pledged to serve? Why, if every other member should turn traitor, you and I would remain, and would wait and work until the good times come again." Seeing tears gathering in the Old Lady's eyes, she patted her affectionately on the shoulder, and quickly left the room.

The following days brought letters full of recrimination and abuse, resignations of members, fear on the part of those who remained. Despite her stated faith, Constance began to think that perhaps The Theosophical Society really was crumbling away under their feet.

Each new incident struck a deeper wound into H.P.B.'s sensitive heart. Sometimes, too, indignation and resentment burst forth in language that would have led a stranger to suppose she was ready to exact the most savage vengeance on her enemies. "It is only those who know her as intimately as half-a-dozen of her closest friends," wrote Sinnett, "who are quite aware through all this effervescence of feeling that if her enemies were really put suddenly in her power, her rage against them would collapse like a broken soap-bubble."

What a strange enigma she seemed! A great compassionate soul in a body through which flowed the fierce, turbulent blood of Dolgorukov princes. Her occult friends sometimes wondered why the soul of a great yogi had chosen such difficult physical and emotional vehicles. Perhaps, they reflected, it was for some karmic lesson she had to learn, certainly a hard lesson though! Perhaps the battle that she still seemed to fight with herself was a reflection of the constant outer battle she fought with the world.

The clear-headed Countess could see through the outer tumult to the noble heart of her friend. That is why she had sacrificed a pleasant holiday with friends in Italy to stay the whole winter in Würzburg, bringing succor and comfort to this tormented, titanic soul in its suffering, swollen body.

In the present crisis she thought the best course would be to treat the ridiculous *Report* of the S.P.R. with the silent contempt it deserved. But she knew that inactivity in the face of attack was something the daugher of the Dolgorukovs could scarcely bear. Especially when the attack was on the thing she held most dear: the Theosophical Movement, the work of her Masters, the advance of the Truth-religion.

She would start for London at once and annihilate her enemies, she declared. She would bring an action for libel against Hodgson and the infamous Committee. She would write to this one and to that one. The Countess knew that such activities would only aggravate and worsen the Old Lady's war with the world. So she counseled restraint.

H.P.B. was fully aware that reactions of anger and hate toward one's enemies are bad yoga. She taught her disciples that the right reaction is ever a Christ-like love and compassion. But she seems to have found it difficult to practice this yoga of restraint. Compassion was always her *final* reaction. But outwardly, to all appearances, it was seldom the *first*. When enemy trumpets sounded an attack on Truth, her warrior blood turned to fire, and her pen became a sword.

CHAPTER 22

Doctor Hübbe-Schleiden's face looked as pale as the winter sky when the Countess showed him into the sitting-room at Würzburg. He had come from Munich especially to see H.P.B., and she sensed that it was about the horrible *Report*.

"How are you, Madame?" he asked politely.

"As well as can be expected."

"Such bitterly cold weather," he remarked, rubbing his hands before the fire.

"Please sit down, Herr Doctor, and give me your honest opinion about that S.P.R. *Report*."

Hübbe, she knew, had good reasons for believing that the Masters were no invention of hers. For one thing he had received a letter from Master K.H. while speeding along in a German train. Only the Colonel was with him, and the S.P.R. judges had declared Olcott honest and innocent of all deceit. The supposed trickster, Madame Blavatsky, was far off in England at the time. Besides, in addition to the fact that the letter had appeared phenomenally by Hübbe's side in the railway carriage, it had commented on some very personal problems he had a moment before been discussing with the Colonel.[1]

These were problems he had never mentioned to the "arch-conjurer" H.P.B. So even if she had a squad of confederates following people around to slip letters into unlikely places as the S.P.R. men implied, how could she have known in advance that Hübbe would be talking on a subject of which she had never even heard?

"The *Report,*" Hübbe answered her question, "is a lot of nonsense. But you, yourself, are in grave danger."

She offered him one of her rolled cigarettes.

"What danger this time, Herr Doctor?"

"Germany is not like England, you know, where the Solicitor-General has nothing to do with a case until a regular complaint is lodged. Here if the charge made by Hodgson that you are a forger gets into the newspapers, you may be arrested on suspicion and put into prison. I advise you to leave Germany at once."

H.P.B. gave a bitter laugh. Wilhelm Hübbe-Schleiden, L.L.D., was an Attorney and Banker, educated at the universities of Gottingen, Heidelberg, Munich, and Leipzig. He must know what he was saying, and she could see that he was very concerned for her welfare—and also concerned for the German branch of The Theosophical Society, of which he was President.

"I am not going to run away. Let them *hang* me if they want to. It would be an appropriate end to such madness," she told him; and no arguments of his were able to change her mind.

Not long after Hübbe's visit the Countess Wachtmeister received a note from Bawaji, begging her to come at once to Elberfeld as she alone, with her psychic powers, could save him; the "Dweller on the Threshold" had come to him, he said, and the consequences would be terrible if she did not help him.

It sounded as though he were raving mad and, with H.P.B.'s agreement, Constance went. When she arrived, Bawaji told her calmly that there was nothing wrong with him. He had written in that manner to get her away from H.P.B. who was "psychologizing her."

The Countess could see that he was having a pernicious influence on the Gebhard family. He was saying outrageous, venemous things about Madame Blavatsky. The great Masters, he said, would never, never condescend to write the letters and perform the phenomena attributed to Them. Therefore, it was all the work of the sorceress, Madame Blavatsky, aided by Colonel Olcott.

Believing that Bawaji was an advanced chela of the Masters, the Gebhards began to believe his stories. The Countess could see that their veneration of him went to his head and made him even vainer, wilder, and more unstable than he might otherwise have been. If not checked, he could do a great deal of harm to the Society, in Germany, and beyond it. Disgusted and depressed, she returned to acquaint H.P.B. with the situation.

Knowing how some European members were inclined to put the Hindu chelas on a pedestal, H.P.B. was very worried about the harm little Bawaji might do. His loyalty to her was probably one of the casualties of the S.P.R. attack. He, like most other Hindus, could not bear to see the names of the Mahatmas desecrated. He was now intent on dissociating her and her phenomena from the Masters by calling her a sorceress who evoked elementals disguised as Mahatmas and performed phenomena for personal gain. The Mahatmas existed, he maintained, but were far above the activities that H.P.B. had associated with their names. It was a mad world!

By letters to Sinnett Madame Blavatsky tried to spike Bawaji's guns before his attack could reach England. The Countess also wrote about him; she was inclined to think that, mixed with his wrongheaded idealism, was a personal ambition to tear The Theosophical Society down, establish a following for himself, and build a new Society.

Some of the old associates were refusing to defend H.P.B., or else damning her with faint praise. Dr. Hartman, planning to compose a *defense* for her, wrote: "You are perfectly innocent of any *wilful* imposture."

"Is he going to make of me an *irresponsible medium?*" she asked Sinnett.

Even Olcott—for whom she had turned the world upside-down when there were only the two of them, spearheading the movement at the old New York lamasery—had sometimes doubted her, although he knew better, the faithless old fool! Yet she could not help loving him, her friend and "chum" ever since they had met on that sunny day at the Eddy Farm more than ten years earlier.

And what about T. Subba Row, for whom she had opened the door to the higher occultism? He would not voice wholehearted support for the genuineness of her phenomena, and he agreed with Hume that The Theosophical Society should not defend Madame Blavatsky's phenomena. Otherwise, he said, the Society's "time and energy will have to be wasted in answering a thousand attacks every day. It is not proper also to attach an undue importance to phenomena." He too, she knew, thought that she had cheapened the names of the Mahatmas and the *Brahma Vidya* that was meant only for the few who were ready for it. Yet she had simply done what her Gurudev directed—attempted to bring part of the Secret Wisdom to a greater number of people.

Perhaps through her unpredictable emotional nature, she had often acted unwisely, but she had never cheated. The great Ones knew that. "I pledge you my word of honour," wrote Master K.H. to Sinnett, "she was never a *deceiver;* nor has she ever wilfully uttered an untruth, though her position often becomes untenable, and she has to conceal a number of things, as pledged to by her solemn vows." And, "She can and did produce phenomena, owing to her natural powers combined with several long years of regular training, and her phenomena are sometimes better, more wonderful and far more perfect than those of some high, initiated chelas."[2]

Perhaps it was because of his long correspondence with the Mahatmas that Sinnett remained her staunch friend throughout this black period of 1886, "the year of the Fridays," as she called it. Sinnett and his wife came and spent three weeks with her at Würzburg early in the year. He was working hard on her *Memoirs,* which he hoped would turn the tide of opinion in her favor. He also drafted a letter in her defense for the London *Times.* H.P.B. and the Countess felt dubious about this, thinking it likely to cause a controversy that would spread the slander to a wider audience. Fortunately, the *Times* refused to become involved and did not print the letter.

But probably the worst shock in the early months of the "year of the Fridays" came from one of Helena Blavatsky's own countrymen.

V. S. Solovyov had seemed to be one of her greatest admirers and staunchest friends during the first period of her exile from India. He visited her several times and considered her an "original and brilliant" writer, whose books, such as *The Caves and Jungles of Hindustan,* written in Russian, "have a respectable place in Russian literature." She was at times, he wrote, "a really inspired prophetess," and it seems to have been the magnet of her mysterious powers that drew him. During his earliest contacts with her he had certainly enjoyed some wonderful extrasensory experiences, including a vision of the Master Morya.

When the S.P.R. *Report* was published, Solovyov considered it not only a slap in the face to H.P.B., but also to himself as one who believed in her powers and who had written favorably of her in the Russian papers. The *Report,* he said, placed him in the false position of being considered either a lunatic or a confederate. He sent in his resignation from the S.P.R. with a strong letter to Frederick Myers, demanding that the latter publish both the resignation and the letter.

What then his motives were in suddenly turning against his countrywoman is one of the mysteries of this stormy period. H.P.B. herself was puzzled. She wrote: "Solovyov has turned round against me like a mad dog—for reasons as mysterious as they can be for me."[3]

But a study of correspondence and of human relationships at this time, suggests some of the factors involved. For one thing it seems that, like many of H.P.B.'s followers, he wanted desperately to be brought closer to the Masters, possibly for the object of developing "powers" himself. For his failure to achieve this he blamed H.P.B., instead of realizing that such a step depended entirely on his own character and stage of spiritual evolution. He was by nature shallow, gossipy, malicious; his failure made him frustrated, jealous, and full of hatred for the one who, he thought, had balked his ambitions.

The spark that fired this explosive material was H.P.B.'s attitude toward a scandal that had blown up regarding Mohini. Lecturing and discoursing in Europe, this brilliant and handsome young Hindu had not only played a part in bringing a new turn of thought to English literature—through such writers as AE (George William Russell), but had also turned the heads of some of the women of Paris and London. One, it seemed, in particular—a Miss Leonard—was very intent on playing Mrs. Potiphar to Mohini's Joseph.

At least H.P.B. regarded this as the situation, feeling quite sure that Mohini, one of the bright lights of the Society and a chela of the Mahatmas, was innocent. She felt that he would be careful to live a strict, morally pure life, as required by his chelaship. But others were saying that he was not so innocent, that he had in fact written many sentimental letters to Miss Leonard. Disapproving Victorian tongues wagged in London and even in Paris. The man who had come to teach them the way to a better life was evidently just an ordinary, morally vulnerable man himself.

H.P.B. protected him vigorously. He may have been foolish enough to write letters, she said, but this did not make him guilty of any misconduct. It was very important to her that he should be innocent, for the sake of the Society and the Masters, and also because she had a great deal of mother love and affection for him.

Solovyov, wallowing in the scandal of Parisian drawing-rooms, accused H.P.B. of purposely screening and protecting Mohini while knowing him to be guilty. This was a cause of the rift between them. H.P.B. wrote to Sinnett on March 3, 1886:

"Solovyov has turned out a dirty gossip, a meddler and a bully. He, whose skirts were dirtier than those of anyone else, arraigned himself as though in *virtue* against

Mohini, sold me like a Judas, without cause or warning; went to Petersburg, got intimate with my sister and her family, set everyone of them against me, learnt all he could learn of the dirty gossips of old (especially about that poor-child story) returned to Paris, sold us all, etc."[4]

From Russia Solovyov brought back a piece of news that shocked Helena; it was that: "Mr. Blavatsky is *not dead* but is a 'charming centenarian' who had found fit to conceal himself for years on his brother's property—hence the false news of his death." Helena had heard long before, from an aunt, that her husband was dead, and so had felt free to marry again in America. Now Solovyov was threatening to expose her to the world as a bigamist.

Furthermore, he immediately did a complete *volte-face* on the matter of her extrasensory and occult powers. He stated that his vision of the Master Morya must have been an hallucination; and he joined forces with the S.P.R. inspired pack that bayed at the heels of the "imposter," as he now labeled her.

From this point on Solovyov reverted to his natural role as a muckraking journalist looking for a good story at any cost to truth. He knew, of course, that exposé stories were easiest to sell and brought the best price. And he made the most of it. But his book, *A Modern Priestess of Isis,* was published after H.P.H.'s death which, writes Colonel Olcott, "made it safe for him to tell his falsehoods about her, shows him to be as heartless and contemptible, though fifty times more talented, than the Coulombs."[5]

In that overwhelmingly terrible year that had dawned with the arrival of the S.P.R. *Report,* Solovyov seems to have been the proverbial last straw for Helena Blavatsky. As she wrote to Sinnett, she felt like the innocent, harmless boar who wanted only to be left to live quietly in his forest. But a pack of hounds come to tear him to pieces and spill his life-blood. He tries for a time to save his life, but finally stops and turns to face his enemies. He knows it is certain that he will be slaughtered. This he accepts, for he can go on no longer. But many of the barking hounds will be disembowelled and killed in the final bloody battle.

She wrote of the same allegory to Solovyov, saying that she would now turn against the overwhelming odds and commit moral suicide. She would confess all, and bring many of her ferocious enemies—ex-friends—down with her. This mood of desperation led to, "My Confession," which she wrote and sent to Solovyov.[6] Much has been made of this by exposé writers.

Actually a reading of it reveals that it does not confess anything damaging. She neither denies the existence of the Mahatmas nor her own psychic powers and occult experiences.

Occult science, she declares, she loved more than the one man (unnamed) whom she loved deeply, and wandered with here and there in three continents. This is no confession to the illegitimate children attributed to her by the scandals. And, as Beatrice Hastings says in her *Defence of Madame Blavatsky,* there is a childlike ingenuousness in anything Helena writes on immorality, as if it is something she has learned *about* from others, but of which she has had no personal experience. So it was most likely true enough that, though she had traveled the world in the company of men, she was, at the age of 55, still a virgin. At any rate the Countess Wachtmeister stated in a letter to Sinnett that Doctor L. Oppenheimer of Würzberg gave her to understand that this was the case.[7]

H.P.B.'s close followers seem to have been anxious to prove that she had lived a life of continence, considered necessary for the special work she had to do.

The long Würzburg winter was coming to an end, and signs of spring were showing, both in the gardens and in H.P.B.'s life. Hübbe's warning of police action and prison had proved unwarranted. Bawaji had written abject apologies to his "Dear and Respected Mother," and was pleading to be allowed to return to India as soon as possible. "I am writing to Colonel Olcott for money to pay my passage back."

H.P.B. knew that the Colonel would send it; he had written earlier that Bawaji should return home as his "epileptomania" was apparently worse, and he could not bear the mental excitements of Europe much longer.

The Secret Doctrine was making progress, despite the long delays caused by emotional turmoil and physical prostration following the Report. Early in March H.P.B. reported to Sinnett that she had completed 300 foolscap pages of the first volume.

Unexpectedly, with April, came an old friend from England. Some ten years earlier H.P.B. had first met Miss Emily Kislingbury when the latter arrived in New York to investigate personally Madame's reputed phenomena. Emily was at the time an ardent Spiritualist. She became an admirer and good friend of H.P.B., staying on in New York, and lending a hand with sketching out the Table of Contents for Isis Unveiled. Then later, when the British branch of The Theosophical Society was formed in London (June 1878), Emily Kislingbury became its first Secretary. But after some time she had dropped out of the movement.

She writes: "I had to encounter almost single-handed the opposition of the English Spiritualists, on account of her [H.P.B.'s] explanations of their favourite 'manifestations'. Finally I left both the Spiritualist and Theosophical Societies, and did not see Madame Blavatsky again for many years; yet so strong and ineffaceable was the impression produced on my mind by her nobleness of character, her truthfulness and honesty, that no sooner had I heard of this Report of the Psychical Society, than I determined to go to H.P.B., if anywhere within reach, if only as a silent protest against the actions of those most unfair and misguided gentlemen who had endorsed so foul a slander. I found her at Würzberg with the Countess Wachtmeister, writing the Secret Doctrine."[8]

"Now that I'm here, how can I help?" Emily asked the Countess.

"I would be very glad if you could accompany H.P.B. to Ostend on your way back to England. She needs a helpful companion," Constance replied. "I, myself, must go home to Sweden for a while."

Ostend had been chosen by H.P.B. for the summer because it was near enough to London for the Sinnetts and any other loyal friends to visit her easily. She hoped to get there before the crowds of summer visitors made apartments expensive and difficult to find.

The Countess accompanied the two ladies, H.P.B.'s maid Louise, and a tremendous pile of luggage to the railway station at Würzburg on May 8. For H.P.B.'s comfort she hoped to be able to secure a compartment for the three travelers on their own. This proved difficult.

Finally, after many protests, the conductor was persuaded to open the door of an empty carriage. The travelers piled in, surrounding themselves with pillows, coverlets, handbags, nine large packages, and the precious box containing the manuscript of *The Secret Doctrine.*

All seemed to be satisfactorily settled when an angry official suddenly appeared at the door and ordered them to remove all the heavy baggage from the carriage and put it in the luggage van. He shouted in German; H.P.B. shouted back in French; Emily looked worried, and Constance pressed her hands to her temples. How could she pacify him and leave H.P.B. in peace?

A shrill whistle sounded, and the train began to glide away. The irate, purple-faced official gave a final splutter; Constance dodged him to run along the platform, waving goodbye to her beloved friend and teacher. Then she walked away, feeling free but somehow empty.

CHAPTER 23

Madame Blavatsky and Miss Kislingbury planned to break their journey at Cologne, resting there one night before continuing on to Ostend. But in the city on the Rhine they met Mr. Gebhard and plans were changed.

"The first news I had of H.P.B.," writes the Countess, "was that the day after she and Miss Kislingbury arrived in Cologne, Mr. Gebhard with several members of his family, persuaded her to go and pay them a visit in Elberfeld. Miss Kislingbury returned to London and Madame Blavatsky went to the house of her kind friends."

The next letter to the Countess told her that H.P.B. "had fallen on the slippery parquet floor of the Gebhard's house . . . and had unfortunately sprained her ankle and hurt her leg. This naturally prevented her from carrying out her plan of continuing her journey to Ostend; she remained, therefore, with her friends, whose kindness was unbounded. They omitted nothing that might alleviate her sufferings and make life pleasant for her. To this end they invited Mme. Zhelihovsky [H.P.B.'s sister Vera] and her daughter to stay with them."[1]

It is evident from this that the Gebhards, despite Bawaji's poison tongue, were still very friendly and affectionate toward the Old Lady. They did not, however, wish to hear any more talk of the Mahatmas. Bawaji was, at the time of H.P.B.'s visit, staying at the home of another German Theosophist.

On July 8, after nearly two months with the Gebhards, Madame Blavatsky was well enough to travel, in the company of her sister and niece, to Ostend. There, after an expensive night in a hotel, Vera searched hard and found a suitable apartment in a side street. H.P.B. was very pleased with this accommodation with its "three splendid rooms on the left and two on the right of the passage . . . and a kitchen downstairs, the whole for a 1,000 francs for the season, and 100 francs a month afterwards."

She had, for herself, a bedroom, a large study and a small drawing-room. The two rooms across the passage she planned to use for the various guests she expected from England and other places. The first guests were, of course, her sister and niece, but they spent most of their time in H.P.B.'s rooms. She was always happy to have members of her family around her, but they did interfere greatly with her writing.

Vera Zhelihovsky was herself a writer and—like so many other scribes at the time and since—she found the inscrutable Helena an inexhaustible source of material for her pen. To this end she challenged her and argued with her more often than was good for the stormy Old Lady. On one occasion she said:[2]

"Well, I've often seen you do *apports,* but I don't believe you can actually *create* a material object."

"That's all right. I'm little concerned about your faith or otherwise in such nonsense!"

"It's not nonsense! If you can create gold and gems, as people say, you should enrich *me*—and yourself. We should not have to search for cheap apartments, for example. We should have nothing but the best."

Helena laughed. "That would be sorcery, black magic, which could bring only harm."

"What's the harm in having enough money?"

Helena reached for her tobacco basket, and her delicate fingers began to roll a cigarette.

"I can only tell you, Vera, that it's your karma and mine to be poor in this life. If I used the sacred powers to enrich us, I would ruin us both, not only in this present life, but probably for long centuries to come."

"Then what about the gifts you are supposed to have given to others—if such things bring harm?"

"My dear, don't you understand? The production of a few trinkets will not make anyone wealthy. But, on the other hand, it might show some thickheaded materialist the potency of the Divine will in man."

Vera was not really convinced with her sister's dictum that occult powers, if used selfishly, were boomerang dynamite. She could not see why Helena should suffer privations for the sake of her ideals. She did not have to use these so-called dangerous occult forces in order to be comfortably off; she could do it through her writings. One Russian paper had offered her a big yearly salary to write exclusively for it.

"I think you are foolish, Helena, for not accepting Katkoff's offer—especially as he said you could write on your favourite psychic subjects for his paper. It could be the end of your money worries."

"I refused because Master told me to; he wants me to concentrate wholly on *The Secret Doctrine*. I must not waste my small reserve of vitality on unimportant things."

"Money has importance. You need good food and proper comfort to give you the energy to write your *Secret Doctrine*."

"All this flapdoodle about money! Master will always see that I have *enough*. It comes in as I want it—a little from America for *Isis* royalties, a little from *The Theosophist* in India, and other places. My worldly wants are very limited, thank God! So why should I sell myself for Katkoff's gold!"

Vera and her daughter left for Russia about the middle of July, and many other visitors came to occupy the rooms across the passage, among them Mohini.

Whatever others may have said about his "scandalous amours," H.P.B. always believed him innocent and pure. It is of interest that, some time later, this supposed philanderer returned to his native Calcutta and opened a home of refuge for destitute "fallen women."

H.P.B. was writing long letters to the Countess Wachtmeister in Sweden urging her to return as soon as possible. She felt that with Constance near her she would be free from many petty annoyances and able to concentrate on her writing. The strong, serene faced Countess evidently acted as a shield against the daily disturbances and was a kind of catalyst, helping to create the correct calm conditions for work on *The Secret Doctrine.*

Their joyful reunion took place in Ostend one day in August, and soon they were settled into the old writing routine, with H.P.B. getting into what she called her "currents" again. "Communications from her Master and from the different chelas were frequent," writes the Countess, "and we lived entirely in a world of our own."

But one day the calm was broken by H.P.B. asking Constance if she would go to London to undertake some private business for her. The Countess agreed, though she hated leaving the Old Lady alone. Then frequent letters between them began again. Madame Blavatsky and Louise were being bothered by the Belgian police: "I am regarded with suspicion even in that affair of a million stolen on the railway between Ostend and Brussels!!!" she wrote.[3]

A parcel of manuscript, sewn up on oil cloth, arrived in London. It was part of *The Secret Doctrine* so far completed, and H.P.B. asked the Countess to send it on to Madras for the criticism and comments of the Colonel and T. Subba Row, "but do insure it for no less than £150 or £200, for if lost—well goodbye!"[4]

And in a letter to the Countess, written about the end of 1886, after *Incidents in the Life of Madame Blavatsky* by A.P. Sinnett was published by George Redway in London, she writes: "You say literature is the only salvation. Well, see the good effect Mme. Blavatsky's Memoirs have produced. Seven or eight French papers pitching into Sinnett, and myself, K.H., etc., on account of these Memoirs. A true revival of Theosophical Society scandals over again, just because of this literature. . . . Your room upstairs with stove is ready, so you will be more comfortable. But you do useful work in London. I feel as lonely as I can be."

Later, "I am as cold as ice and four doses of digitalis in one day could not quiet the heart. Well, let me only finish my *Secret Doctrine.* Last night instead of going to bed I was made to write till 1 o'clock. The *triple Mystery* is given out—one I had thought they would never have given out—that of . . ."[5]

Apart from private business for Helena Blavatsky, the Countess was doing good theosophical work in London, sorting out members' difficulties, answering their queries, explaining concepts, re-establishing faith in H.P.B., the Masters and their great project. She was, though she did not then know it, helping to prepare the ground for a new beginning. A Western window was beginning to raise its blinds to the slow dawn.

Master Morya gave H.P.B. her instructions. The writing of *The Secret Doctrine* was not the only work he wanted her to do during the short time she had left. Her new project, which would dovetail well with the writing chore, was to teach a small band of dedicated, faithful disciples in London. This was the tiny handful of wheat left after the chaff had been blown away by the winds of public scandal and calumny.

Whether Helena would have to go to London in person, or could operate from Ostend or somewhere else near at hand, was not yet certain. But it was certain that her work was now here in the West, not in India. The esoteric, world-challenging, world-changing doctrines of spiritual evolution and true brotherhood must be taught right at the heart center of power politics—imperial, Victorian England.

Toward the idea of living there she was ambivalent. In one way she had affection for the land where she had first come face to face with her great Master, and where staunch friends like the Sinnetts lived. In another way she loathed the place.

She thought of England as the land of snobbery and hypocrisy, the land from which certain S.P.R. "gentlemen" had dealt her a cruel, unjust blow, the land where even now the traitor Solovyov was displaying to her enemies his lying, misleading translation of her Russian correspondence with him, especially the "Confession."

What evil slanders against her name and work were poisoning the London mists? It did not seem to her the kind of atmosphere in which tender theosophical plants might flourish and strengthen. But, of course, the Master knew best.

PART III

Westward Glimmerings

The Secret Doctrine is the accumulated Wisdom of the Ages. . . . The fundamental Law in that system, the central point from which all emerged, around and toward which all gravitates, and upon which is hung the philosophy of the rest, is the One homogeneous divine *Substance-Principle,* the one radical cause. . . . It is the omnipresent Reality: impersonal, because it contains all and everything. *Its impersonality is the fundamental conception* of the System. It is latent in every atom in the Universe, and is the Universe itself. . . . The Universe is the periodical manifestation of this unknown Absolute Essence. . . . The Universe is called, with everything in it, *Maya,* because all is temporary therein, from the ephemeral life of a firefly to that of the Sun. . . . Yet, the Universe is real enough to the conscious beings in it, which are unreal as it is itself. . . . Everything in the Universe, throughout all its kingdoms is *conscious*: i.e., endowed with a consciousness of its own kind and on its own plane of perception. . . . There is no such thing as either "dead" or "blind" matter, as there is no "Blind" or "Unconscious" Law. . . . The Universe is worked and *guided* from *within outwards.* As above so it is below, as in heaven so on earth; and man—the microcosm and miniature copy of the macrocosm—is the living witness to this Universal Law and to the mode of its action. . . . The whole Kosmos is guided, controlled, and animated by almost endless series of Hierarchies of sentient Beings, each having a mission to perform, and who . . . are "messengers" in the sense only that they are the agents of Karmic and Cosmic Laws . . . each of these Beings either *was,* or prepares to become, a man, if not in the present, then in a past or a coming cycle. . . . They are *perfected,* when not *incipient,* men. . . . The whole order of nature evinces a progressive march towards *a higher life.* There is design in the action of the seemingly blindest forces. The whole process of evolution with its endless adaptations is a proof of this. . . . what is called "unconscious Nature" is in reality an aggregate of forces manipulated by semi-intelligent beings (Elementals) guided by High Planetary Spirits (Dhyani-Chohans), whose collective aggregate forms the manifested *verbum* of the unmanifested *Logos,* and constitutes at one and the same time the *mind* of the Universe and its immutable *law.*

—*The Secret Doctrine,* Vol. I, pp. 272-278.

CHAPTER 24

One winter's evening toward the close of 1886, H.P.B.'s "year of the Fridays," five men and a woman were gathered in a London drawing-room, studying and discussing Theosophy. They had come to an impasse on some point. Though they could all speculate brilliantly on it, none could offer an explanation satisfactory to the others.

This kind of thing happened too often. They were all keen, serious students of the Ancient Wisdom, believing fully in the reality of the Mahatmas. They wanted to revive the Theosophical Movement in London, but seemed to be getting nowhere. They had written letters to H.P.B. in Ostend, and she had answered generously; the Countess Wachtmeister, when in London, had thrown some light on *some* problems, but that was not enough.

Twenty-five-year-old Bertram Keightley pulled at his brown, drooping moustache. A keen thinker, a mathematician and graduate of Cambridge University, he enjoyed these challenging metaphysical problems, but he knew when the equation was beyond him. He looked at his bearded uncle, Dr. Archibald Keightley, who was tacitly regarded as the leader of the group, though he too was only in his mid-twenties.

"What we need," said Bertram, "is to sit at the feet of a real leader—a teacher who can speak with authority."

"Who can lead us to the Masters," added Mabel Collins, daughter of novelist, Mortimer Collins, herself a writer and a clairvoyante. "Yes, it would be wonderful if we could have H.P.B. here."

"I have spoken to Sinnett about asking her to come and live in London," Bertram told them. "He's dead against it. Seems to think she'll stir up trouble among the members of his Lodge."

"Pooh! What would that matter!" exclaimed Mabel.

Archibald Keightley had no vanity about the idea of his own leadership. He knew his limitations. If they were to revive Theosophy in London, it was true that they needed H.P.B. among them.

"What, indeed!" he answered Mabel. "We must go and beg her to come over."

"What about the London climate?" queried Dr. Ashton Ellis.

"The climate is not much worse than in Ostend," said Archibald, determinedly.

After some further discussion, the six agreed to invite the precious Old Lady over and to take good care of her. But someone should go in person to ask her.

"Who?" Archibald looked around the group, "I can't go immediately, myself, unfortunately."

"I can—straight after New Year," volunteered Bertram.

And so it was agreed.

Actually, both Bertram and Archibald made several trips over to Ostend. At first Madame Blavatsky would not give a definite answer to them; then, finally, she agreed, but would not name an exact date for the move.

About ten days after Archibald's last visit to her, a telegram arrived in London for Dr. Ashton Ellis. It was from the Countess Wachtmeister, asking him to come over to Ostend as quickly as he could; Madame Blavatsky, it said, was seriously ill and her Belgian doctor could do no more for her.

Dr. Ellis felt sure that, although the lady had many ailments, the main seat of her trouble was in the kidneys. So before leaving, he called to see a leading London specialist. Armed with all the professional advice he could get from this man, Ellis set off for Ostend.

The Countess and Madame Gebhard, who had come to Ostend to help in the nursing, were overjoyed when Dr. Ellis rang the front door bell. He had brought some medicine prescribed by the London specialist, who had also recommended massage to stimulate the paralyzed organs. But a consultation between the English and Belgian doctors dashed the ladies' hopes again.

"I have never known a case," said the Belgian doctor, "with kidneys in such a condition, to live as long as Madame has."

"It is exceedingly rare for anyone to survive so long in such a state," agreed Dr. Ashton Ellis.

"No medicines or massage can make much difference now. Nothing can save her, I'm afraid," the Belgian concluded gloomily.

"She has not made a will, and I think she should," suggested Madame Gebhard. "Dying intestate in a foreign country can bring no end of annoyance and confusion."

H.P.B., in one of her periods of consciousness, agreed to sign a will for the disposal of her estate: clothes, a few books, some jewelry, and a few francs in cash. She would leave it all, she said, to the Countess, who must be careful with the manuscript of *The Secret Doctrine*, and hand it over to Colonel Olcott with directions to have it printed.

"I think the Master might let me be free at last, Countess," H.P.B. murmured. "I will be so glad to die."

All that day Dr. Ellis worked at the massaging until he was exhausted. But as the Countess sat alone by Madame Blavatsky's bed that night, she was horrified to detect the peculiar faint odor of death which sometimes precedes dissolution. She felt then that the woman, whose noble character she had learned to love, would not survive the night.

Yet *The Secret Doctrine* was unfinished, and H.P.B. had told her of the Master's plan for a circle of earnest students in London. The Keightleys had come and H.P.B. had agreed to go. But now, what was the use of all the poor woman's self-sacrifice, all the agony she had gone through for so long, if she were to die before her work was done? It did not make sense.

Yet how could one presume to judge of such inscrutable, imponderable things as life and death and karma. "I do not even begin to understand," she thought, "the enigma lying there in the bed—her strange powers, her marvelous knowledge, her mysterious life spent in regions unknown to ordinary mortals, so that though her body might be near, her soul is often away communing with others. How often have I seen her thus, and known that only the shell or body was present!"

As the slow hours ticked by, the blank despondency of the Countess intensified. Her soul rose up in rebellion at the thought of how empty life would be without the presence and affection of Helena Blavatsky. The Master had saved her before, could he not do it again?

"My Master is a white Magician and a Mahatma too," H.P.B. had once told her, meaning a great worker of miracles and a great soul. So if it was for the best, he would work the miraculous cure. Whether through overwhelming emotions, fatigue, or some occult reason (most likely the latter), the Countess slipped away into unconsciousness.

When she opened her eyes the early morning light was stealing into the room. Her first appalling thought was that she had failed in her watch, and her dear friend had probably died in the night. She stood up and looked across the bed. There, to her utter amazement, she saw two clear, blue eyes watching her calmly, and heard a firm voice say:

"Countess, come here."

Constance flew to the bedside, and asked: "Whatever has happened, H.P.B.? You look so very different from what you did last night!"

"Yes," replied the patient, "I am. Master has been here. He gave me my choice to die and be free, or live and finish *The Secret Doctrine*. He warned me of further great sufferings and calumnies if I chose to live."

"Nevertheless, you did so choose, H.P.B.! That's wonderful. I am so glad."

"Well, when I thought of those earnest students waiting for me to help them, as a channel to the Masters, when I thought of the poor, storm-tossed Society, of *The Secret Doctrine* that could be its firm anchor. . . ."

Constance stroked back the mass of silver "African wool," and kissed the broad forehead. The Old Lady's eyes filled with tears, and she said, brusquely:

"Now fetch me some coffee and something to eat—and give me my tobacco box."

In a letter on her recovery to William Judge, H.P.B. wrote, with the flippancy she often adopted: "Anyhow *saved* once more, and once more stuck into the mud of life right with my classical nose. Two Keightleys and Thornton (a dear, REAL new Theosophist) came to Ostend, packed me up, books, kidneys, and gouty legs, and carried me across the water, partially in steamer, partially in invalid chair."[1]

She made this sea voyage on the first of May, 1887. The crossing was calm, and at Dover several of her new disciples were waiting. The ship arrived at low tide, and there were steep, slippery steps to be negotiated at the pier. But the strong, young arms carried her ashore to the train for London.

Her new home was a tiny house, called "Maycot," at Crown Hill, Upper Norwood, London. It belonged to Mabel Collins. "When there are three people in my two rooms (half the size of my Ostend bedroom) we tread uninterruptedly on each other's corns," wrote H.P.B. to the Countess in Sweden. Mostly there were many more than three, and when G. H. Thornton (a wealthy young bachelor, six-and-one-half feet tall) arrived with his five Great Danes, they were all indeed, as H.P.B. said, "like herrings in a barrel."

Actually, they were more like busy bees than herrings, buzzing in and out, while the queen bee sat at the center, writing and directing during the daylight hours, and in the evening talking, discussing, teaching. In less than three weeks after her arrival the enthusiastic young people had organized and established a new lodge around her. They insisted on calling it—in spite of her protests—the Blavatsky Lodge. There were fourteen members.

Archibald and Bertram were spending all their spare time helping with the manuscript of *The Secret Doctrine*, typing, editing, and rearranging the material into sections, according to plans agreed upon by H.P.B. They were careful not to alter any of the writing except the foreign sounding idioms, and this only after considerable conflict.

"For me," writes Archibald Keightley, "Life was one long wrestle in the mazes of *The Secret Doctrine,* with the effort to suggest a grouping and arrangement and the correction of foreign turns of language, at the same time retaining Mme. Blavatsky's very distinctive style." When asked about the wording of a phrase, she would say:

"Make it as you see best, my dear. It's your job to put it into right English."

But others, called in to help, would disagree with his alterations: "The original language must be left," they would insist, "so that readers will have the chance of taking their choice about the writer's actual meaning."

But remembering H.P.B.'s dire threats if the English was not correct, Archibald chose the "deep sea" of her favor to "the devil" of his friends' attacks, and edited the language as he thought necessary.[2]

One day H.P.B. said to the group:

"At the rate we are going it will take a year or more to finish *The Secret Doctrine.* Meantime you are all learning, but what of the larger public?"

"Does that deserve anything?" someone asked, pointedly.

"Yes, it's the field from which we must draw for the movement to grow as the Masters wish it to," she answered; and then went on: "We must have a channel to the general public. *The Theosophist* is no longer any use for the purpose. The very mention of the Mahatmas is taboo at Adyar, and Madame Blavatsky is suspect—particularly to Cooper-Oakley who seems to be in charge of editorial matters, with Olcott away traveling so much."

"Why don't we start our own magazine here in London?" someone asked.

The idea seemed to meet with excited general approval, and after some further discussion, the matter was decided.

"A Theosophical Publishing Company has been formed . . . and not only have we started a new Theosophical journal, but they [the Blavatsky Lodge group] insist on publishing themselves *The Secret Doctrine,*" H.P.B. wrote a little later to the Countess.

Lucifer was to be the name of the new journal. While this was appropriate, remembering the true meaning of the name—the Light-Bringer—it was not calculated to promote good public relations with the Christian churches to whom *Lucifer* was synonymous with Satan.

A great deal was accomplished that summer; some positive beginnings were made; and there was steady progress on the time-absorbing manuscript, despite the difficulties of the crowded little house.

But all, the Keightleys in particular, realized that a change of residence was necessary. They must find a less cramping place where the Blavatsky Lodge could expand, where the Old Lady could write in more comfort, and so that her many visitors would not have to travel so far from the center of London.

All searched hard, and soon H.P.B. was able to write to the Countess that a suitable place had been found. The plan was for the expenses of the house to be shared between H.P.B., the two Keightleys, and the Countess, if the Countess agreed.

"I have chosen two rooms for you, which I think you will like, *but do come and do not put off for mercy's sake.* Yours ever, H.P.B."

CHAPTER 25

The Countess Wachtmeister arrived in London early in September 1887, in time to help with the packing and supervise the move. On a morning three days later she stepped into a carriage and escorted Madame Blavatsky to the new abode at 17 Lansdowne Road, Holland Park. This was nearer to the hub of London and in the vicinity of the Sinnett and Arundale homes.

The Countess describes their arrival:

"There the two Keightleys were hard at work making the house comfortable for H.P.B. I could but admire . . . the tender devotion and eager thought for her comfort, even down to trivial details, which these two young men have always shown. . . .

"H.P.B.'s rooms were on the ground floor, a small bedroom leading into a large writing-room where furniture was so arranged around her, that she could reach her books and papers without difficulty; and this room again led into the dining-room."[1]

From her writing room a wide window opened onto leafy Holland Park, and the back of the house faced a small private compound common to the occupants of the houses surrounding it.

They had hardly settled in before the house became a busy writing workshop. The Keightleys, sleeping in bedrooms upstairs, spent their days as secretaries, personal assistants and subeditors, slaving happily on *The Secret Doctrine* and the production of *Lucifer*. The Countess, now relieved of secretarial work for H.P.B., devoted her time to the management of household affairs. From Sweden she had brought two domestic servants, called by Madame Blavatsky the "Swedish virgins."

Lucifer, as was to be expected, brought some shadows along with the Light. To her old chum at Adyar it brought much irritation; he thought it competed for circulation with *The Theosophist*. What if it did, thought H.P.B. The journal they had started together some eight years earlier in India was now "like a series of dull sermons unenlivened by the smallest spark of human wit and poetry," she wrote to Olcott. Let it go its safe, timid way; she needed something more vital, something with which to attack error, complacency, hypocrisy wherever she found them, and with no respect for personalities.

She would undoubtedly stir up a great deal of mud in the complacent compounds of Christendom. But only by churning up tons of mullock could one find the gold and precious stones beneath. The last great stir-up had unearthed the three gems who now lived with her at Holland Park, and others were awaiting the miner's exploring shovel. Anyhow, it was her way, her role, her *dharma* to attack, and her Masters evidently approved.

So Helena Blavatsky, now right in the camp of "the enemy," pulled no punches. She led the attack right to the very citadels of the entrenched establishment—for instance, to the palace walls of the Head of the Church of England. Her 6,000-word *Open Letter to the Archbishop of Canterbury* would shock no one today, when so many journals have trumpeted the death of the God of the Victorians, but it shocked a great many people then.

She attacked the theology and dogma of the Church as belonging to the Middle Ages and not to the dawn of science and reason. She quoted the philosopher Herbert Spencer: "The damning of all men who do not avail themselves of an alleged mode of obtaining forgiveness, which most men have never heard of, and the effecting of reconcilation by sacrificing a son who was perfectly innocent, to satisfy the assumed necessity for a propitiating victim, are modes of action which ascribed to a human ruler, would call forth expressions of abhorrence."

The Christian churches were certainly not, she said, propagating the word of Jesus Christ who taught "love your enemies". . . . "the world has become one huge battlefield, on which 'the fittest' descend like vultures to tear out the eyes and the hearts of those who have fallen in the fight". . . . "Religion does not weigh a feather in the world today, when worldly advantages and selfish pleasures are put in the other scale."

It was small wonder, she pointed out, that physical science was emptying the church pews when all that the pulpit could offer were dogmas once enforced by the rack and the faggot, but holding no nineteenth century logic. The "mysteries of the kingdom of Heaven," the *secret doctrine* of Jesus, given to his apostles alone, might have satisfied the thirst of man's renascent mind; but they had been suppressed, thrown away, lost. Now without them, the Church was barren—a time-server of the materialists.

Modern Theosophy had come to teach again the *secret doctrine* that lay hidden, or half-hidden, at the heart of all great religions, including Christianity, she said. It was "no pioneer of the Anti-Christ, no brood of the Evil one, but the practical helper, perchance the saviour, of Christianity . . . it is only endeavouring to do the work that Jesus, like Buddha, and other 'sons of God' who preceded him has commanded all his followers to undertake."

Some few churchmen may have understood her message and warning, but the majority simply regarded The Theosophical Society as the "brood of the Evil one." So ministers of the churches were generally conspicuous by their absence among the many seekers who found their way to 17 Lansdowne Road, though there was a Salvation Army captain, and sometimes a priest of the Greek Orthodox

Church, who came.

It was a mixed and interesting crowd: curiosity-seekers and serious investigators, cranks and celebrities, the little-known and the well-known. Among the latter were: England's leading scientist William Crookes, F.R.S., himself a member of The Theosophical Society, an occultist and psychic investigator; G. J. Romanes, W. T. Stead, editor of the *Pall Mall Gazette* and perhaps England's best-known journalist; Lord Crawford, Earl of Crawford and Balcarres, F.R.S., keen student of occultism and cosmogony and a pupil of Lord Lytton. Beauty combined with talent in the Princess Helena Racovitza, "a living Titian of ineffable charm, as when the now-forgotten Lassalle duel thrilled all Europe, and George Meredith wrote his 'Tragic Comedians' around her," recalled the American artist Edmund Russell who was himself of the Lansdowne Road company.

Russell wrote also that the discourses were Upanishadic, and thought H.P.B. knew the whole 108 main Upanishads. "One felt if he did not understand what she was talking about, she at least did. Which can hardly be said for the jargon of most spiritual leaders."[2]

She talked, too, of the many occult subjects she was writing about in her *Secret Doctrine,* such as the pre-Adamic races of man which were androgyne.

"The story of Adam is the separation of the sexes," she would explain.

Russell, who liked to tease her, once said:

"Yes, I understand all that, Madame, but I am sure that when the cutting-in-two came, the knife sometimes slipped . . . *You* are all woman, but have more than your share of man. Somewhere a poor little creature wanders—demi-masculine—the left-over scrap of Blavatsky."

Madame laughed. There was always a thread of humor running through the most serious discourse. But there were mysteries and seeming contradictions about her that puzzled some, and one dared to ask her:

"Why is it that you, a natural clairvoyant, a reader of the minds and hearts of men, cannot even tell your friends from your foes—the Coulombs, for instance?"

There was no anger, only great sadness, in the "amber eyes streaked with turquoise."

"Ah, my friend, a person's cloudy, forbidding aura may fill me with misgivings, but there is *always* the divine spark I see within. Who am I to deny anyone the chance of profiting by the truths I can teach, and entering upon the Path? It does not matter that I, personally, risk the consequences of deception, hatred, vengeance—while there is hope for the other's redemption. The Lord Buddha has enjoined us not to fail to feed even a starving serpent, scorning all fear that it might turn and strike the hand that feeds it."

Emboldened by this compassionate reply, another one said:

"Madame, you preach control of temper, but you yourself go into outbursts now and then."

"That," she replied, "is my loss and your gain. If I did not have that temper, I should have become an Adept by this time, and no longer be here among you."

A knock came at the door. "Come in," she called in a voice that "broke the door panels like Katie Fox's raps."

The new-arrival was a sharp but shallow journalist who began to ask questions designed to trap her. This she recognized at once and gave him her Socratic treatment. Putting on a stupid look, she questioned him, leading him on to play out all his rope and reveal the weakness of his arguments. Then regaining her ground step by step, she finally mopped the floor with him. Her eyes shone with the victory; then with a hearty laugh, she grasped his hand:

"You are a splendid fellow—come again—come often!"

It was nearly midnight and the gathering broke up. As Edmund Russell strolled away with poet W. B. Yeats, he asked,

"Have you heard her play the piano? Friends of her New York days tell me she was then a wonderful musician—with bursts of savage improvisation, like nothing else in the world?"

"It does not surprise me," replied Yeats; "She calls herself a Russian savage. To me she's still an interrogation mark, but wonderful in every way. Yet when she's gone, the fellow who opens the door will think he can take her place."

Yeats who, according to Russell, was one of H.P.B.'s "Esoterics," was very interested in magic. It was, he said, next to poetry the most important pursuit of his life. To John O'Leary he wrote: "If I had not made magic my constant study, I could not have written a single word of my Blake book nor would *The Countess Kathleen* have ever come to exist. The Mystical life is the centre of all that I do, and all that I think, and all that I write. . . . I have always considered myself a voice of what I believe to be a greater renascence—the revolt of the soul against the intellect—now beginning in the world."[3]

H.P.B. evidently had a strong influence on his thinking and his work.

It was a rule of Madame Blavatsky's life and conduct —recognized by Olcott and Judge in the New York days —that the test of people's closeness to her, and their worthiness as pupils, was the severity and harshness she meted out to them.

And now the two young Keightleys were going through the hard tests. It is a measure of their occult understanding that, though their nerves were sometimes raw with the apparent injustices of her lashing tongue, they took it as training, as a tempering of their metal, and were— like Olcott before them—complimented by it. At least, that is what their *Reminiscences,* written some years later, indicate.

But Bertram reports one occasion on which his control broke down under the great strain. H.P.B. had sent for him before breakfast, and she immediately began to abuse, scold, and scarify him pitilessly, hitting all his weakest and tenderest spots. The whole matter about which she was carrying on with such apparent anger was something in which Bertram had played no part; he knew nothing whatever about it.

But he could not get a word in edgeways, and his sense of injustice and self-pity began to swell like a balloon ready to burst. He had been already somewhat overwrought with the heaviness of the work and some personal worries. Now he felt his temper suddenly break and his eyes flash.

Madame Blavatsky, who had seemed almost raving with fury, stopped, dead silent and absolutely still. There was not one vibration of anger emanating *from her*. It was as if she had just been putting on a big act, and actually felt no emotion whatever. Her eyes looked him up and down coldly; she said:

"And *you* want to be an occultist."

He writes: "Then I saw and knew, and went off deeply ashamed: having learnt no small lesson."

But nothing was ever remembered by her against her disciples.

"Everything was just wiped clean out and wholly forgotten once it was past."

As the months of 1887 merged into those of 1888, threatening storm clouds banked higher and higher on the eastern horizon. For one thing T. Subba Row seemed to be turning against her—writing against her in *The Theosophist,* refusing to help her with *The Secret Doctrine,* despite his earlier praises of the work. This she could not at first understand; she had loved, admired, and trusted him and now his growing hostility cut very deep.

Second, there was her old partner, Olcott. Him too she loved and trusted, though he sometimes acted foolishly when she was not at hand to guide him. Now he was being more than ever obtuse, and his angry opposition to her was mounting. In fact, a war of nerves was being waged between them.

Reluctantly, he had accepted the journal *Lucifer*; but he ignored it completely, as if it did not exist. Then the real thunderclap from Adyar came when she intimated her intention of forming an Esoteric Section in London. This went right against the Colonel's grain. An *imperium in imperio,* an empire within an empire, he called it. It would divide the Society, he said.

Also, as she had learned by experience, his frank, trusting "New World" mind loathed the very idea of secrecy. Everything should be open to the public and democratic. Even though he had recently seen where that policy led, he was still strongly against esotericism. He would not have such a section in The Theosophical Society, he said.

Well, he would have to have it. It was Master's orders. Master knew, and she knew, and Olcott *should* know, that it is dangerous to let any Tom, Dick, or Harry into a school of special training in high Occultism—the kingly yoga. The majority are not ready, are not prepared to live the life that will make them ready; they will simply turn and publicly rend their teachers, like the proverbial swine, incensed at the sight of pearls.

Lectures on Theosophy were all right for the general public. Some people would sneer, some would agree, *in theory*; a very few would really understand and be prepared to practice the self-discipline, the strict way of life, the study, the meditation, the *sadhana* that would lead them toward the superhuman consciousness of the Great Brotherhood.

Yet that few must be given the chance. They would provide the heart, the steam power, the continuity for the Masters' great project to change the world. Around her in London there *were* a few ready. Individually, most would fail to reach the altitudes—even of high chela-hood —in this incarnation. But their sincere efforts, their steps forward, would keep the great movement alive and raise the whole consciousness of humanity to a higher level.

The Colonel was proud of the Society he had helped create, rightly so. He was a little proud, too, of his position and authority as Founder-President—understandably, if not rightly, so. But the Society, the organization, was created for the Cause. Not the other way around. The spread and growth of true Theosophy must come first. Anything that impeded *that* must be broken.

Many of her followers in England had wanted her to assume the headship, in name as well as in reality—and, they said, let the Old Man at Adyar stew in his own fustian Executive Orders.

But she had remained staunchly loyal to the headquarters flag.

Even so, if he would not now accept this new, this vital development, she would split the Society asunder, and each of them must go his own separate way. She wrote and told him so.

But she hoped it would not turn out that way, for she loved her old Yankee friend dearly, and he *was* a fine organizer.

Then she heard that he was on his way to London, breathing enough dragon fire to boil the seven seas and singe the green of Holland Park. The Foundation of the Esoteric Section was planned to take place soon after his expected date of arrival, and the proofs of *The Secret Doctrine* would be rolling off the press. The autumn of 1888 bade fair to be a lively season.

CHAPTER 26

As proofs of *The Secret Doctrine* poured into the big writing room at Holland Park, H.P.B. went to work on them with a ruthless pen—after the manner of Balzac. Like all true artists, she was never completely satisfied with her work and kept altering, cutting, adding—even to the final page proofs. The people around her gnawed the nail of anguish for the slender finances of their publishing company. The bill for the corrections would be staggering, maybe crippling.

But the grand hand of genius swept aside such petty commercial considerations, and the workers-cum-shareholders in the new publishing venture carried out her orders with scarcely an audible murmur. Most of them had seen enough inexplicable things connected with the book's production to make them feel that here was something really out of the ordinary, something that would echo down the ages. "Not many of this generation will understand it," H.P.B. had told them, "but next century will see the beginnings of its acceptance and appreciation."

The Secret Doctrine had had its beginnings over four years earlier, before Madame Blavatsky left India for Europe and the snares of the S.P.R. Her Master had given her an intimation of the project but, even when later she began working seriously on it in Paris and Enghien, she still had only a vague idea of what exactly it was to be. There William Quan Judge had given her whatever help she asked and had seen some strange phenomena.

Once, for instance, he asked her if she intended to say much on the subject of elementals in the proposed work.

"I might," she replied, thoughtfully, "but it's not a quiet or harmless part of the thing—so I must await orders concerning it."

She knew that Judge was very interested in this subject, so she asked him to write down all he thought he knew about it.

"Then if it's all right, I will see if that much can be used," she told him.

Judge wrote a long chapter on elementals. The afternoon on which he finished it and handed it to her was warm, but suddenly the air in the room seemed to drop to a temperature below freezing point. The cold seemed to blow out from H.P.B. as if she were a channel to some huge refrigerator.

Judge remarked: "It's like as if a door is open on the Himalayas, and the frozen air is blowing into this room." Madame Blavatsky smiled: "Perhaps it is so."

Judge began to shiver and picked up a rug from the floor to wrap around himself.

About three days later she told him that it had been decided not to put much, if anything, on the subject into *The Secret Doctrine*. And when the work was published, he found that nothing he had written had been included.[1]

Two years later, in March 1886, H.P.B. wrote to him from Würzburg, telling him that she would like him to come for two or three months to help her with the arrangement of material for *The Secret Doctrine*. "I have some money now and could easily pay your fare out and back. There's a dear, good fellow, *do* consent to it. . . . Such facts, *such facts,* Judge, as Masters are giving out will rejoice your old heart."

Judge reminisces: "I could not accept because of certain circumstances, but on looking back at it, I am sorry that it was let slip by."

According to many witnesses, and to H.P.B. herself, the *methods* by which the material from the Masters came through the pen of Helena Blavatsky were various. Some of it was dictated, either clairaudiently or by other means. Some of it appeared in the Mahatmas' own scripts. Dr. Hübbe-Schleiden, who had come to Würzburg in 1886 to advise Madame Blavatsky to leave Germany, writes later about his experiences there: "I know I saw a good deal of the well-known blue K. H. handwriting as corrections and annotations on her manuscripts [of *The Secret Doctrine*] as well as in books that lay occasionally on her desk. And I noticed this principally in the morning before she had commenced work. I slept on the couch in her study after she had withdrawn for the night, and the couch stood only a few feet from her desk. I remember well my astonishment one morning when I got up to find a great many pages of foolscap covered with that blue pencil handwriting lying on her own manuscript at her place on the desk. How these pages got there I do not know, but I did not see them before I went to sleep, and no person had been bodily in the room during the night for I am a light sleeper."[2]

Much of the material came to her in what she calls the "astral light," either by conscious concentration or by other means. To Sinnett she once wrote: "There's a new development and scenery, every morning. *I live two lives again.* Master finds that it is too difficult for me to be looking consciously into the astral light for my S.D., and so, it is now about a fortnight, I am made to see all I have to as though in my dream. I see large and long rolls of paper on which things are written and I recollect them. Thus all the Patriarchs from Adam to Noah were given me to see—parallel with the Rishis; and in the middle between them, the meaning of their symbols—or personifications."[3]

But even for one of her occult development, peering clairvoyantly into the astral light was not completely free from error. The trouble was, she said, that sequences were reversed as in a mirror, so that she sometimes copied down numbers and words wrongly. Her secretaries and personal assistants in the work often had the job of checking quotations from rare old books, very difficult of access.

Once the Countess, for instance, had the task of verifying a passage from a manuscript in the Vatican. She finally managed to do so through an acquaintance who had a relative in the Vatican. It was found that only two words were wrong in H.P.B.'s quotation and, strangely, these two words were considerably blurred and hard to decipher on the original manuscript.

Both Archibald and Bertram Keightley verified passages for her after many hours of search—sometimes in the British Museum—for a rare book. They have both remarked on the curious, but understandable, fact that numerical references were sometimes reversed by Madame Blavatsky. For instance, "page 321" might be written down by her as "page 123."

A young Cambridge Master of Arts, George Mead, who came into the work later than the Keightleys and added a picturesque note to the household with his red-brown pointed beard and black velvet jacket, confirms what other witnesses say about H.P.B.'s quoting from rare but known sources, not available in the ordinary way.

"But," he says, "what I have been most interested in, in her writing, is precisely that which she does not quote from known sources, and this it is which forms for me the main factor in the enigma H.P.B. I perpetually ask myself the question: whence did she get her information—apparent translations of texts and commentaries, the originals of which are unknown to the Western world? . . . One of the most interesting facts in the whole problem is that she was herself as much delighted with the beauty of these teachings and amazed at the vastness of the conceptions as anyone else."[4]

One of the scientists who often talked with H.P.B. at Holland Park was Dr. C. Carter Blake, zoologist, geologist, and anthropologist, of London. He, like some other scientific men, was astounded at the extraordinary knowledge of this sickly old lady whose formal education in Russia had not even reached English High School level. He found that she often knew more than he did on his own particular lines of study. "For instance," he writes, "her information was superior to mine on the subject of the Naulette Jaw."

On some matters she made statements which he at first thought were wrong, but found later to be correct. "I remember in conversation with her in 1888, in Lansdowne Road, at the time she was engaged on *The Secret Doctrine*, how Madame Blavatsky, to my great astonishment, sprung upon me the fact that the raised beaches of Tarija were pliocene. I had thought them to be pleistocene—following the line of reasoning of Darwin and Spotswood Wilson.

"The fact that these beaches are pliocene has been proven to me since from the works of Gay . . . and other works. . . .

"Madame Blavatsky certainly had original sources of information (I don't say what) transcending the knowledge of experts on their own lines."[5]

But many of the experts, in that last decade of the nineteenth century, could not agree that their knowledge or their concepts had been transcended. Science, as it stood, was right, they maintained, and Madame Blavatsky was writing fantasy.

Yet in the century since *The Secret Doctrine* first saw the light of day, many of the "enduring misconceptions" of the men of science have been proved to be the fantasy, and much—though not all—of what H.P.B. wrote has already been vindicated by science. It begins to seem, as one scientist of today writes, that "modern science is in fact rediscovering that which has been known to earlier civilizations whose very existence we have forgotten."

The Secret Doctrine has thus become a door-opener for many modern research scientists, groping for light at the dead-end of materialism. One of them writes it "has been a source of inspiration and information to a growing number of seekers for understanding . . . its influence on world thought has steadily increased . . . the aspirant for truth receives illuminating insights into basic realities of man and nature. . . . In the light of the *Secret Doctrine*, modern materialistic concepts are recognized as crude dogmas unrelated to the facts of science and to ordinary human experience."[6]

But this growing fulfillment of H.P.B.'s prophecy was still in the closed hand of Time when, in the early autumn of 1888, the "Theosophical Twins" sat together once more at a table, correcting proofs. It was like the old days when they worked on *Isis Unveiled*, except that they were both now twelve years older, and through the windows was a London park instead of a New York street.

By all the Colonel could learn from witnesses, the two works had been produced through similar occult methods. Who could name all the Great Ones who had contributed something to this second and fuller revelation of the Ancient Wisdom? though it was certain that the Masters Morya and K.H. had done so. What a pity that T. Subba Row had not given his assistance as expected! The rift between the young Brahmin and the Old Lady had been caused largely by third parties, yet there was something inexplicable about it all, thought Olcott.

H.P.B. showed him a letter she had received some time before from a Bombay Theosophist, Tookaram Tatya. It said that T. Subba Row had informed him (Tookaram) that he was quite ready to help H.P.B. with *The Secret Doctrine* provided she took out from it every reference to the Masters.

"Does he mean that I should deny the Masters, or that I garble the facts? Surely he knows that the Masters, themselves, have approved the contents of the book," H.P.B. protested.

"I don't know, chum. But I do know that he blames you for desecrating the names of the Mahatmas. One of his terms for helping was that your name should not appear on *The Secret Doctrine*, as its author."

"It was the Hodgson and Myers flapdoodle that started him off. After that he began saying I was a shell abandoned by the Masters," H.P.B. retorted.

The Colonel stroked his beard. "Yes. I've heard that. . . ."

Helena interrupted: "When I took him to task, do you know what he said?"

"No."

"I can remember his words almost exactly. 'You have given out the most sacred secrets of Occultism—never meant for European minds. So it's better that you be sacrificed. People had too much faith in you; now they must doubt you. Otherwise they would pump out of you all that you know.' His actions since have been based on that principle."

"Well, it's a pity. But never mind, Latchkey," Olcott soothed her. After putting a match to his pipe, he went on: "*Isis Unveiled* made an epoch, as I said at the time, but *The Secret Doctrine* is much greater; it's a book for eternity."

Helena smiled happily, and packed the last of the corrected proofs into a cardboard box.

"But what are *those* proofs?" the Colonel pointed to a pile at the end of the table.

"*Lucifer*," she replied, expecting a hostile reaction.

"Pass them to me; I'll go over them for you."

The unexpected cooperation and benignity of the venerable beard on the questions of both *Lucifer* and the Esoteric Section delighted H.P.B. What had happened? What sea had quenched the dragon fire he had been breathing out when he left Bombay?

Actually, it was on the blue Ionian, east of Brindisi, that the change had taken place. There, with the calm, shining sea all around the good ship *Shannon,* and with no one else in his cabin, an envelope had suddenly appeared on his table. It was in Master K.H.'s handwriting. The Colonel was thrilled with its arrival under such impeccable conditions; one moment it was not there, the next it was! No one around, no postage stamp, no messenger!

Inside the envelope was a long letter which, among other things, solved his vexing dilemma. It made clear to him that the proposed Esoteric Section was necessary, and that he must leave such occult matters to H.P.B. He, himself, should, however, play his accustomed role as organizer and administrator.

So Henry Olcott worked hard in England to help H.P.B. organize the new venture on a sound footing. Then on October 9, 1888, he issued a carefully worded order officially forming an Esoteric Section of The Theosophical Society. The new Section had, he wrote, "no official or corporate connection with the Exoteric Society save in the person of the President-Founder." And so, he hoped, the potentially dangerous matter of an "empire within an empire" was safely settled, but he did not feel altogether sure.

While in England the Colonel attended the wedding of Charles Johnston—friend of Yeats and son of the Irish member of parliament for South Belfast—to Madame Blavatsky's niece Vera, daughter of H.P.B.'s sister Vera.

Late in October Olcott left overland for Naples where he planned to embark on the *Arcadia* for India. He wrote to Madame Blavatsky from Rome that, while traveling by train through Italy, he had had the most unexpected and splendid astral visit from their Guru, Master Morya. "I felt so rejoiced I could almost have jumped out of the window. He was so kind so loving and compassionate; despite all my faults and shortcomings, he bears with me and holds to me because of the useful work I have now and then done, and of my fervent desire to do my duty." The Colonel signed his letter with the old nickname Helena had pinned on him in New York—"Maloney."

From Naples he had Charles and Vera Johnston as shipmates to India. Charles had passed brilliantly for the Indian Civil Service. So that famous arm of imperial Britain was about to receive a member who, through Theosophy, had learned to appreciate the culture of "the natives." There had been others, but their numbers were few.

Back in England during October 1888, the first impression of *The Secret Doctrine* came off the press. A review copy was sent hopefully to Mr. W. T. Stead, the famous London editor who had shown himself sympathetic toward the Theosophical Movement.

Stead turned over the pages of the two thick volumes. They would be, he knew, packed with profound metaphysics and arcane knowledge—a forbidding job for any reviewer! Who could do it properly? Where was the penetrating mind, the freedom from religious bias, the breadth of vision?

Suddenly a name came into his mind: the name of a woman he admired, one who, though married to an orthodox minister of religion, had mentally reached out beyond the confines of church Christianity, and had had the courage to break the bonds. Now she was a leading figure of the rebels, the Freethinkers who were known as "Secularists." She was broadminded and fair-minded, but an avowed agnostic and very busy with her social reform work. Would she be interested in this great tome of occult lore? He doubted it. Yet something made him send it to her and ask for a review.

And so it was that *The Secret Doctrine* came into the hands of Annie Besant.

CHAPTER 27

"An admirable review, the best I think I have ever seen of the work, appeared in Stead's *Review of Reviews*," writes Bertram Keightley in his *Reminiscences*. The review was by Annie Besant. "Soon afterwards, a few days only I think," Bertram continues, "Mrs. Besant herself came to 17 Lansdowne Road to see H.P.B."

The great agnostic had discovered in *The Secret Doctrine* something to change her outlook and her life, and she was applying to join The Theosophical Society.

Helena Blavatsky looked at her visitor and knew that, here before her, was a truly great soul. But she wanted no more bitter disappointments. From her bookshelf she took down a copy of the S.P.R. *Report,* and handed it to Mrs. Besant. "Study this well before you take the important step of joining us," she said.

It did not take Annie Besant a great time to read, analyze, and appraise the *Report,* weighing it in the balance against the genius, and power revealed through both *The Secret Doctrine* and, in her own judgment, the woman at Lansdowne Road.

Edmund Russell describes a visit he made there a little later. Madame Blavatsky was sitting at her table playing Patience, her accustomed form of relaxation. "On the floor beside her was a little grey woman who pressed one of the 'Card Dealer's' hands close to her cheek, who only inclined at the introduction, who did not speak, whose name I did not catch.

"All the evening she held the hand, as if this time the shipwrecked mariner was drawing force from the giant octopus to whose tentacles he clung.

"Walking home I happened to mention this simile.

" 'Do you know,' said Mrs. Coues, 'that your *little grey woman* was the great Annie Besant?' "[1]

Another visitor to Lansdowne Road describes Mrs. Besant's appearance at that time ". . . in a black frock with elbow sleeves—a slim youngish woman with short grey hair surmounting a thoughtful brow."

Madame Blavatsky was still struggling with her sick, troublesome body. "Never before has a patient been known to live even for a week under such conditions of renal disorder as have been chronic with her for very many months past," wrote a physician. She said herself that she felt well only when she was sitting writing, that walking and even standing were difficult.

How much longer must she live, she wondered. All her life she had been half in love with death, who from the days of her infancy in plague-ridden Russia, had often brushed close to her.

Through the years there had been her constant, terrible struggle against her turbulent nature, inherent, no doubt, in her Dolgorukov blood. And there had been the long struggle to master the uncontrollable psychic envelope that had haunted and plagued her youth. It was some twenty years now since she had gained control of the psychic forces, but did she always use them with necessary moderation? In a large measure she had also risen above the violent emotions of the turbulent blood, but they still played through her psychophysical vehicle.

To what extent her bodily diseases were scars of these old battles, and to what extent they were karmic (the harvest of earlier lives) she did not know. But she did know that they were mortal, held at bay only by her Master, for a time and for a purpose. She also knew that she was getting very tired of the pain, discomfort, and restrictions of the creaky old physical carriage.

But to most of the new disciples around her in London it seemed that the quiet, dignified mantle of the great

Teacher had fallen upon her; that she was like old Plato when he sat late at a party with young friends, watching their strange human antics with more tolerance than one might expect.

But she taught that a serious aspirant to the Path must merely exist in the fleshy capsule that covers him while his real life is in the spirit. Yet a calm acceptance of life, and nonattachment to its joys and sorrows, was not enough. To a neophyte she wrote:

"The 'Kingdom of Heaven', which I need not tell you is but the dominion of man's immortal spirit over the inner forces of the Universe, must be taken by violence. I am sorry to be compelled to tell you that the prize of Wisdom and Power must be won through danger, trial, temptation, the allurements of sense, and all the besetments of this world of matter whcih they counterpoise."[2]

Group harmony among her esotericists was something on which she insisted as the most vital condition for success. Twice that harmony had been broken, and she wrote that if it happened a third time, the teaching of the Group —*as a group*— would cease and not be resumed. "Individual members, who are worthy, will be taught, but all class teaching—where the haters and the hated are promiscuously gathered—will be put an end to at once."

Her pupils in Occultism had to live according to a strict code and those who broke it were expelled without the slightest hesitation. Yet H.P.B.'s compassion for the weak, downtrodden, or unfortunate had grown, if possible, even greater with the passing years, and she was always ready to give unstintingly from her "widow's mite." When, for instance, a Russian priest of the Eastern Orthodox Church would call at her London home to collect alms for his poor, she would point to a drawer where she kept her little stock of money and simply say, "Help yourself."

Once she wrote to Annie Besant who did welfare work among the destitute: "I have but 30 shillings of *my own* money, of which I can dispose (for as you know I am a pauper and proud of it), but I want you to take them, and *not say a word.* This may buy 30 dinners for 30 poor little starving wretches."[3]

Her compassionate heart also led her back sometimes to the old phenomena. Her "miracles" had caused such bad reactions in the world that now she seldom performed any publicly.

But her close disciples tell interesting tales of strange happenings. One of the best is given in Dr. Archibald Keightley's *Reminiscences.* The London group was discussing the needs of a man who at the time was "in actual want of food." Madame Blavatsky grew silent during the conversation, and at last exclaimed suddenly:

"Well, I will!" She turned to Archibald and asked:

"Have you a £25 note?"

He did not think so, but he finally found one and brought it to H.P.B. She refused to handle it.

"No," she said, "I want you to fold the note closely and put it in my tobacco basket over there. Bury it deep into the tobacco."

Archibald did as instructed and then placed the basket on the arm of her chair. She rested her hand on the top of the closed lid, and seemed to go into "a brown study." In a minute or two she said, with a sigh: "Open the basket and take your note."

As he unfolded it, Archibald found a second £25 note rolled up with it. Examining it, Archibald found that it had a different number from his own note. The "materialized" £25—not counterfeit but good in every way—was posted to the man in need.

Later Archibald queried her: "Why did you need my note in order to precipitate the other one?"

"Well, it's easier with a mould to work from. It then does not require such a precise astral picture on which to build the physical particles."

"Where did those physical particles come from—the ones you used to materialize the second note?" he wanted to know.

She tried to explain to him the hidden forces behind the phenomena. "You see, there are funds at certain centers, guarded by my occult friends. To aid people, under certain circumstances, I have the right to call on those funds. When I do so, the money there, at the other end of the line, is disintegrated and sent; then I re-integrate it here."

More than once the dark recesses of the tobacco basket seem to have made a good focus for materializations. Bertram Keightley writes in his *Reminiscences* about another occasion.

On a Saturday night H.P.B. received a letter from a woman who had done her a great injury. It was a piteous appeal for financial help in an extremity of distress.

H.P.B. took five sovereigns from her purse and asked if anyone present could give her paper money in exchange. No one could. Madame's Ceylon grass basket of tobacco was going the rounds of those who wanted to make cigarettes. When it came to her, she dropped the five sovereigns inside, closed the lid, and went on talking.

After a while Bertram begged for a cigarette, and she pushed the basket over to him. Noticing the absence of the gold coins, he said:

"Hallo, H.P.B., what have you done with those five sovereigns? I thought you put them in here."

"So I did."

He searched through the tobacco again and found—a five pound note!

"So, up to your little games again!" remarked Bertram, handing her the note.

She just smiled, then, writing a kindly letter to the "enemy," she enclosed the five pounds and handed the envelope to Bertram for posting.

"I went out and posted it at a nearby pillar box in time for the midnight collection," he writes.

A good deal of the material written for *The Secret Doctrine* had been put aside as not fitting into the scheme of the first two volumes. In her preface to the first edition, H.P.B. commented: "Should the present volumes meet with a favourable reception, no effort will be spared to carry out the scheme of the work in its entirety. The

third volume is entirely ready; the fourth is almost so."[4]
However, her immediate task was concentrating on writing
two other books: *The Key to Theosophy* and *The Voice
of the Silence.*

There were also, as always, many long letters to be
written, not only to India and other places, but now particularly to America where something good was building up.

The Light in the West was growing but—perhaps inevitably—a shadow was forming. "A shadowy darkness
passes always along with the philosophic body moving in
its own light until it is thoroughly purified from sensual
defilements," says an old book on the Hermetic mysteries.

The good thing in America was the vigorous new
growth of The Theosophical Society there. The movement had been dormant for some years after H.P.B. and
Olcott left New York in 1878; then, following William Q.
Judge's visit to Europe and India in 1884, fresh green
shoots had appeared. This was very largely due to Mr.
Judge's zealous gardening. Previously he, her old pupil
in Occultism, had been too busy with his professional affairs to give adequate time to the theosophical garden.
Also he had felt somewhat neglected when the two "Elders"
had gone off to India, where he himself longed to go and
live.

But now he was different. He realized that his *dharma*
was in America. He had become H.P.B.'s representative
of the Esoteric Section there, and he was doing great work,
too, in building up the exoteric Society. In 1888 he held
his first big national Convention. To that H.P.B. sent
Dr. Archibald Keightley as her emissary, bearing a long
message to be read out at the Convention. Dr. Keightley
enjoyed the experience—his first journey outside England
—and was asked to go to the second annual Convention
in 1889.

The shadow that now was seen to be moving along with
the growing Light was a very busy man called Professor
Elliott Coues. He was a member of the Smithsonian In-
stitution, and considered himself a person of importance

in the community. His main aim was to increase that importance—by almost any means available.

His interest in Theosophy had begun several years earlier; in fact he was one of the many who visited Madame Blavatsky when she was at Elberfeld in 1884. But she had been rather suspicious of him from the beginning. She saw too much ego, vanity, personal ambition. Furthermore, he used foolish flattery on her and, annoyingly, the manner of one ready to intrigue with her. She began to believe that he considered her the great impostor as labeled by Hodgson & Co. but admired her for it. He showed signs of being eager to join forces with her in making the public dance to the drumbeats of the most brilliant deception of the century.

But his first object was to get full power in America; Judge stood in his way and must be superseded or eliminated. International power, he believed, would come later as Olcott would not be difficult to thrust aside. Overtones of such dreams and schemes began to appear in his letters to Madame Blavatsky, and soon an open quarrel between Coues and Judge began.

H.P.B., despite her early suspicions, had felt that Coues must be given his chance. There was the possibility, the hope, that he might overcome his lust for personal prestige and power. If so, he would become a very useful member of the Society, and a strong force in the movement. He had great possibilities for either good or evil. She hoped it would turn out to be the former.

But, alas, the evil was coming more and more to the front. In a letter written at the end of 1888 to Dr. J. S. Buck, a great Theosophist in America, H.P.B. said of Coues: "He acted like Satan, offering to the meek Nazarene all the Kingdoms of Earth, if I would only help him *secretly,* and recognise him the sole Head of the T.S. in America, throwing out Olcott and Judge altogether. To make a long story short, he [Coues] would force America to recognise and *worship* me as the Sole Representative of Theosophy on the Continent, and I would make (!) K.H. write a circular letter to the Americans telling them

Coues alone was His (K.H.'s) representative, etc., etc. It made me sick with disgust. . . .

"I told him that never *never* would I turn traitor to Olcott and Judge, my two best and trusted friends, for all the glory and vindication of character in the world. I said that if he (Coues) would turn himself and Hodgson against me, and finally ruin my character in the U.S., it would make no difference. . . . that I *would not* countenance any *bogus* letters from K.H., nor help him [Coues] to bamboozle the public."

H.P.B. felt sure by this time that Dr. Elliott Coues did not believe in the actual existence of the Masters, that he considered her the leader of a brilliant international fraud and desired to become the chief lieutenant of the Machiavelli in petticoats.

In a long letter to Coues in April 1888, rejecting his schemes, H.P.B. wrote: "No bitterest enemy of mine has ever misunderstood me as you do." She exhorted him: "Work for the Society and show me that you can do it, real good, and my life will be at your service." And she warned him: "You can create lots of scandal, turn against Judge and myself and the whole Society; but believe me even were you to upset a few Fellows, you will never upset the Society. . . . A Persian proverb says: 'He who spits against the wind receives it back in his face'."

Even at this late hour she was urging Coues to choose the right road, but she felt sadly that he would take the wrong one, and soon be plotting a vicious revenge on the "ingenious and interesting imposter" who had spurned his proffered help.

CHAPTER 28

In July, 1889, Annie Besant attended the great Labour Congress in Paris, accompanied by Herbert Burrows, a co-worker in social reform, and now also one of H.P.B.'s devoted disciples. While in France both took the opportunity of visiting Madame Blavatsky who was staying in the beautiful forest of Fontainebleau at the home of an American Theosophist.

They found her translating from memory some fragments of an archaic volume she had studied long before at one of the Tibetan Monasteries.

"She wrote swiftly," said Mrs. Besant, "without any material copy before her, and in the evening made me read it aloud to see if the 'English was decent'. . . . The translation was in perfect and beautiful English, flowing and musical, only a word or two could we find to alter, and she looked at us like a startled child, wondering at our praises—praises that anyone with the literary sense would endorse if they read that exquisite prose poem."

The ancient manuscript volume from which H.P.B. had selected the fragments was called, she said, *The Book of the Golden Precepts*. It will not be found in any of the world's great libraries outside Tibet. The English prose poem that she composed from it's teachings is entitled *The Voice of the Silence*. It is now well-known, as it has been through many editions, including one " 'under the auspices of the Chinese Buddhist Research Society,' which contained a portrait of, and some benedictory verses by, the late Tashi Lama of Tibet (1883-1937), 'written with his own hand specially for the reprint.' " Bhikshu Sangharakshite, an Englishman well versed in the literature of both the Hinayana and Mahayana Schools of Buddhism, says, "*The Voice of the Silence* seeks to awaken Wisdom by appealing to the heart—not a physical organ but a transcendental faculty—and by encouraging the disciple to adopt an attitude in which the intellectual will be subordinated to the spiritual."[1]

He considered it a beautiful mixture of poetry and Buddhist paradox; the paradox that transcends the narrow bounds of logic—the poetry that is rich in both imagery and mantra-like vibrations.

H.P.B. seems to have written this little gem mainly as a daily guide in essential self-disciplines. She knew there was a need for such an inspirational guide on the narrow and thorny path of true Occultism, especially as she, herself, would not much longer be there to give personal guidance to her beloved disciples.

She had felt the need for another book, too. More and more new people were flowing into the Theosophical Movement. Her two large books in double volumes—*Isis Unveiled* and *The Secret Doctrine*—were hard for beginners to digest, and also too expensive for many of them. The need was for a compendium of the teachings, something that would be easier to buy, handle, and understand. And so she wrote *The Key to Theosophy*.

Sending a copy of it to Mr. Stead, she wrote, "This work at least, you will understand, and metaphysics are absent from it. Mr. Oscar Wilde gave me his *word of honour* to review it but—this does not go far, nor do I care for it. What I do care for is that you should read it."

Both the new books were published in 1889 after her return to England.

In the fall of the same year a Theosophist named Annie M. Jaquess came to Lansdowne Road to see H.P.B., prior to leaving for America.

"Well, 'Little One'," said H.P.B., looking at her visitor intently, "we will never meet again in these bodies."

Miss Jaquess was startled: "Will I soon pass on, then?" she exclaimed.

"Not *you,* but when you return, *I* shall be gone."

Miss Jaquess was silent for a while, her eyes moistening. Then she asked: "Who will take your place, H.P.B.?"

The Old Lady looked at her earnestly a full minute, and said: "Annie Besant. But do not speak of this. I have the word from the Master."

"But—but, how can that cold, intellectual woman ever fill your place?"

Madame Blavatsky smiled and replied: "She will unfold in spirit and become soft and beautiful, and she will be able to reach the people and do a greater work than I could ever do, as she has command of languages, especially English."

Miss Jaquess shook her head. She could not agree—but no doubt the Masters knew best.

The members of the household at Lansdowne Road began to scatter—some temporarily, some permanently. The Countess had to return for periods to her home in Sweden. Archibald Keightley went to New Zealand on family matters, and then to America for theosophical work. H.P.B. sent Bertram Keightley on a trip to America and then to India to assist the Colonel. He stayed on there and became the first General Secretary of the Indian National Section of the Society.

Madame Blavatsky herself left Holland Park and moved to the home of Annie Besant at 19 Avenue Road, St. John's Wood, London. This was a large house set in pleasant gardens. H.P.B. had her workroom on the ground floor, her large desk near a window through which she could see the front grass plot and trees. A door on one side led to her small bedroom, and on another to the office of her private secretary, George Mead. He was also General Secretary of the European Section of The Theosophical Society.

The whole layout was designed to save the Old Lady's failing legs as much as possible. Without climbing stairs she could walk to the hall for Blavatsky Lodge meetings

and to the spacious chamber that had been built specially
for the Esoteric Section.

But the old Russian warrior still had her battles to
fight. Skirmishes with the Colonel at Adyar continued
despite the fact that he had been over to England to settle
their differences in 1888, then again late in 1889, when
the two old friends and fellow workers had spent a happy
Christmas together—their last.

When they were together the Colonel's diplomacy and
the old camaraderie prevailed, and all went well. But
when they were apart, third parties set up tensions, mis-
understandings, and conflicts between them. Basically
the problem lay in the fact that H.P.B.'s followers in
Europe looked upon her as the head of the Society. This
was natural enough as she was the channel through which
the teachings came; she was the specially trained messenger of the Mahatmas. But her keen London disciples desired also that she should be, as European President, quite
independent of the international headquarters and the
President-Founder (Olcott) at Adyar.

About the middle of 1890 the Council of the British
Section passed a resolution "vesting permanently the
Presidential authority for the whole of Europe in H.P.
Blavatsky." When the Resolution reached Adyar, the
Colonel cancelled it publicly through *The Theosophist*
". . . as contrary to the Constitution and By-laws of the
Theosophical Society, a usurpation of the Presidential
prerogative, and beyond the competence of any Section
or fragment of the Society to enact."[2]

In his personal diary for the day the Colonel wrote:
"That may mean a split, but it does not mean that I
shall be a slave." While President of the Society, he was
determined to *be* President in *fact* as well as in name.
He believed that it was for this role, as executive head and
chief administrator, that the Masters had called him
away from his prosperous law business in New York a
dozen years before. At times throughout those years they
had confirmed that his job was to take care of all exoteric
affairs, leaving the esoteric to H.P.B. Surely she was

being badly advised now by the young hotheads around her, he thought. She had always made a mess of practical matters, and she always would.

Finally, he outmaneuvered his old friend by threatening to resign and leave the whole of the Society's affairs, national and international, to her.

In a letter to him, saying how by this act he would prove a traitor to the Masters, to India and to the world, she wrote: "Put aside your miserable personality, and its petty squabbles and competition with that other wretched, dirty old rag, called H.P. Blavatsky. Listen to the words of H.P.B. who has ever been true to you, so long as you were true (even only the best you knew how) to the Masters."

A later letter offered to make any sacrifice necessary to keep him in office. He consented to stay, but one of the conditions he insisted on was an alteration in "the form of obligation which candidates for the E.S. were then taking." It had been worded so as to exact the promise of perfect obedience to H.P.B. in matters that Olcott considered were in fact T.S. affairs. This, he said had been giving her, "quasi-dictatorial powers, and quite nullifying the basis of membership upon which the movement had been built up, and which left each member the most absolute freedom of conscience and action."[3]

H.P.B. agreed to his suggestion and altered the pledge to which he took such strong exception. Thus the possible disintegrating effects of what he called a "Star Chamber" and an "empire within an empire" were nullified. Moreover, the European Section, with Madame Blavatsky at its head, remained—nominally at any rate —under the leadership of the international headquarters at Adyar, India.

The trouble from another direction was much more serious. Dr. Elliott Coues had apparently given up all hope of collusion with Madame Blavatsky in what he believed her chicanery, and decided to have his revenge by attacking her publicly. He gathered together all the defamatory rumors, old and new, and approached *The Sun,* a New York daily, widely circulated, and edited by the well-known Charles Dana.

Coues was apparently regarded as a trustworthy citizen in Washington society. He had been a surgeon in the United States army and was considered an authority on the subject of ornithology. He evidently persuaded Charles Dana that his material on Madame Blavatsky was reliable and provable—because it was certainly libelous.

His press attack opened with an article on June 1, 1890, entitled "The History of a Humbug." This was followed on Sunday, July 20, by a full-page spread in the form of an interview given by Coues to the *Sun's* correspondent in Washington, D.C.

In this feature, illustrated by photographs of the two Founders, Elliott Coues reveals that his concept of H.P.B., her main helpers, The Theosophical Society and the Great Ones behind it was as he had suspected. It was all, he stated, a gigantic imposture, used first as a cover for Russian espionage and then to make money for Blavatsky and other knaves engaged in it.

As people often do, he saw a reflection of himself in his mental image of Madame Blavatsky. The character traits he imputes to her are largely the ones he had revealed in himself through his private correspondence when striving to rise to greater power in her promising organization.

"The ingredients of a successful charlatan," he says, "are no conscience, some brains, much courage, great industry, the corrosive sublimate of selfishness, vainglorious ambition, vivid imagination, good address, ready resources, monumental mendacity and a pious, living faith in the love of mankind for being humbugged. Blavatsky had all these."

In his unrestrained, vindictive attack on her moral character, he says that Madame Blavatsky had been a member of the demimonde in Paris, that she had borne an illegitimate, deformed son to Prince Emil von Wittgenstein, and he implies (on the authority of Emma Coulomb) that she was either the mistress or the bigamous wife of Mitrovitch. Madame Blavatsky was, he states, expelled by the police from Egypt in the early 1870s, and he claims that this could be confirmed from the records there.

Olcott, Judge, and other leading members of The Theosophical Society were aware of the Blavatsky chicanery and assisted her in it, maintains Coues. The rest, he says, are fools and content to be so. The whole thing is nothing but fraud and folly. The so-called worthy objects of the Society—universal brotherhood, promotion of the study of Aryan and Eastern religions, and so on—are simply blinds to enable knaves to make money.

By the razzle-dazzle of flamboyant journalism, Coues and the reporter managed to twist facts into falsehoods, and presented assumptions and rumors as if they were facts, easily proved if necessary. This whole newspaper page on a colorful career of criminal imposture must have provided some enjoyable Sunday reading for the man in the street. But to the serious Theosophists it was a slap in the face.

Mr. W.Q. Judge in New York cabled H.P.B. for permission to file a suit for libel in her name.

Helena no longer cared very much about the whips and knives of malicious calumny. She had by now learned to master the anger and resentment that flared up in her, and she could practice, herself, the ideal she taught her pupils—"a courageous endurance of personal injustice."

But, on the other hand, public slanders against *her* reflected on the Society and the work of the Masters. And, moreover, Coues had attacked the whole movement as well as herself. If she sued for libel, *The Sun* would spare none of its great resources in trying to prove the defamatory charges against her and her work. As these were false, the paper would fail to prove them. So perhaps this was her chance to squash those old, evil tongued rumors forever. She gave her consent for the suit for libel.

As her suit was against Elliott Coues as well as the newspaper, the daring doctor must have given all the assistance he could to *The Sun's* investigators and lawyers. After all, he had implied strongly that the necessary documents, records, and witnesses to prove his case could be readily found.

The months passed. The calendars of 1890 were replaced by those of 1891. How were the defendants progressing in their worldwide search for evidence? wondered the Theosophists around the world. In March 1891 *The Path*, the magazine of the American Section, edited by lawyer W.Q. Judge, carried a statement on progress headed, "The Libel Suits against the N.Y. *Sun* and Elliott Coues." The case had not yet come up for trial, but an important victory had already been won, the magazine reported. The lawyers for *The Sun* had confessed in open court (where a question of law had been argued before Judge Beach) their inability to prove the charge of immorality on which the suit lay. They asked permission to retain a mass of irrelevant matter in the defense. But, as this could only have been meant to prejudice a jury, Judge Beach "ordered the objectionable matter to be stricken out."

"The case now looks," *The Path* prophesied hopefully, "merely like one in which the only question will be the amount of damages, and everything must now stand until the case is reached in the Trial Term."

Dr. Elliott Coues must by this time have been a very worried, if not, indeed, a surprised man—beginning to think that perhaps he had, in the words of Madame Blavatsky, spat against the wind.

CHAPTER 29

In the year 1891 the term "electron" was first used. A few scientists, like the great Russian, Butleroff, were beginning to doubt the age-old concept of the atom as something solid and indivisible. But they admitted that this was tantamount to doubting the very existence of matter.

Three years earlier—and over a decade before science had actually established the divisibility of the atom—Madame Blavatsky had written in *The Secret Doctrine:* "The atom *is* elastic, ergo the atom is divisible, and must consist of particles, or of sub-atoms. . . . It is on the doctrine of the illusive nature of matter, and the infinite divisibility of the atom, that the whole science of Occultism is built. It opens limitless horizons to *substance* informed by the divine breath of its soul in every possible state of tenuity."[1]

But people at large cared little about these occult truths and scientific trends that would change the face, and fate, of the world. Edwardian society, around the Prince of Wales, was still immersed in hunting, house parties, adulterous amours and baccarat for high stakes. The masses were buried in the apathy of poverty and industrial hells.

In 1891 the German Kaiser formed the Triple Alliance with Austria and Italy and visited London; the *Adventures of Sherlock Holmes* began in the *Strand* magazine, and Oscar Wilde published *The Picture of Dorian Gray*. In the spring of the year, when Theosophists were rejoicing about the almost certain defeat of defamer Elliott Coues in New York, a mild epidemic of influenza came to London.

Theosophist E.T. Sturdy went down with it toward the end of April, and at about the same time the Old Lady at 19 Avenue Road had to take to her bed with a temperature of 105 degrees.

A Doctor Mennell, perhaps influenced by the presence of the epidemic, pronounced her illness to be influenza. Aware, however, of the poor state of her general health, he took her illness quite seriously. A responsible member of the household must be constantly on hand, he instructed, to make sure that both medicine and food were given punctually.

The bulk of this duty fell to Laura Mary Cooper, a young lady of good family, her father being Frederick Cooper, C.B., of the Indian Civil Service. Laura Cooper has left us the fullest account of H.P.B.'s last illness.[2]

Although the Old Lady was feeling very ill indeed, she wanted to know all that was going on, and when she heard about Mr. Sturdy's sickness, insisted on his being brought at once to 19 Avenue Road to be properly nursed.

H.P.B. herself began to get worse, but neither the doctor nor her disciples were unduly worried; they reminded one another that she had been through critical illnesses several times before, but that the Master's hand had always pulled her through; why should it be different this time?

As the days passed and she got no better, Dr. Mennell asked Madame Blavatsky if she would mind seeing his partner Dr. Miller. She consented. Dr. Miller came and examined her chest. After consultation the two doctors called the sisters, Laura Cooper and Isabelle Cooper-Oakley.

"Madame Blavatsky is suffering from bronchitis, and is in extremely weak condition. The case is most serious," Dr. Miller said, adding that she should be given a table-spoonful of brandy every two hours—more if she became weaker.

H.P.B. had always hated any form of alcoholic beverage, but agreed to take the stimulant prescribed. Breathing she found very difficult while lying in bed and seemed better sitting, propped up with pillows, in her big armchair. She alternated between bed and chair. On the night of May 7 she even spent a few minutes at her desk, pen in hand. But she soon laid it aside.

That night she suffered greatly. At seven o'clock the morning of the 8th someone relieved Laura Cooper, who had been watching the patient all night. But before she could lie down the doctor came and examined the patient. There seemed to be no immediate danger, he told Laura, as the stimulant was having a good effect, and Madame's pulse was stronger. He advised Laura to get a few hours rest.

"About 11:30 a.m.," she writes, "I was aroused by Mr. Claudfalls Wright, who told me to come at once as H.P.B. had changed for the worse, and the nurse did not think she would live many hours; directly I entered the room, I realized the critical condition she was in. She was sitting in her chair and I knelt in front of her, and asked her to try and take some stimulant."

H.P.B. could not hold the glass herself, but her attendants managed to get some brandy, and some nourishment, through her lips.

"She might linger a few more hours," the nurse decided, but even then Laura detected a further change. She writes: "The dear eyes were already becoming dim, though she retained full consciousness." She noticed also that H.P.B. was moving one foot about, a habit that had always been a sign of mental concentration.

The nurse, evidently feeling that she could do no more to help, left the room, and Helena Blavatsky was alone with three of her close disciples. Laura stood with one arm supporting her beloved Teacher's head. Walter Old and C.F. Wright knelt in front of her, each holding one of her hands. Thus the three remained, motionless and silent for many minutes, during which Helena Blavatsky, sitting in her work chair, finally broke the link with her disease-ridden body.

"A great sense of peace filled the room," said Laura, "and we knelt quietly there until first my sister, then the Countess arrived."

"Her right hand grew cold in mine," remembers Walter Old, who was General Secretary of the English Section, and an astrologer known to the public as Sepharial. "Those moments of exquisite pain, when self-compassion, and a joy for the rest that had come to one I loved, tore my being in twain with their wild contest, will ever remain among the sacred memories of my life."

Far away in the drawing-room of a house in Odessa two anxious old ladies sat reading a letter from the Countess Wachtmeister. One was the loving Aunt Nadyezhda who, sixty years earlier at the age of three, had set fire to the priest's robe at the baptism of baby Helena. The other was prim Aunt Katherine de Witte who, in all her 75 years, never did approve of her niece's "wild ways." Still, family was family, and now she was worried about the reports of Helena's illness.

Aunt Nadyezhda felt particularly concerned because the moss agate ring from India, which Helena had sent her some twelve years earlier, had turned completely black. The transparent yellowish stone had been darkening for about a month, and now she could not even see the sprig of moss embedded within it. Surely this must mean that something terrible had happened!

Because mails took so long to reach Odessa from London, the old aunts were unaware of the fact that their niece was already dead. The letter that Nadyezhda was reading aloud to Katherine merely told them that things were getting worse.

"I am sure she will recover," Katherine tried to comfort her sister.

As she said this there came a tremendous crash as if a wall of the room had shattered and fallen, or a table laden with glasses had crashed to the floor. The frightened ladies ran about the house to see what had happened. But there was not a sign of any breakage.

This crash was the worst of all the strange sounds they had been hearing about the house—snappings and blows on the furniture, as it had been in the long ago when young psychic Helena was at home.

It was, however, oddly the disapproving Katherine who had the strongest clairvoyance. As the sisters sat in their large drawing room in the evening trying to read, Katherine suddenly whispered: "I see her! There she is!" She pointed to a dark, distant corner of the room. Nadyezhda could see nothing, so Katherine described her vision of Helena "clad in white, with great white flowers on her head."

This was in fact how she had been laid out in her coffin two days earlier, but the aunts had not yet received the news.

After word of Helena's death came by ordinary means, there were no more strange noises in the house, and the moss agate ring returned to its normal color.

It was at Woking in Southern England on May 11, 1891, that the mortal remains of Helena Petrovna Blavatsky were cremated. Her funeral oration was delivered by twenty-eight-year-old George Mead of the red pointed beard. Son of Colonel Robert Mead, George was an intellectual mystic. He had been H.P.B.'s private secretary since 1887, and was later to write some profound books on Christian origins, Gnosticism, Hermetic teachings and other religious subjects, and to marry Laura Mary Cooper.

In the funeral oration he said: "H. P. Blavatsky is dead, but H.P.B., our teacher and friend, is alive, and will live for ever in our hearts and memories. In our present sorrow, it is this thought especially that we should keep ever before our minds. It is true that the personality we know as H.P. Blavatsky will be with us no longer; but it is equally true that the grand and noble individuality, the great soul that has taught all of us men and women to live purer and more unselfish lives, is still active. . . .

"Her unvarying fidelity to her great mission, from which neither contumely nor misrepresentation ever made her swerve, was the keynote of her strong and fearless nature."

The urn of ashes was brought back and placed temporarily in her room at 19 Avenue Road, where an unfinished editorial lay on her desk.

Later the ashes would be divided into three parts for the three main world centers of Theosophy. One part would be kept in Europe, and for this the eminent Swedish sculptor Sven Bengtsson had offered—through the Countess Wachtmeister—to design an appropriate urn. Another part would go to America by the hand of William Q. Judge, now on his way to England. The other third was for India.

Colonel Henry Steel Olcott, busy lecturing in far-off Sydney, Australia, had received a telepathic sign—a deep feeling of sorrow, loss, and emptiness. "Had an uneasy foreboding of H.P.B.'s death," he wrote in his private diary.

Then had come a press cablegram announcing her death. The Colonel canceled all further programmed tours of the Antipodes, and was soon steaming across the seas to England.

The partnership that had meant so much to him, and —he believed—would mean much to mankind, was finally, irretrievably broken. All he would find back there in the room in Avenue Road would be a handful of grey ashes. What connection could that have with the great soul, the fascinating, mysterious Light-bringer known as H.P.B.? Even to him, who had known her so long, she was an enigma. But he knew that she was too great an occultist for most men to measure her moral stature.

Ashes! They were perhaps a symbol—a religious symbol, as the ancients taught. He would bear them back to the Sacred Land, to Mother India, whose divine, Eternal Light Helena Blavatsky had struggled so long, and suffered so much, to bring to the world's reluctant windows.

EPILOGUE

Under the laws of New York Madame Blavatsky's death in 1891 automatically terminated the lawsuit for libel brought by her against *The Sun* and Dr. Elliott Coues. They had escaped, and need have done no more about it.

But through its efforts to find evidence in support of the press statements, the editors of *The Sun* were convinced that a great wrong had been perpetrated through its columns. Without any legal necessity or compulsion, they published an editorial article (on September 26, 1892) repudiating the Coues interview. At the same time the paper opened its columns to a long report by Mr. W. Q. Judge on the life work and character of H.P. Blavatsky.

In part *The Sun* editorial said: "We print on another page an article in which Mr. William Q. Judge deals with the romantic and extraordinary career of the late Helena P. Blavatsky. We take occasion to observe that on July 20, 1890, we were misled into admitting into *The Sun's* columns an article by Dr. E. F. Coues of Washington, in which allegations were made against Madame Blavatsky's character, and also against her followers, which appear to have been without solid foundation. Mr. Judge's article disposes of all questions related to Madame Blavatsky, as presented by Dr Coues, and we desire to say that his allegations respecting the Theosophical Society and Mr. Judge personally are not sustained by evidence, and should not have been printed."

Publication of the retraction was an honorable act by a great newspaper to clear the dead woman's name of

WHEN DAYLIGHT COMES

slanders unsupportable by factual evidence.

The reactions of Elliott Coues are not on record. No doubt he had been pleased when the death of his adversary had saved him from the effects of the lawsuit; but *The Sun's* retraction and apology, implying that his attack had been malicious and based entirely on falsehood, must have been a bitter pill to a man so ambitious for public prestige and power.

Some glowing obituaries on H.P.B. were written by her pupils who had known her well. But perhaps of most interest to the general reader of today are the effects Madame Blavatsky and her work had on some people— thinkers, writers, social reformers, and community leaders —active and known beyond the perimeter of the Society she founded.

The social reformer, Herbert Burrows writes, in part: "I went to her a materialist, she left me a Theosophist, and between these two there is a great gulf fixed. Over that gulf she bridged the way. She was my spiritual mother, and never had child a more loving, a more patient, a more tender guide.

"It was in the old Lansdowne Road days. Beset with problems of life and mind that our materialism could not solve, dwelling intellectually on what are now to us the inhospitable shores of agnosticism, Annie Besant and I ever craved more light . . . and so on an ever-to-be remembered evening, with a letter of introduction from Mr. W.T. Stead, then editor of the *Pall Mall Gazette,* as our passport, we found ourselves face to face . . . with the woman we afterwards learned to know and to love as the most wonderful woman of her time. . . .

"If those who talk so foolishly about her magnetizing people, could but know how she continually impressed upon us the absolute duty of proving all things and holding fast only to that which is good!

"Sitting by her when strangers came, as they did come from every corner of the earth, I have often watched with the keenest amusement their wonder at seeing a woman who always said what she thought. Given a prince she would probably shock him, given a poor man and he would have her last shilling and her kindliest word."[1]

"Saladin" (Stewart Ross), who called himself an agnostic, wrote a long eulogy of H. P. Blavatsky, for the *Agnostic Journal.* Here are some extracts from his articles:

"She was simply an upright and romantically honest giantess, who measured herself with the men and women with whom she came in contact, and felt the contrast, and was not hypocrite enough to pretend she did not feel it. But she did not call even those who reviled and wronged her by a more bitter epithet than 'flapdoodles'. Such assailants as even the Coulombs and Dr. Coues she referred to with expressions equivalent to, 'Father forgive them, for they know not what they do.' . . . 'Impostor' indeed! She was almost the only mortal I have ever met who was *not* an impostor. . . . Ye sneerers of cheap sneers, read *Isis Unveiled, The Secret Doctrine,* and *The Key to Theosophy,* and you will find that Theosophy is, most likely, something too high for your comprehension, but something that is immeasurably removed from the possibility of being assisted by the legerdemain of a charlatan or the jugglery of a mountebank. . . .

"Hers had been a life of storm, toil and unrest which had left their autographs written cruelly upon her face, and had originated or accentuated incurable illness. . . . She was cheerful and sociable, incapable of an ungenerous thought, and she had not a mean drop of blood in her veins. . . .

"She had none of that restrained precision in utterance in regard to friends and contemporaries which ladies in society adopt. She meant no ill, and so it did not occur to her that she could speak any evil. . . .

"The Madame Blavatsky I knew is *dead* to me. Of course, all that might be permanent or impermanent of her still whirls in the vortex of the universe; but she lives to me only as do others on the roll of the good and great, by the halo of her memory and the inspiration of her example. Her followers are gnostic on grave issues of teleology on which I am only agnostic. They have unbroken communion with their dead; but I am left to mourn."[2]

An editorial in the New York *Tribune* of May 10, 1891, gave some perceptive thoughts on H.P.B. and her work:

"However Utopian may appear to some minds an attempt in the nineteenth century to break down the barriers of race, nationality, caste and class prejudice, and to inculcate that spirit of brotherly love which the greatest of all Teachers enjoined in the first century, the nobility of the aim can only be impeached by those who repudiate Christianity. Madame Blavatsky held that the regeneration of mankind must be based upon the development of altruism. . . .

"In another direction . . . she did important work. No one in the present generation, it may be said, has done more towards reopening the long-sealed treasure of Eastern thought, wisdom and philosophy. No one certainly has done so much toward elucidating that profound wisdom-religion wrought out by the ever-cogitating Orient. . . .

"Her steps often led, indeed, where only a few initiates could follow, but the tone and tendency of all her writings were healthful, bracing and stimulating. The lesson which was constantly impressed by her was assuredly that which the world most needs, and has always needed, namely the necessity of subduing self and of working for others. . . .

"Careful observers of the time . . . long since discerned that the tone of current thought in many directions was being affected by it [H.P.B.'s lesson]. A broader humanity, a more liberal speculation, a disposition to investigate ancient philosophies from a higher point of view, have no indirect association with the teachings referred to. Thus Madame Blavatsky has made her mark upon the time."[3]

The great editor, W. T. Stead, wrote on the significance of H.P.B.'s teaching: "To begin with it has at least the advantage of being heretical. The truth always begins with a heresy. In every heresy there may be the germ of a new revelation. Then, in the second place, it brought

back to the scientific and skeptical world the great conception of the greatest religions, the existence of sublime
beings, immeasurably superior to the pigmy race of men,
who stand, as it were, midway between the Infinite and
ourselves. . . .

"Madame Blavatsky also reinforced and almost recreated
in many minds the sense of this life being a mere probation. In this respect her teaching was much more in ac-
cord with the spirit of the New Testament than much
of the pseudo-Christian teaching of our day. She widened
the horizon of the mind, and she brought something of the
infinite sense of the vast, illimitable mystery, which char-
acterises some of the Eastern religions, into the very heart
of Europe in the nineteenth century."[4]

Mahatma M. K. Gandhi is revered as a saint as well as
a national hero in India. He played the leading role in
freeing India from foreign domination and, by his own
inspiring example, led the minds of his countrymen
toward the divine truths of their ancient spiritual culture.

In his *"Autobiography: or, The Story of My Experiments with Truth,"* he relates how, when he was a law
student in London, he met two Theosophists whom he
took to be brothers. These were probably Archibald and
Bertram Keightley, mistaken for brothers by many people.
They introduced him to the *Bhagavad Gita,* and Gandhi
felt ashamed that he had never before touched this glowing heart of Hinduism.

"They also," he writes, "took me on one occasion to
the Blavatsky Lodge and introduced me to Madame Blavatsky and Mrs. Besant. The latter had just joined the
Theosophical Society, and I was following with great interest the controversy about her conversion. . . . I recall
having read, at the brothers' insistence, Madame Blavatsky's *Key to Theosophy*. The book stimulated in me
the desire to read books on Hinduism, and disabused me
of the notion fostered by the missionaries that Hinduism
was rife with superstition."

At this time Gandhi was becoming keenly interested
in comparative religion: "My young mind tried to unify

the teaching of the *Gita,* the *Light of Asia* and the Sermon on the Mount."

"During my first sojourn in South Africa it was Christian influence that had kept alive in me the religious sense. Now [i.e. after his return from England] it was theosophical influence that added strength to it. Mr. Ritch was a theosophist and put me in touch with the Society at Johannesburg."

It was the *Bhagavad Gita,* brought to him by H.P.B.'s close disciples, that finally became Gandhi's "infallible guide of conduct."

"I understood the Gita teaching of non-possession to mean that those who desired salvation should act like the trustee who, though having control over great possessions, regards not an iota of them as his own. It became clear to me as daylight that non-possession and equability pre-supposed a change of heart, a change of attitude."

The fact that it was Madame Blavatsky's influence that first led Gandhi to the Ancient Hindu spiritual Wisdom is interesting and perhaps little known.

The results were tremendous. Gandhi not only absorbed the culture but lived by it—as H.P.B. always taught her pupils to do. And so the inspiration of his teachings, life and death brought indelible changes to the world, and a new ray of Light to brighten the Eastern windows.

REFERENCES AND NOTES

Publisher's Note: *Inevitably many titles appear repeatedly in these refer-ences and notes. Publishing information is given in the Blavatsky Biblio-graphy; to avoid needless and tiresome repetition, only identifying information appears in the references. Sources not included in the bibliography are given here in full.*

Introduction
[1] New York: Carlton Press, Inc., 1969.

[2] Hastings: *Defence of Madame Blavatsky,* Vol. II, p. 20.

[3] Solovyov: *A Modern Priestess of Isis,* pp. 176-181. No original Russian text available.

[4] From a letter in the Archives of The Theosophical Society, Adyar, Madras, India.

[5] Blavatsky: *H.P.B. Speaks,* Vol. II.

[6] *Proceedings of the Society for Psychical Research,* December 1885.

[7] Jinarajadasa: *Letters from the Masters of the Wisdom,* First Series, Letter No. 29.

[8] See Adyar *Notes and News,* Vol. I, No. 30, October 25, 1928.

[9] Richet: *Thirty Years of Psychical Research,* pp. 31, 410.

[10] Sinnett: *The Mahatma Letters to A. P. Sinnett,* Letter No. 54.

Ch. 1
[1] Now called Dnyepropetrovsk.

[2] See *Adventures in Czarist Russia,* by Alexandre Dumas.

[3] Zhelihovsky: *When I Was Small.*

Ch. 2
[1] See *The Theosophical Forum,* Point Loma, California, August 1948, p. 452.

[2] Hommaire-de-Hell: *Travels in the Steppes.*

[3] Blavatsky: *H.P.B. Speaks,* Vol. II, p. 62.

[4] *The Theosophist,* Adyar, Vol. 32, May 1911.

Ch. 3
[1] *The Word:* "Letters from H.P.B. to Alexander Wilder, M.D.," Vol. VII, No. 3, June 1908.

Ch. 4
[1] Blavatsky: *H.P.B. Speaks,* Vol. II.

[2] Ibid., p. 66.

Ch. 5
[1] Blavatsky: *H.P.B. Speaks,* Vol. II, p. 66.

[2] Sinnett: *Incidents in the Life of Madame Blavatsky,* pp. 50-51.

[3] Hastings: *Defence of Madame Blavatsky.*

[4] Blavatsky, op. cit. Vol. II, p. 20.

Ch. 6
[1] See *The Theosophist,* Adyar, August 1959, pp. 295-6.

[2] Sinnett: *Incidents in the Life of Madame Blavatsky,* pp. 59-60.

[3] Ibid., p. 108.

Ch. 7

[1] Nikolayeff: "Reminiscences of Prince A. I. Baryatinsky," *Istoricheskiy Vestnik*, Vol. VI, December 1885.

[2] Blavatsky: *H.P.B. Speaks*, Vol. II, pp. 152, 156.

[3] From a letter in the Archives of The Theosophical Society, Adyar.

[4] Footnote added by H.P.B. to her English translation of her sister's account entitled "The Truth About H. P. Blavatsky" and published in *Rebus* (St. Petersburg), Vol. II, Nos. 40-48, 1883.

[5] Blavatsky: *The Letters of H. P. Blavatsky, to A. P. Sinnett*, Letter No. LX.

[6] Ibid.

[7] Ibid.

[8] Blavatsky: *H.P.B. Speaks*, Vol. II, p. 65.

Ch. 8

[1] Jinarajadasa: *Letters from the Masters of the Wisdom*, Second Series, Letter No. 1.

[2] *The Mahatma Letters to A. P. Sinnett*, Appendix, Letter No. 140.

[3] Blavatsky: *The Letters of H. P. Blavatsky to A. P. Sinnett*, p. 127.

[4] Sinnett: *Incidents in the Life of Madame Blavatsky*, p. 127.

[5] After Guiseppe Mazzini (1805-1872), Italian patriot and revolutionary.

[6] Blavatsky, op. cit. Letter No. LXXVIII.

[7] Ibid.

[8] Ibid.

[9] Ibid.

[10] From a letter written in New York on December 26, 1875, to Colonel H. S. Olcott of that city.

[11] Research so far has revealed nothing concerning the name of the ship and the date of the journey, although it has been stated that Madame Blavatsky arrived in New York on July 6 or 7, 1873. The shipping news of the New York *Times* for July 6 gives, as the only arrivals from Havre that day, the passenger ship, *Pereire*, and the cargo ship, *St. Laurent*. The latter did carry 120 passengers, but it is unlikely that it had steerage accommodations. The same paper gives no passenger arrivals for July 7. On the other hand, Lloyds of London states that its records show the *Pereire* arriving in Brest *from* New York on July 7, 1873, and at Havre on the following day. It gives the *St Laurent* as arriving in New York on July 7, a day later than reported by the New York *Times*.

Ch. 9

[1] *The Theosophist*, Adyar, Vol. LIII, Part I, pp. 257-266: "A Reminiscence of H. P. Blavatsky, in 1873."

[2] From a letter in the Archives of The Theosophical Society, Adyar.

[3] Rice, Louise: "Madame Blavatsky" in *Flynn's Weekly*, May 21, 1927.

[4] Olcott: *Old Diary Leaves*, First Series, p. 440.

[5] Blavatsky: *Collected Writings*.

Ch. 10

[1] For more details of these phenomena see Olcott: *People from the Other World* and Murphet: *Hammer on the Mountain*.

[2] For H.P.B.'s statement concerning her problem with regard to Spiritualism, see her "IMPORTANT NOTE" on page 73 of H.P. Blavatsky *Collected Writings*, Vol. I, to end of paragraph: ". . . posterity will learn to know me better." This is from her *Scrapbook*, Vol. I, pp. 20-21.

[3] Olcott: *Old Diary Leaves*, First Series, p. 56.

[4] Flint: *Memories of an Active Life*.

[5] Racowitza: *An Autobiography*.

Ch. 11

[1] Corson, Eugene Rollin: *Some Unpublished Letters of H.P.B.*
[2] Ibid.
[3] Ibid.
[4] See for instance letters to General F. J. Lippitt in *H.P.B. Speaks,* Vol. I.
[5] *Proceedings of the Society for Psychical Research,* March 1964, p. 46.
[6] Ibid., p. 47.
[7] Ibid., p. 54.
[8] Corson, op cit.

Ch. 12

[1] Corson, Eugene Rollin: *Some Unpublished Letters of H.P.B.,* pp. 176-77.
[2] An interpolated note for a new edition of his book, *Incidents in the Life of Madame Blavatsky.*
[3] From a letter to her sister Vera, published in *The Path,* December 1894.
[4] Hastings: *Defence of Madame Blavatsky.*
[5] Blavatsky: *Isis Unveiled,* Vol. 2 p. 264.

Ch. 13

[1] Olcott: *Old Diary Leaves,* First Series, p. 368.
[2] The *Mahatma Letters to A. P. Sinnett,* Letter No. 54.
[3] Now, nearly a century later, the turban is still intact, though frail, in the Archives of The Theosophical Society, Adyar.

Ch. 14

[1] Olcott: *Old Diary Leaves,* Second Series, p. 78.

Ch. 15

[1] See "Statement by H.P.B." in *The Path,* March 1893.
[2] Spear: *History of India,* Vol. II, p. 156.
[3] Olcott: *Old Diary Leaves,* Second Series, p. 288.
[4] Sinnett: *Incidents in the Life of Madame Blavatsky,* pp. 185-6.
[5] Blavatsky: *H.P.B. Speaks,* Vol. II, pp. 64, 67.

Ch. 16

[1] Olcott: *Old Diary Leaves,* Second Series, Ch. XXIII.
[2] Ibid.
[3] Blavatsky: *The Letters of H.P. Blavatsky to A. P. Sinnett,* Letter No. XVIII.
[4] *The Mahatma Letters to A. P. Sinnett,* Letter No. 24b, p. 188.
[5] Ibid., Letter No. 46, p. 266.

Ch. 17

[1] Blavatsky: *The Letters of H. P. Blavatsky to A. P. Sinnett,* Letter No. XIX, dated October 9th.
[2] Jinarajadasa: "How a Chela Found His Guru," *Letters from the Masters of the Wisdom,* Second Series, Appendix A.
[3] Ibid.
[4] Blavatsky: op. cit. Letter No. XXII, p. 44.
[5] Ibid., pp. 44, 65.
[6] Ibid., Letter No. XXX.
[7] Ibid., Letter No. XXXI.

Ch. 18

[1] This story was republished in *The Theosophist* (Adyar), Vol. V, Supplement to February 1884, p. 31, and carried an introductory paragraph expressing some reservations about the authenticity of the incident.
[2] Wachtmeister: *Reminiscences of H. P. Blavatsky and The Secret Doctrine,* pp. 14-15.
[3] Miss Francesca Arundale writes of an episode of this period: "I was sitting one afternoon in the drawing room at Elgin Crescent, when

Mr. Frederick W. H. Myers was announced. He asked if she [H.P.B.] would show him some phenomena. 'It will be perfectly useless,' said Madame Blavatsky, but at last consented. She told me to place a finger-bowl with water on a small wooden stool, just before us, and while her hands were quietly resting on her lap, the astral bells sounded clearly on the bowl which was about three feet away from her.

"Mr. Myers made every examination, under, and over, and all around, and then, turning to me, said, 'Miss Arundale, I shall never doubt again.'

"In less than a fortnight he was as great a skeptic as ever."

[4] Jinarajadasa: *Letters from the Masters of the Wisdom*, First Series, Letter No. 18.

[5] From a letter to the Coulombs dated Paris, April 1st, 1884. Reproduced in Mme. Coulomb's pamphlet, "Some Accounts of My Association with Mde. Blavatsky."

Ch. 19

[1] Arundale, Francesca: *Mde. Blavatsky and Her Work*, pp. 141-5. See also *In Memory of Helena Petrovna Blavatsky* by some of her pupils.

Ch. 20

[1] Oakley, Isabel Cooper: "At Cairo and Madras" from *In Memory of Helena Petrovna Blavatsky* by some of her pupils.

[2] From a letter to Mr. Sinnett in Appendix to *The Mahatma Letters to A.P. Sinnett*.

[3] Oakley, op. cit.

[4] Olcott: *Old Diary Leaves*, Third Series, p. 223.

Ch. 21

[1] See *The Theosophist*, March 1925, Vol. XLVI, p. 783.

[2] Blavatsky: *The Letters of H. P. Blavatsky to A. P. Sinnett*, Letter XLV.

[3] Solovyov: *A Modern Priestess of Isis*. (A letter from V. Solovyov to H.P.B from Paris, Oct. 8, 1885.)

[4] Later published as *Incidents in the Life of Madame Blavatsky*, compiled and edited by A. P. Sinnett.

Ch. 22

[1] Olcott: *Old Diary Leaves*, Third Series, Ch. 13.

[2] *The Mahatma Letters to A. P. Sinnett*, Letter 54, pp. 307-311.

[3] Blavatsky: *The Letters of H. P. Blavatsky to A. P. Sinnett*, Letter No. LXXII.

[4] Ibid., Letter No. LXXX.

[5] Olcott: *Old Diary Leaves*, Third Series, p. 178.

[6] This "Confession" is not available in the original Russian sent to Solovyov, but only in translation. Hence it could have been considerably altered by Solovyov. Even so, it is not a very damaging document, revealing nothing more than sheer desperation with the world's attitudes.

[7] Blavatsky: *The Letters of H. P. Blavatsky to A. P. Sinnett*, enclosure with Letter No. LXXXIII. See also Introduction p. xxiv.

[8] Kislingbury, Emily: "At New York and Würzburg" from *In Memory of Helena Petrovna Blavatsky* by some of her pupils.

Ch. 23

[1] Wachtmeister: *Reminiscences of H. P. Blavatsky and The Secret Doctrine*.

[2] Zhelihovsky: "Helena P. Blavatsky: Biographical Sketch."

[3] Wachtmeister, op. cit.

[4] Ibid.

[5] Ibid.

Ch. 24

[1] *The Path*, November 1892.

[2] Keightley: *Reminiscences of H. P. Blavatsky*.

Ch. 25

[1] Wachtmeister: *Reminiscences of H. P. Blavatsky and The Secret Doctrine*, p. 81.

[2] See "As I Knew Her" by Edmund Russell in *Herald of the Star*, London, May-June 1916.

[3] Yeats: *Some Letters from W. B. Yeats to John O'Leary*, pp. 13-14.

Ch. 26

[1] Judge, William Q.: "About *The Secret Doctrine*"; see also Wachtmeister: *Reminiscences of H. P. Blavatsky and The Secret Doctrine*, pp. 103-4.

[2] Wachtmeister, op. cit. Letter from Dr. Hübbe Schleiden, pp. 112-113.

[3] Blavatsky: *The Letters of H. P. Blavatsky to A. P. Sinnett*, Letter LXXX.

[4] Mead, G.R.S.: *Concerning H.P.B.*, pp. 13, 14, 18.

[5] Wachtmeister, op. cit., pp. 119-120.

[6] Hanson (Ed.): *H. P. Blavatsky and The Secret Doctrine:* "H. P. Blavatsky Brings to Mankind the Light of the Timeless Wisdom," by Alfred Taylor, Ph.D., formerly head of cancer research in the Biochemical Institute of the University of Texas.

Ch. 27

[1] "As I Knew Her" by Edmund Russell, in *Herald of the Star*, London, May-June, 1916.

[2] *Theosophical Forum*, Vol. XV, No. 1, July 1939: "Blavatsky's Instructions to a Neophyte."

[3] *The Theosophist*, Vol. LIII, Part I, p. 633.

[4] It is not known precisely what material H.P.B. intended for the third and fourth volumes of her major work. In 1897, six years after her death, a new edition of *The Secret Doctrine* was published and a third volume was added. Careful analysis of this volume shows it to be a collection of miscellaneous essays written by H.P.B. at various periods of her literary career.

Ch. 28

[1] From a lecture given under the auspices of the Indian Institute of World Culture, Bangalore, India, 1958.

[2] Olcott: *Old Diary Leaves*, Fourth Series, p. 257.

[3] Ibid., p. 270.

Ch. 29

[1] Blavatsky: *The Secret Doctrine*, original edition, 1888, Vol. 1, pp. 519-20.

[2] "H.P.B.", *In Memory of Helena Petrovna Blavatsky* by some of her pupils.

Epilogue

[1] Extracts from the collection, "H.P.B.", *In Memory of Helena Petrovna Blavatsky* by some of her pupils.

[2] Ibid.

[3] Ibid.

[4] Ibid.

BLAVATSKY BIBLIOGRAPHY

Titles preceded by an asterisk (*) indicate Source-Material, i.e., accounts and records by eyewitnesses or participants, upon which subsequent writings are based.

*Arundale, Francesca, *My Guest—H.P. Blavatsky*. Adyar: Theos. Publ. House, 1932, ix, 81 pp. Foreword by C. Jinarajadasa. Front. F. Arundale.

Barborka, Geoffrey A., *H.P. Blavatsky, the Light-Bringer*. The Blavatsky Lecture of 1970. London: Theos. Publ. House, 1970, 68 pp., Glossary, Illustr.

—————, *H.P. Blavatsky, Tibet and Tulku*. Adyar: Theos. Publ. House, 1966, xxix, 476 pp., Index, Illustr.; 2nd ed., 1970.

—————, *The Divine Plan*. Written in the Form of a Commentary on H.P. Blavatsky's *The Secret Doctrine*. Adyar: The Theos. Publ. House, 1961, xxvi, 564, incl. copious Index.

—————, *The Mahatmas and Their Letters*. Adyar, London, Wheaton, Ill., The Theos. Publ. House, 1973, xviii, 422 pp. Index.

Bechhofer-Roberts, C.E., *The Mysterious Madame*. New York: Brewer & Warren, Inc., 1931, 332 pp. *Hostile*.

*Besant, Dr. Annie, *H.P. Blavatsky and the Masters of the Wisdom*. Issued as a Transaction of the H.P.B. Lodge, London. London: Theos. Publ. Society, 1907, 57 pp. Repr. at Krotona, 1918.

Blavatsky, H.P., *Isis Unveiled*. Original edition, New York: J. W. Bouton; London: Bernard Quaritch, 1877. Two Volumes: xlv, 628, & ix, 692 pp. Index. Currently: (as part of the *Collected Writings*) Madras, London, Wheaton,

Ill., The Theos. Publ. House, 1972, Two Vols.; Pasadena, Calif., Theos. University Press, 1950, Two Vols.; Los Angeles, Calif., The Theosophy Co., latest pr., 1968, Photographic reproduction of the orig. ed.; both volumes under one binding.

—————, *The Secret Doctrine.* Original edition, London: The Theos. Publ. Co., 1888. Two Volumes: xlvii, 676, & xvi, 798, xxx pp., Index. Currently: Sixth (Adyar) Edition, 1971. In Six Books, as in all editions since 1938. Includes "Volume III" of 1897.—
Pasadena, Calif., Theos. University Press, 1963, Two Volumes; Los Angeles, Calif., The Theosophy Co., 1925; latest pr., 1968. Photographic reproduction of the orig. ed.; both volumes under one binding.—
An Abridgement of The Secret Doctrine. Edited by E. Preston and Christmas Humphreys, London: 1966 & 1967.

—————, *The Key to Theosophy.* Orig. ed., London: The Theos. Publ. Society, 1889, xii, 307 pp.; 2nd ed., 1890, with Glossary. Many editions since, one of the best being: London, The Theos. Publ. House, 1968.

—————, *The Voice of the Silence.* Being Chosen Fragments from the "Book of the Golden Precepts." Orig. ed., London, 1889, xii, 97 pp. Many subsequent editions published by various Theosophical and allied bodies.

—————, *Collected Writings,* Volumes I through XI. Compiled by Boris de Zirkoff. Madras, London, Wheaton, Ill.: The Theos. Publ. House. *In progress.*

—————, *Transactions of the Blavatsky Lodge of The Theosophical Society.* Discussions on the Stanzas of the First Volume of *The Secret Doctrine.* London: The Theos. Publ. Society. Part I (January, 1889), 1890; Part II (Feb. & March, 1889), 1891. Contained in Vol X of the *Collected Writings.*

—————, *Gems from the East.* A Birthday Book of Precepts and Axioms. Compiled by H.P.B. and Illustrated by F.W., London: Theos. Publ. Society, 1890.

—————, *The Theosophical Glossary.* London: Theos. Publ. Society, 1892, 389 pp. Based primarily on various Encyclopaedias of the XIXth century and data furnished by Orientalists. Only a small portion of the text is H.P.B.'s. Edited by G.R.S. Mead.

—————, *Nightmare Tales.* London: Theos. Publ. Society, 1892. Included now in the *Collected Writings.*

——————, *From the Caves and Jungles of Hindostan.* A partial translation of the Russian Serial story originally published in the *Russkiy Vestnik* (Russian Messenger). London: Theos. Publ. Society, 1892, 318 pp. Complete English translation to appear in the *Collected Writings.*

——————, *The Mysterious Tribes from the Blue Hills.* Partial translation of the Russian Serial story from the *Russkiy Vestnik.* Wheaton, Ill.: Theos. Press, 1930. Complete English translation to appear in the *Collected Writings.*

——————, *The Durbar in Lahore.* Complete English translation of the Russian text from the *Russkiy Vestnik* published in *The Theosophist,* Vol. 81, August, 1960 — March, 1961. To be published also in the *Collected Writings.*

——————, *The Letters of H.P. Blavatsky to A.P. Sinnett.* Transcribed, Compiled, and with an Introduction by A.T. Barker. New York: Frederick A. Stokes Co.; London: T. Fisher Unwin, 1925, xvi, 404 pp. Index.

——————, *H.P.B. Speaks.* Letters written by H.P.B. to various people, such as General Lippitt, Prince A.M. Donukoff-Korsakoff, her own relatives, etc. Edited by C. Jinarajadasa. Adyar: Theos. Publ. House; Vol. I, 1950, xii, 248 pp.; Vol. II, 1951, xx, 181 pp.; facsimiles, portraits.

——————, *Some Unpublished Letters of Helena Petrovna Blavatsky.* With an Introduction and Commentary by Eugene Rollin Corson. London: Rider & Co., 1929, 255 pp. Facs. & Ill. Letters addressed to Professor Hiram Corson of Ithaca, N.Y.

Bragdon, C., *Episodes from an Unwritten History,* Rochester, N.Y.: The Manas Press, 1910, 109 pp.

Butt, G. Baseden, *Madame Blavatsky.* London: Rider & Co. Preface dated December, 1925, x, 269 pp.; front.

Carrithers, Walter A., Jr., The *Truth about Madame Blavatsky.* An Open Letter to the Author of *Priestess of the Occult.* Covina, Calif.: Theos. University Press, April, 1947, 27 pp.

——————, (pseud.: Adlai E. Waterman), *Obituary: The "Hodgson Report" on Madame Blavatsky—1885-1960.* Preface by N. Sri Ram. Adyar: The Theos. Publ. House, 1963, xx, 92. Two folded Plates.

*Cleather, Alice Leighton, *H.P. Blavatsky—A Great Betrayal,* Calcutta: Thacker, Spink & Co., 1922, viii, 97 pp.

*——————, *H.P. Blavatsky—Her Life and Work for Humanity,* Calcutta, Spink & Co., 1922, 124 pp.

*————, *H.P. Blavatsky as I knew Her,* Calcutta & London: Thacker, Spink & Co., 1923, ix, 76 pp.

*Coulomb, Emma, *Some Account of my Association with Madame Blavatsky from 1872 to 1884,* etc. Madras: Higginbotham & Co., 1884; London: Elliot Stock, 1885; ii, 112 pp. *Hostile.*

*Dharmapala, Anagarika Devamitta. Autobiographical Sketch, including description of H.P.B., etc. *The Theosophist,* Vol. LIV, July, 1933.

Eek, Dr. Sven, *Damodar and the Pioneers of the Theosophical Movement,* Adyar: The Theos. Publ. House, 1965. Preface by N. Sri Ram; xvi, 720 pp. Illustrated.

Eek, Dr. Sven & B. de Zirkoff, *William Quan Judge: Theosophical Pioneer,* Wheaton, Ill., Theos. Publ. House, 1969, 96 pp., front., facs.

Endersby, Victor A., *The Hall of Magic Mirrors,* New York: Carlton Press, 1969, 351 pp., ill.

*Evans, Thomas H., "Blavatsky's Instruction to a Neophyte," *The Occult Word,* Rochester, N.Y. December, 1885. Reprinted in *The Theosophical Forum,* Point Loma, Calif., Vol. XV, July, 1939.

*Flint, Charles R., *Memories of an Active Life.* New York & London: G.P. Putnams Sons, 1923, xviii, 349 pp., ill.

*Gandhi, Mohandas K., *Autobiography: or, The Story of my Experiments with Truth.* Translated from Gujarati by Mahadev Desai. 2nd ed., Ahmedabad, 1940; repr. 1945, viii, 422 pp., ill.

Hahn, Helena Adreyevna von, *The Ideal,* 1837 (Russian text).

Hanson, Virginia (Edited by), *H.P. Blavatsky and The Secret Doctrine.* Commentaries on her Contributions to World Thought, by various Writers. Introd. by Joy Mills. Wheaton, Ill.: Theos. Publ. House, 1971 (Quest Book), 227 pp.

Harris, Iverson L., *Mme. Blavatsky Defended.* Refutations of Falsehoods, etc. San Diego, Calif.: Point Loma Publications, Inc., 1971, 174 pp. Index.

*Hartmann, Dr. Franz, *Report of Observations Made during a Nine Months' Stay at the Hdqrts. of The Theosophical Society at Adyar (Madras), India.* Madras: Scottish Press, 1884, 60 pp.

Hastings, Beatrice, *Defence of Madame Blavatsky.* Worthing: The Hastings Press. Vol. I, April, 1937, 60 pp.; deals with various attacks on H.P.B.; Vol. II, August, 1937, 105 pp.;

deals with the "Coulomb Pamphlet."

—————, *New Universe—"Try."* A Review Devoted to the Defence of Madame Blavatsky. Worthing, England. Vol I, Nos. 1 through 5, July, 1937, through July, 1938. No more published.

*Holloway, Laura C. Langford. "Helena Petrovna Blavatsky: A Reminiscence," *The Word,* Vol. XXII, December, 1915. Portrait.

*Holt, Elizabeth G.B., "A Reminiscence of H.P. Blavatsky in 1873," *The Theosophist,* Vol. LIII, December, 1931.

*Hommaire-de-Hell, Ignace-Xavier Morand (1812-48), *Travels in the Steppes,* etc. English translation of French text. London: Chapman & Hall, 1847.

*H.P.B. — *In Memory of Helena Petrovna Blavatsky,* by some of her Pupils. London: Theos. Publ. Society, 1891. Collection of articles originally published in *Lucifer,* Vol. VIII, following H.P.B.'s passing. *Important Source Material* by eyewitnesses and friends. Second edition publ. by The Blavatsky Association, London, John M. Watkins, 1931, contains a few additional essays and illustrations.

Humphreys, Christmas, *The Field of Theosophy.* The Teacher, The Teaching and The Way. London, Adyar, Wheaton, Ill.: Theos. Publ. House, 1966, 64 pp.

*Jinarajadasa, C., *The Personality of H.P. Blavatsky.* The Blavatsky Lecture for 1930, London, England. Adyar: Theos. Publ. House, 1930, 25 pp., ill.

—————, *Did Madame Blavatsky Forge the Mahatma Letters?* Adyar: Theos. Publ. House, 1934, 55 pp., 30 facs.

*—————, *Letters from the Masters of the Wisdom, 1870-1900.* Compiled by C. Jinarajadasa. First Series. Fourth edition. Adyar: Theos. Publ. House, 1948. — Second Series. Adyar: Theos. Publ. House, 1925. Facsimiles in both.

*Judge, William Quan, *Dr. Elliott Coues in His Letters.* New York, June 14, 1889; another ed., July 28, 1890.

*Keightley, Dr. Archibald, "Reminiscences of H.P. Blavatsky," *The Theosophical Quarterly,* Vol. VII, October, 1910.

*Keightley, Bertram, *Reminiscences of H.P. Blavatsky.* Adyar: Theos. Publ. House, 1931, ill. (Orig. publ. in *The Theosophist,* Sept., 1931.)

*Kingsland, William, *The Real H.P. Blavatsky.* A Study in Theosophy and a Memoir of a Great Soul. London: John M. Watkins, 1928, xiv, 322 pp., portraits.

Kuhn, Alvin Boyd, *Theosophy: A Modern Revival of Ancient Wisdom.* New York: Henry Holt & Co., December, 1930, viii, 381 pp.; extensive bibliography.

Lillie, Arthur, *Madame Blavatsky and her "Theosophy".* A Study. London: Swan Sonnenschein & Co., 1895, x, 228 pp. *Hostile.*

*Morgan, General Henry Rhodes, *Reply to a Report of an Examination by J.D.B. Gribble,* 1884; 2nd ed., Ootacamund: Observer's Press, 1884.

Müller, F. Max, *Theosophy or Psychological Religion.* Gifford Lectures, 1892.

Murphet, Howard, *Hammer on the Mountain.* Life of Henry Steel Olcott (1832-1907). Theos. Publ. House: Adyar, London, Wheaton, Ill.: 1972, xii, 339 pp.

Neff, Mary K., *The "Brothers" of Madame Blavatsky.* Adyar: Theos. Publ. House, 1932, vi, 125, ill. & facs.

—————, *Personal Memoirs of H.P. Blavatsky.* Compiled by M.K. Neff, New York: E.P. Dutton & Co., 1937, 323 pp. Index, ill.; also London: Rider & Co., 1937. Quest Book paperback edition, Theos. Publ. House, 1967.

*Nikolayeff, Gen. P.S., "Reminiscences of Prince A.I. Baryatinsky," *Isotoricheskiy Vestnik* (Historical Messenger), St. Petersburg, Vol. VI, December, 1885. Speaks of H.P.B.'s visit to the Fadeyeffs and her fascinating travel stories. (Transl. in *Theosophia,* Los Angeles, Vol. IV, May-June, 1947.)

*Olcott, Col. Henry Steel, *People from the Other World.* Hartford, Conn.: American Publ. Co., 1875. The Colonel's account of meeting H.P.B. at the Eddy Homestead. *Scarce.*

*—————, *Old Diary Leaves. The True Story of The Theosophical Society.* This Series was inaugurated in *The Theosophist,* Vol. XIII, March, 1892.

*—————, *Diaries.* Col. Olcott's actual *Diaries* cover 30 Volumes and are preserved in the Adyar Archives.

Psaltis, Lina (compiler), *Dynamics of the Psychic World.* Comments by H.P. Blavatsky on Magic, Mediumship, Psychism and the Powers of the Spirit. Notes by the Compiler; Index. Quest Book. Wheaton, Ill.: Theosophical Publ. House, 1972, xviii, 132 pp.

Purucker, G. de, *H.P. Blavatsky: The Mystery.* In collaboration with Katherine Tingley. San Diego, California:

Point Loma Publications, Inc., 1972. xviii, 242 pp.

*Racowitza, Princess Helen von, *An Autobiography*. Transl. from the German by Cecil Mar. London: Constables & Co., 1910, xiii, 421, front. Pages 349-55 & 391 concern H.P.B.

Ransom, Josephine, *Madame Blavatsky as an Occultist*. London: Theos. Publ. House, 1931.

Rice, Louise, "Madame Blavatsky," *Flynn's Weekly*, May 21, 1927.

Richet, Charles (1850-1935), *Thirty Years of Psychical Research*. London: Collins, 1923. (Transl. from the French by Stanley De Broth of Richet's *Traité de métapsychique*.)

Ryan, Charles J., *H.P. Blavatsky and the Theosophical Movement*. Point Loma, Calif.: Theos. University Press, 1937, xxii, 369, ill., index.

*Sinnett, Alfred Percy, *The Occult World*. London: Trübner & Co., 1881, 172 pp.; 2nd ed., 1882.

*————, *Esoteric Buddhism*. London: Trübner & Co., 1883; many subsequent editions.

*————, *Incidents in the Life of Madame Blavatsky*. London: George Redway; New York: J.W. Bouton, 1886, xii, 324 pp., front. Schmiechen's portrait of H.P.B.; 2nd edition, London: Theos. Publ. Society, 1913, 256 pp.; this edition is abridged, with many important items eliminated.

*————, *The "Occult World Phenomena" and the Society for Psychical Research*. With A Protest by Madame Blavatsky. London: George Redway, 1886, 60 pp.

*————, *The Early Days of Theosophy in Europe*. London: Theos. Publ. House, 1922, 126 pp. Issued by Sinnett's Literary Executor.

*————, *The Mahatma Letters to A.P. Sinnett*. From the Mahatmas M. and K.H. Transcribed, Compiled and with an Introduction by A.T. Barker. London: T. Fisher Unwin; New York; Frederick A. Stokes, December, 1923, xxxv, 492 pp. — 3rd and revised edition. Edited by Christmas Humphreys and Elsie Benjamin. Adyar: Theos. Publ. House, 1962, xliv, 524 pp. New Index.

*Society for Psychical Research, *Report of the Committee appointed to investigate Phenomena connected with the Theosophical Society*. *Proceedings*, Vol. III, Part IX, December, 1885. Some 300 pages, facsimiles. — In December, 1884, a Preliminary Report was circulated among members, but not published. It consists of 130 pages and is rather scarce.

*Solovyov, Vsevolod S., *A Modern Priestess of Isis.* Original Russian text in *Russkiy Vestnik* from Feb. through Dec., 1892. Publ. in book form by N.F. Mertz, St. Petersburg, 1893 and 1904. — English ed., abridged and translated by Walter Leaf, with Appendices. London: Longmans, Green & Co., and New York, 1895, xix, 366 pp.

Spear, Thos. G. Percival, *A History of India.* 1965.

Symonds, John, *Madame Blavatsky: Medium and Magician.* London: Odhams Press Ltd., 1959, 254 pp., ill. Published in U.S.A. as *The Lady with the Magic Eyes,* by Thos. Yoseloff, New York, 1960. *Hostile.*

Vania, K.F., *Madame Blavatsky: Her Occult Phenomena and the Society for Psychical Research.* Bombay: Sat Publ. Co., 1951, xvi, 488 pp.

*Wachtmeister, Countess Constance, *Reminiscences of H.P. Blavatsky and The Secret Doctrine.* London: Theos. Publ. Society: New York: *The Path;* Madras: Theos. Society, 1893, 162 pp. Includes accounts by Bertram Keightley, Dr. Archibald Keightley,, William Quan Judge, Vera P. de Zhelihovsky, Vera V. Johnston, Dr. Franz Hartmann, Dr. Wm. Hübbe-Schleiden, and other rare items.

Whyte, G. Herbert, *H.P. Blavatsky: An Outline of Her Life.* London: Percy Lund, Humphries & Co., 1909, iv, 60 pp.; also London: Theos. Publ. House, 1916.

Williams, Gertrude Marvin, *Priestess of the Occult: Madame Blavatsky.* New York: Alred A. Knopf, 1946, x, 345 pp.; Index. *Hostile.*

Witte, Count Serguey Yulyevich. *The Memoirs of Count Witte.* Translated from the original Russian MSS., and edited by Abraham Yarmolinsky. New York: Doubleday, Page & Co.; London: Heinemann, 1921, xi, 445 pp. — An edition in three volumes publ. by "Izdatel'stvo sotzial' noekonomicheskoy literaturi," Moscow, 1960. Witte's remarks about H.P.B. are in Vol. I, covering period of 1849-94. *Unfriendly.*

*Yeats, W.B., *Four Years.* Churchtown, Dundrum: The Cuala Press, 1921, 92 pp. Pages 69-80 contain reminiscences about H.P.B.

*————, *Some Letters from W.B. Yeats, to John O'Leary and his Sister.* Edited by Allan Wade. New York, 1953.

—————, *The Countess Kathleen.*

—————, *Autobiography.*

*Zhelihovsky, Vera P. de. "The Truth About H.P. Blavatsky," *Rebus,* St. Petersburg, Vol. II, Nos. 40-48, 1883. This authoritative account was translated into English by H.P.B. herself to provide A.P. Sinnett with data about herself. H.P.B. has added some passages and footnotes to it. Mr. Sinnett used only parts of that material. H.P.B.'s own translation-manuscript is in the Adyar Archives.

*—————, "Helena P. Blavatsky: Biographical Sketch," *Russkoye Obozreniye* (Russian Review), Vol. VI, Nov., & Dec., 1891 (Russian text). Of considerable historical value. Free translation in *Lucifer,* London, Vols. XV & XVI, Nov., 1894 — April, 1895.

*—————, *My Adolescence,* St. Petersburg, 1893, 295 pp.; 4th ed., A.F. Devrient (1902). (Russian text.)

*—————, *When I was Small.* 2nd rev. & enl. ed., St. Petersburg, A.F. Devrient, 1894, 269 pp., fig., pl.; 3rd ed., 1898. [Russian text.]

INDEX

SOME QUEST BOOK TITLES

MAN VISIBLE AND INVISIBLE by C. W. Leadbeater

THOUGHT-FORMS by Annie Besant and C. W. Leadbeater

THE MYSTERY OF HEALING edited by Adelaide Gardner

THE FUTURE IS NOW by Arthur W. Osborn

THE PSYCHIC SENSE by Phoebe D. Payne and Laurence J. Bendit

THE ETHERIC DOUBLE by A. E. Powell

SCIENTIFIC EVIDENCE OF THE EXISTENCE OF THE SOUL by Benito F. Reyes

THE DOCTRINE OF THE SUBTLE BODY IN WESTERN TRADITION by G. R. S. Mead

MEDITATION: A PRACTICAL STUDY by Adelaide Gardner

CONCENTRATION: AN APPROACH TO MEDITATION by Ernest Wood

PSYCHISM AND THE UNCONSCIOUS MIND, edited by H. Tudor Edmonds

For a complete list of all Theosophical Publishing House Books write to:

P. O. Box 270, Wheaton, Ill., 60187

2216